Yes, Minister

Yes, Minister

Christopher Finlayson

Attorney-General
2008–2017

ALLEN & UNWIN
SYDNEY • MELBOURNE • AUCKLAND • LONDON

First published in 2022

Allen & Unwin
Level 2, 10 College Hill, Freemans Bay
Auckland 1011, New Zealand
Phone: (64 9) 377 3800
Email: auckland@allenandunwin.com
Web: www.allenandunwin.co.nz

83 Alexander Street
Crows Nest NSW 2065, Australia
Phone: (61 2) 8425 0100

A catalogue record for this book is available from the National Library of New Zealand.

ISBN 978 1991006 1 03

Design by Katrina Duncan
Cover photo by Nicola Edmonds
Set in Adobe Garamond Pro and Gotham
Printed and bound in Australia by Griffin Press

10 9 8 7 6 5 4 3 2 1

MIX
Paper from responsible sources
FSC
www.fsc.org
FSC® C009448

The paper in this book is FSC® certified. FSC® promotes environmentally responsible, socially beneficial and economically viable management of the world's forests.

For Jody Wilson-Raybould,
Attorney-General of Canada 2015–2019.
A real example of principle in politics.

Contents

Preface

WHEN I LEFT PARLIAMENT IN EARLY 2019, I decided to write several books. The first one, published in 2021, is *He Kupu Taurangi*. It discusses my work as minister for Treaty of Waitangi negotiations between 2008 and 2017, and talks more generally about the importance of the treaty settlement work begun by Doug Graham and Jim Bolger in the early 1990s.

This book is a sketch of my time in politics. I initially thought it would be a general overview of the Key government from 2008 to 2017 but, as I worked on it, I saw that there was an opportunity to talk about the office of attorney-general and the contribution made by the attorney to ensuring that the business of government is conducted in accordance with the rule of law. Throughout the book there is much discussion around the rule of law. I refer to the excellent book by the late Lord Bingham, *The Rule of Law*, where he explains the essence of 'the rule of law', that all persons and authorities within the state, whether public or private, should be bound by, and entitled to, the benefit of laws publicly made, taking effect (generally) in the future and publicly administered in the courts.[1] The importance of the rule of law goes beyond lawyers and legal academics. One need only refer to the famous question put to Alan Greenspan, the former chair of the Federal Reserve of the United States of America (and an economist): 'What do you consider the single most important contributor to economic growth?' Greenspan's answer? Quite simply, 'The rule of law'.[2] In his book, Lord Bingham also refers to an article published many years ago in *The Economist*, which said: 'The rule of law is usually thought of as a political or legal matter . . . but in the past ten years the rule of law has become important in economics too . . . the rule of law is held to be not only good in itself, because it embodies and encourages a just society, but also as a cause of other good things, notably growth.'[3]

I also endeavour to talk about my involvement in the National party for many years, and the ups and downs of political life. I am not a professional historian. This is not a comprehensive history of the Key government, and I acknowledge that there are many gaps in the narrative. I have not even tried to address some of the major social initiatives advanced during these years, such as Bill English's idea of social investment. This material will need to be analysed by a professional historian or, preferably, by Bill himself. Instead, this book is narrowly focused on my term as attorney-general, and spends some time looking at the other portfolio responsibilities I held, including minister responsible for the Government Communications Security Bureau and minister in charge of the New Zealand Security Intelligence Service (2014–17), minister for arts, culture and heritage (2008–14), and associate minister for Māori development (2011–17). Several important themes emerge:

- For the first few years, the Key government operated in conditions of extreme austerity given the financial circumstances we inherited when we assumed office. Throwing money at projects was not an option for any minister, and I was not exempt.
- My experience (which I hope is shown in the book) is that you don't need to spend large sums of money to do innovative and exciting things. In the chapter 'Minister for arts, culture and heritage', for example, I talk about things such as New Zealand's stellar performance at the Frankfurt Book Fair as the guest of honour. That did not cost a lot of money. Money is not a prerequisite for success.
- The law needs to be constantly kept under review. During my time in the various portfolios I held, I was responsible for modernising intelligence law, most of our cultural legislation, and many of what could be called black-letter law statutes but that are nonetheless very important to all New Zealanders. If the law is not constantly upgraded, it becomes out of date very quickly indeed. That is why I applaud the intention of former Minister of Conservation Kiri Allan to begin the enormous task of updating all the statutes in her conservation portfolio. Many of them, such as the Wildlife Act 1953, are hopelessly out of date. Reform is needed.
- The National party has been a very successful party in government for many years since it first attained office in 1949, and has known great highs and dreadful lows. Having been a party activist for many years, I talk about some of those times, particularly the lows. One of the disappointing aspects of my involvement is that lessons learnt have had to be relearnt as a result of bitter defeat. I suppose that is inevitable in any human institution, but many of the errors — such as those committed between 2017 and 2020 — were avoidable.

Some years ago a news organisation contacted me asking whether I could write a brief article for them setting out any regrets I had from my time in public life. I wrote an article, but for some reason they never published it. So here it is now.

Do I have any regrets? I have three. My greatest regret in politics has to be that I never mastered the essential art of self-promotion. I have recently been reading the third volume of Charles Moore's magnificent biography of the late, great Margaret Thatcher, who once complained that politics used to be about doing something, but now it's about being someone. Looking back, I certainly wasted far too much time on doing things. I used to get excited about things like settling as many treaty claims as I could and reforming intelligence legislation. The day that the Legislation Act 2012 came into force was a genuinely happy day — a true banner day for black-letter law. At the time, some cynics said this stuff wasn't sexy. I disagreed then, but now I realise they were right. In modern politics, just doing the job you've been given as well as you can is old hat. If you really want to get ahead, you have to self-promote. My tongue might have been sharp from time to time, but my elbows were never sharp enough. Now I think of all the times I could have posed for the cover of *Woman's Day* and shared my feelings. They could have hired a dog for me to walk down a beach for a photoshoot. I could have learnt to emote properly (although I admit this would have taken a lot of empathy training). I could finally have proven Annette King wrong when she claimed that the more people I met in Rongotai every election campaign, the higher her majority would be. I could have approached repealing the foreshore and seabed legislation through a kindness and well-being lens. People might have shouted at me less during public meetings.

My second regret is that I wish I had learnt an essential lesson earlier: never assume background knowledge on behalf of the person you are talking to, no matter who they are. Jacinda Ardern copped some flak at Waitangi Day in 2019 when she couldn't recite the three articles of the treaty. Some months later, the prime minister gave a speech in Australia where she referred to 'the Treaty of Waitangi partnership between Māori and Pākehā New Zealanders'.[4] This is a legally and historically incoherent description: the treaty is an agreement between Māori and the Crown, not Māori and Pākehā. It is difficult to try to comprehend New Zealand through Ardern's conception of things, and she's the prime minister! So never assume anything.

My final regret is that I sometimes allowed myself to be pigeonholed. It's all about identity politics these days. But the truth is that people are more complex than the labels that get placed on them. 'Conservative', 'gay', 'Catholic', 'cold', 'intellectual' — these descriptions were made of me from time to time. The result was that on issues such as the marriage equality debate, I chose to sit it out rather than engage in it. I should have done the opposite. Being in the 'no' vote column alongside a number of people whose views I found frankly repellent belied the fact that I was delighted same-sex couples could have equal status under the law. My objection was to the state being involved in marriage at all; I saw it as a law reform issue. But try explaining that by emoting.

CHAPTER 1

Getting involved in politics

IN LATE SEPTEMBER 1973, one of my schoolfriends and I were preparing for a debate at St Patrick's College on foreign affairs, and we decided to visit Parliament to obtain some information. Those were the good old days — one could wander around the corridors relatively freely, so we decided to visit the area occupied by the then National opposition. Peter Gordon, the late MP for Clutha, noticed us and asked what we were up to. I said we were looking for information to prepare for a debate on foreign affairs. He said he knew exactly who we should talk to and took us to the office of Sir Keith Holyoake, the former prime minister and at that time the opposition MP for Pahīatua. My friend and I spent half an hour chatting with Sir Keith, not so much about foreign affairs but more about him and his illustrious career. I wrote a thank-you letter to Sir Keith a few days later, and on 16 October was thrilled to receive a reply from him, where he said: 'I am delighted to learn that you had a resounding victory in the first round of your debating competition and am equally pleased to know you feel your discussion with me helped you towards your objective. I do hope that you go from success to success and if at any time you think that I might be able to help you, please do not hesitate to call me.'

A few weeks later, we had another debate and decided to visit John Marshall, my local MP and then opposition MP for Karori. We had a brief discussion with Marshall, who was a little more reserved than Sir Keith. He was nonetheless friendly and helpful.

After my experiences with Gordon, Holyoake and Marshall, I decided I really liked National politicians, and it was about then that I decided I would join the party. My friend was not so impressed; I think he joined the Labour party a couple of months later. Anyway, that was my introduction to MPs, and when my time at St Pat's was over I immediately joined the National party as a member of the Khandallah branch.

It was not as though I had any particular dislike of Labour party MPs. The then prime minister, Bill Rowling, lived in my street in Khandallah (as did the great, self-proclaimed child of Wainuiomata, Trevor Mallard). Rowling was an extremely pleasant and neighbourly man. At one stage I held the exalted position of caretaker of Cashmere Avenue School and was responsible for, among other things, maintaining the swimming pool. Rowling and his children used to swim in the pool on many occasions. I always felt sorry for the Rowling children, particularly during the 1975 campaign when a lot of nastiness was being directed at their father about his being a mouse or a shiver looking for a spine to crawl up. I thought he was treated badly by Robert Muldoon and others and did not deserve it. His family suffered greatly as a result.

In the early 1970s the Karori electorate was one of the jewels in the crown of the National party, with more than 5000 members spread across a number of branches. The Karori branch, for example, which ran from the Karori Cemetery to the mall, had over 1500 members and the Khandallah branch over 1000 members. The leaders of the electorate were important figures in the community — business-people, lawyers and other professionals. The chair of the Karori branch, for example, was Dan Stevenson, then a senior partner at the Wellington law firm Izard Weston. In 1975 the electorate was preparing for a new candidate because Sir John Marshall had announced his intention to retire after 29 years in Parliament, 21 of which had been as MP for Karori. Sir John had a very interesting approach to constituency work. I once asked him whether he did much and he responded, 'Of course not; those people can look after themselves.' As a list MP, I had a particular interest in the Chatham Islands (in truth, the only area of the Rongotai electorate that really interested me). I spent a lot of time over in the Chathams working to obtain a new barge for Pitt Island (Rangiauria), a new wharf at Waitangi and other such projects. Day-to-day constituency work, however, was not my strength.

The final selection in the Karori electorate was held in the hall of the teachers' college on Donald Street. It was considered a significant event in the life of the National party and more than 300 people were present, many of whom were voting delegates. The final four nominees were very impressive. There was Hugh Templeton, former Rhodes Scholar and diplomat, who had been the MP for Awarua from 1969 until his defeat in the 1972 land-slide, after which he worked for the National party. Then there was Julian Watts, a partner in the leading law firm Watts and Patterson. Watts had a postgraduate degree from Cambridge University and was very highly respected in the law and in politics. He had stood for National in Western Hutt in 1972 and did very well in what was a bad year for the party. Doug Catley, a very respected and successful businessperson, was the third nominee, and the final nominee was Bill Nathan, a very highly regarded rangatira of Wellington. After the candidates had given their speeches, the delegates voted. Such was the strength of the National party in Karori that the delegates' position was much sought after, and head office did not need to appoint any additional delegates to bring up the number. One of the great weaknesses of the National party in recent years has been that the electorate organisations are so run-down that there either have to be board appointments because the electorate does not have 200 members, or the regional chair has to appoint supplementary delegates because there aren't enough members in the electorate to fill the delegates' slate. One can only hope that, after the 2020 calamity, the party now recognises the need to build good local structures.

There was great excitement when Egan Ogier, the party's divisional chair, announced that Templeton had won on the first ballot. A few days later, the local newspaper had an interesting headline: 'Watch out Rob, Hugh is on the way'. Templeton did not get to the top, but he was an outstanding — indeed probably *the* outstanding — cabinet minister from 1975 to 1984, when he lost Ōhāriu in the Labour landslide of that year. It was a privilege to get to know him in those years. He made a significant and enduring contribution to New Zealand, the most notable of which was as the author of the Australia–New Zealand Closer Economic Relations Trade Agreement in 1983. Politics is a funny business. Templeton should have been minister of education from 1978 to 1981 instead of Merv Wellington, who proved to be a disaster, and he should have been minister of foreign affairs from 1981 to 1984 instead of minister for trade and industry, which was a strange appointment given his lack of commercial experience. The reason for that is that his leader was Robert Muldoon, who didn't build on people's strengths but made appointments for different reasons, most notably loyalty to him. As can be seen from those years, loyalty to Muldoon did not result in good ministerial appointments. People like Colin McLachlan should never have been in cabinet; they held office not based on merit, but on blind loyalty to the leader.

I have already alluded to the 1975 campaign. It was a nasty campaign overall, and unnecessarily so. Bill Rowling was no mouse; he was a decent man and a middle-of-the-road social democrat. Despite this, the campaign in Karori was fun. We used to distribute pamphlets after advertisements were shown on television, including the now infamous 'dancing Cossacks' advert. The electorate was divided between teams, and as soon as the advertisement was broadcast we would put a hard copy of it into people's letterboxes. It was the most efficient way of doing things in the pre-internet age. Another pamphlet we produced and distributed widely had Templeton's face on the front with the caption 'Hugh Templeton: just what Karori needs'. In it there was a somewhat arrogant quote based on something published in *The Economist* in 1972: 'National is our government, Labour is our opposition. Occasionally they change places briefly — and nobody enjoys the experience.'

Once I had finished my university exams I played quite an active role in canvassing, not only in Karori, but also in Miramar for Bill Young. One evening I was canvassing in Maupuia when some very nice Labour party people detained me for a chat. They told me that Australian Governor-General Sir John Kerr had fired Prime Minister Gough Whitlam. I said that was impossible because a governor-general could never fire a prime minister. They were, however, correct. That was a constitutional outrage, and so I was delighted some years later to meet Whitlam in Canberra on the occasion of the twenty-fifth anniversary of the dismissal. There were a number of speeches at a public law conference held at the Australian National University about the dismissal and the reserve powers of the Crown. I was standing next to someone as I was listening to Whitlam give his speech, and said to him that I thought I recognised him. He responded that he had been Whitlam's last minister of defence and told me, 'I have been through this speech with Gough; it's going to be a beauty.' A few minutes later he leaned over and said to me, 'We'll be here for hours. The old bastard has lost his way.'

I had the chance to talk to Whitlam, who was very engaging. He said that he was the great winner of the dismissal because Kerr had died an alcoholic and had been shamed for his behaviour, and Malcolm Fraser, his Liberal successor, had not achieved anything as prime minister. He was correct on both counts.

In 1976 I continued to be active in the Khandallah branch, although I was very busy doing second-year law subjects at Victoria University of Wellington. Among my lecturers was Geoffrey Palmer, who taught me the law of torts. He had been a 'Citizen for Rowling' (a group of well-known and influential New Zealanders who expressed concern about Robert Muldoon becoming prime minister) and was unsuccessful in his quest to become the MP for Nelson when Stan Whitehead died suddenly in 1976. My other lecturers that year included Kenneth Keith, who went on to be a judge of the Supreme Court and then the International Court of Justice, and Robert Quentin-Baxter, who was a member of the International Law Commission. In 1976, Quentin-Baxter taught us all about the reserve powers of the Crown. He said that in the previous year the students had been fast asleep when he taught that subject, and then Whitlam had been fired by Kerr, so he suggested we pay close attention to what were considered to be arcane and irrelevant topics. It was interesting, given my subsequent career, to observe that in 1976 there was not a single mention of the Treaty of Waitangi in constitutional law. How times change.

An early sign that the National party under Robert Muldoon was going off the rails came towards the end of that year. I was studying one night and turned the radio on to listen to Parliament, only to find there appeared to be commotion in the House. That was the night of the Moyle incident, when Muldoon made some outrageous allegations against the then MP for Māngere, Colin Moyle. He had accused Moyle of participating in homosexual activity in Wellington streets late at night. The subsequent events are well known and I need not dwell on them in this book. I can recall, however, that I was part of a canvassing team in Khandallah the following Saturday. People were disgusted with what had happened in Parliament, and doors closed on the National party that were never opened again. The rot had started.

The rot in western Wellington continued after the 1977 boundary changes. Khandallah was taken out of the Karori electorate and placed in Wellington Central, and the refigured Karori seat — which brought in Newlands and Paparangi — was renamed Ōhāriu. Templeton's majority was more than halved and it became a marginal seat. I was the last branch chair of the Karori branch (in 1981) to achieve 1000 members. It wasn't easy but we met our target. The following year membership fell off, largely because of Muldoon's approach to economics, which as David Lange once said was akin to commissars running a Polish shipyard. The boat tax, and subsequently the wage and prices freeze in 1983, were too much and people were not interested in becoming members of the party.

Then in March 1983, Templeton delivered a speech at the AGM of the Ōhāriu electorate. He was perturbed by the intention of Bob Jones to contest the seat as an independent. The speech was entitled '1983: The pursuit of happiness' and it was incredible, especially these lines: 'Mr Jones is a man who seems to hate. Mr Jones is a man who despises many people — bureaucrats, civil servants, politicians, women, Jews, professionals. Doesn't it sound familiar? The politics of hatred.' I was sitting next to my old friend Sid Moses, former chair of the Decimal Currency Board. Like me, he could not believe what he was hearing and was muttering under his breath, 'Jesus Christ, Hugh, stop it.' Meanwhile, Sid's wife, Dorothy, was remonstrating with him, telling him not to say 'Jesus Christ' because I was a Catholic and would be offended. I wasn't offended by Sid's mutterings, but I was amazed at Templeton's speech, which I thought would bring with it all sorts of consequences — as indeed it did. A few days later, Jones published what I consider to be the funniest ever advertisement in the *Independent Herald*, where he said something along the lines that he admitted it: he hated not only Jews, bureaucrats and women, but also Rosicrucians, muesli and getting up in the morning, and that he had not only killed the Crewes but also Cock Robin. He continued by commenting that as his character was no longer an issue, could the real issues please be discussed. Then he sued Templeton for defamation.[1] The speech heralded the formation of the New Zealand party and Jones stood as the candidate in Ōhāriu in 1984, attracting a lot of support, particularly in areas such as Churton Park. I never attended any of the candidates' meetings, but understand that Jones's performance as a stand-up comic proved popular. The same was true of other New Zealand party candidates in Wellington, one of whom was Mike Bungay, a leading barrister who had represented Bill Sutch in the espionage trial of 1975. Bungay told a friend of mine, George Barton, that winning was not supposed to be part of the agreement. He had wanted to stand to have a bit of fun. He was, however, attracting so much support at one stage that he was fearful he might actually win the seat.

These were awful times for the National party. Support had dried up, the electorate was looking for something different and the administration appeared to be tired. Walking to work at around this time was always an exciting experience, because in the early 1980s some very clever left-wingers started posting billboards around the city with slogans such as 'Rooting pig shot in Ngaio — PM safe' and 'What's the difference between a leader and a deputy leader? The deputy leader lies about the land while the leader lays about the land'. The latter was published shortly after the Marginal Lands Board inquiry, where former Deputy Prime Minister Duncan MacIntyre had been criticised over a loan that had been granted to a member of his family. No one ever determined who the authors of these billboards were, but they certainly amused Wellington commuters at the time.

I did not play an active role in the 1984 election, thank goodness. I had reluctantly agreed to go back as chair of the Karori branch in 1984, having had a break from active involvement in 1983. It was a foolish thing for me to do. The electorate was in disarray, membership was hard to get, money had gone and Templeton was rightfully panicking about his prospects at the general election. This was to be held in November, although subsequently of course it was held on 14 July following Muldoon's crazy decision to call a snap election. One morning Templeton called on me, told me I wasn't doing enough work and asked me to resign. Looking back now, it was one of the best things that ever happened to me. I was able to concentrate on my work and finishing my Master of Laws, and avoided being part of the train wreck that was the National party campaign in 1984.

For the next few years I was more interested in work than involvement in the National party. I helped the party out in the early 1990s, as counsel for the caucus when Winston Peters was thrown out.

I always recall the day he appeared before the National party executive. My major task that day was to fill his glass with water. His was a rambling and incoherent defence of his actions, and it came as no surprise when my secretary brought me in a note saying, 'Geoff Grant telephoned to advise he has been advised by National executive that their decision was to exclude Winston Peters from being the National party candidate for the 1993 election by a substantial majority.'

I can't emphasise enough the importance of political parties. I think the Conservative politician Douglas Hurd, in his brilliant biography of Robert Peel, got it right when he said:

> The question . . . is whether political parties are any longer the acceptable vehicle for political thought and action. Today's intelligent citizens remain deeply interested in political issues, but do not see why they have to be discussed in the raucous way normally adopted by political parties. They turn instead to pressure groups outside Parliament which offer a clear though narrow message. Supporters of Greenpeace or Amnesty International or the World Development Movement would have felt at home in the Anti-Corn Law League or O'Connell's Catholic Association. But pressure groups cannot balance out the different arguments and interests; only Parliament and politicians can do that.[2]

Membership of political parties is not what it used to be, and I think this is unfortunate. When the National party in Karori was strong and the leading lights of the community were active in it, it could make a substantial contribution to politics. I cannot speak for the Labour party, but I can say that National electorate organisations these days are very weak and do not contain the leaders of the community. That weakness has consequences — in particular, the branches too often select mediocrities as their candidates.

I referred to the selection in Karori in 1975 to show what the National party used to be capable of achieving. I don't think that there have been many selections of that quality since. So many selections, as I said, are made by the board because of the weakness of the local electorate, or the regional chair has to supplement the delegates because the local organisation is so weak. In 1987 and 1990, weak candidates were chosen to carry the National banner in Ōhāriu. I mean no disrespect to the candidates, but they simply were not up to it. This meant that Peter Dunne's majority in 1987 was about 1000 more than it should have been, and it also meant that in 1990, when National should have won back the Ōhāriu seat, it continued to be held by Labour. In early 2005 I was asked by the president of the National party, Judy Kirk, to stand for the Ōhāriu seat. I was very happy to do so because it was my tūrangawaewae. The local organisation, however, did not like me for various reasons, principally because I was a lawyer. They preferred Katrina Shanks, who went on to serve for five or six years before she left in early 2014. She was succeeded by Brett Hudson, who lost the seat to Peter Dunne, then Greg O'Connor. The National party will get truly good candidates only when it rebuilds its grassroots membership, rebuilds its branches and takes an excellence approach to candidate selection.

When I first joined the National party, members used to sneer at Labour party selections. It was felt that most Labour candidates were either teachers, trade unionists or ex-student association presidents. The National party always considered itself superior in terms of getting people with experience in the law, business or otherwise. But some years on, is the National party any better than the Labour party? We no longer have enough candidates with experience and knowledge of the outside world and who are active in their communities. The concern was expressed very well by Douglas Hurd, when he said about Westminster:

> Forty years ago there was no ladder which went upwards from university or school directly into national politics. In practice, a young man or woman interested in politics had to go and do something else for 15 years before they could seriously be considered as an MP. That has changed. The palace of Westminster is thronged with eager young men and women who have done nothing but politics all their lives. The highly professional politician is particularly vulnerable to the single issue and the pressure group. They have not learned in practical work-a-day careers how to balance conflicting interests before they reach a decision. The number of MPs with outside experience who could provide a counterweight to the more professional politicians has greatly reduced, even in my political lifetime. This narrowing of experience also threatens to unbalance the relationship between ministers and civil servants. A minister should complement the analytical skills of the permanent officials. He should not be an official with an ideology.[3]

I have looked at some of the selections for the National party in recent years and cannot understand how people such as Jami-Lee Ross, Andrew Falloon, Jake Bezzant (Paula Bennett's 'game changer') and others were ever selected. In my opinion, people like that can make no contribution to the National party or to politics in New Zealand. The gross negligence of the party in allowing its base to run down so that these sorts of people are selected can be tolerated no longer.

Kirk became president of the National party after the 2002 calamity, and was very compassionate and wise in the role. She started the candidates' college, the purpose of which was to introduce candidates or would-be candidates to the National party and give those people the chance to understand it. It operated very well, but under Peter Goodfellow's leadership, I don't think the candidates' college was made enough use of. I hope that the initiative is revived and selects very strong candidates for the 2023 election. It seems the mistakes of one generation have to be relearnt the hard way by the next generation.

Some of my comments may appear to be extreme criticism of the National party. In fact, they are the observations of someone who has been active in the party for many years and who cares about its future. When I joined the National party in the mid-1970s it was a very strong organisation led by community figures who gave of their time, even though they were very busy. Elections of candidates, even in strong Labour seats such as Island Bay, were often contested because the branches were active and people were ambitious for New Zealand rather than for themselves. How can the mistakes of the past twenty or so years be addressed? I think the prescription is as follows:

- The party needs to rebuild electorate structures and build branches up once again, even in urban electorates. That will enable it to connect more effectively with individuals.
- The party needs to re-establish the candidates' college and make it a requirement that, in order to stand, any potential candidate must have graduated from this college.
- The board must vet candidates properly before they are permitted to run. Failure to check the credentials of potential candidates has, in the past, caused huge embarrassment to the party. This vetting will involve rigorous financial assessments, proper inquiries of a candidate's curriculum vitae and thorough reference checks.
- Anyone who has worked in Parliament as a policy adviser or executive assistant should not be eligible to stand unless they have had a job in the real world for at least five years. The board

could have the ability to grant an exemption in exceptional circumstances.

- Finally, some active involvement in the National party should be mandatory. There is no substitute for having been a branch or electorate chair. There are many people who have become MPs because they are careerists and not because they actually care about the National party. People need to learn loyalty to party and not loyalty to self. They also need to understand that when they enter Parliament they are stewards of brand National and must do whatever is necessary to protect that brand. In the penultimate chapter of this book I will talk about the nauseating experience of the years 2017–20, when people destroyed the brand of the National party because they were selfish and self-serving.

After the disaster that was the 2002 election, the National party regrouped and went on to make massive advances in 2005. Much of what I have discussed in this chapter was addressed in 2003 and 2004. Because those lessons were not learnt properly, however, the party had to endure the humiliation of the 2020 election and start over. One hopes that these fundamental lessons will not be ignored again.

CHAPTER 2 Early days in the law

AFTER COMPLETING MY UNIVERSITY STUDIES, I entered the legal profession. Over the course of the next twenty or so years, I was lucky to be an employee and/or partner in two very fine law firms. In 1980 I joined Brandons, which is the oldest law firm in the country, established by Alfred de Bathe Brandon in Wellington in 1841. When I joined, the firm had a strong practice in banking and public law. It acted for most of the local authorities in the Greater Wellington region, as well as the Bank of New South Wales and the National Bank. I was fortunate to have Peter McKenzie as my first boss. Peter had been a senior lecturer in company law at Victoria University before joining Brandons. He is a great New Zealander, and the thing I most associate with him is his commitment to social justice. Every Tuesday afternoon, he would go to Porirua East to help underprivileged members of the community in Cannons Creek, and I remember a number of occasions when senior officers of the Bank of New South Wales had to wait outside his room because he was dealing with the immigration concerns of a local family. In 1982, he had an extended sabbatical from Brandons so that he could work in the East End of London and establish an immigration centre there. These days lawyers produce glossy publications proclaiming their commitment to pro bono work and social justice; Peter did it without the self-promotion. He is also an outstanding company lawyer and an original thinker. During my time as minister for Treaty of Waitangi negotiations, I would suggest to officials that if ever there was a difficult conceptual issue to be addressed, they should speak to him. In addition, Peter was chair of the Securities Commission of New Zealand for some years, in recognition of which he was awarded Companion of the New Zealand Order of Merit.

I was fortunate to do some wonderful work in my years at Brandons. In 1984 the firm merged with Beyer, Christie, O'Regan and Dunning. The senior partner of that firm, Colin Beyer, gave me some very interesting files. Perhaps the most intriguing was a case brought by the English television personality Hughie Green against the Broadcasting Corporation of New Zealand (BCNZ) for breach of copyright of the format of his television talent quest programme *Opportunity Knocks.*[1] Green was unsuccessful in the New Zealand High Court and Court of Appeal, and in 1989 appealed to the Privy Council in London. Peter McKenzie had been lead counsel in the Court of Appeal, but Green decided that he wanted to instruct Hugh Laddie — probably the most distinguished copyright barrister in England — to act on his behalf in the Privy Council. I juniored to Laddie. Unfortunately, the Privy Council decided that the majority in the Court of Appeal were correct, and that Green was not entitled to claim copyright in something as remote as the format of a talent quest programme. After his loss, the *Daily Mail* ran the headline, 'For Hughie Green Opportunity Flops'.

Some years later, Hughie Green died. At his funeral at the Golders Green Crematorium, one of his friends stood up and declared that he had promised Green he would get on the front page of the newspapers one more time. To the astonished congregation, the eulogist declared that Green had a love child. As it turned out, that love child was Paula Yates, who had been married to Bob Geldof. It was a very interesting case involving a strange man.

At about the same time, Colin Beyer gave me another case involving Cathy Wilson, the former deputy leader of the Values party. Wilson had created a 57-page feasibility study for a television show about a physically disabled boy and girl who performed magic acts. She submitted a study to the BCNZ in the hope that the corporation would produce a television series. They failed to reach an agreement, but while watching television one night Wilson subsequently saw that the defendant had created a television series following her format. She sued the corporation for copyright as well as breach of confidence and was successful.[2]

One of the strangest cases I ever worked on during my time at Brandons involved Porirua City Council and Sir Gerard Wall, the former speaker of the House of Representatives and MP for Porirua. Wall was prosecuted by the council (with me acting for the council) because he would not demolish his builder's shed. Time and time again he was asked to remove the offending building but refused, and when he retired from politics in 1987 the council had had enough and instructed Brandons to prosecute him. Wall represented himself in court before Judge David Ongley. It was a virtuoso performance. In his cross-examination of the town clerk, he accused the clerk of never liking him and claimed the clerk always wanted the nomination for his seat. I objected to that line of questioning, complaining to the judge that every question Wall asked had been irrelevant, repetitious or offensive, and had those questions been asked in the House, Wall would have ruled them out of order. Ongley adopted a very emollient approach, saying that, as Wall was representing himself, he proposed to be lenient.

The prosecution was successful, and Wall was required to demolish the offending structure.[3] Some weeks later, I saw Frank O'Flynn, the former MP for Island Bay, in the street and he said to me, 'I saw your name in the paper in some case the other day.' When I told him that I'd been prosecuting his former colleague Gerry Wall, he said, 'Ah yes, that bloody idiot.'

Peter McKenzie also had many interesting clients, but one of the more absorbing involved the then Social Credit Political League, which was a force in New Zealand politics from the mid-1950s to 1987. The party tasted electoral success on only a few occasions, in Hobson, Rangitīkei and, unbelievably, East Coast Bays. It became involved in much litigation when its former leader, John O'Brien, was dismissed in 1972. There were a number of interesting decisions (from a procedural point of view) involving O'Brien, represented by Bill Gazley of Wellington, and the Social Credit Political League, represented by Peter.[4] In 1983, the Representation Commission was undertaking its five-yearly review of electorate boundaries. Rangitīkei's boundaries were changed and Marton, a very strongly Social Credit town, was taken out of Rangitīkei and moved into the new seat of Waitōtara. This had the effect of making Rangitīkei marginal for Bruce Beetham, the Social Credit leader. Peter acted on that matter, and I helped him — although, of course, I could not appear as I was a member of the National party. The new boundaries were confirmed and Beetham lost in the 1984 general election.

Mention of Bill Gazley reminds me of the time I was with the law firm Bell Gully in the late 1980s, and Bill Wilson and I acted for Gazley when an attempt was made to remove him from a case based on a conflict of interest because he was acting against a former client. The case went to the Court of Appeal, and Gazley was told that he could no longer act, with several of the judges making critical comments about him.[5] Those comments enraged Gazley, and I rang him after judgment was released suggesting that he not do anything too precipitate. He replied, 'Oh Chris, it's a little bit late for that advice.' After the judgment had been released, he had marched down to the High Court and filed a proceeding in which the judges of the Court of Appeal were named as defendants. Gazley was a feisty and strongly independent lawyer, and he was not going to be told by judges that he could not act.

In 1988, Colin Beyer asked me to junior to Jim Farmer QC in a case being brought by the Commerce Commission against Brierley Investments (for whom Brandons acted) and Fletcher Challenge, involving the sale of Winstones by Brierley to Fletcher. Looking back now, I marvel at the way the case was conducted in the High Court. It began in May 1988, and Justice Andrew McGechan supervised the case through all of its interlocutory stages and presided at the trial. Justice McGechan is probably the best trial court judge I ever appeared before. The case proceeded at an amazing pace; Justice McGechan never reserved any judgments but gave oral judgments at the end of argument. The case was set down in early 1989 for a six-week trial. Within a short period, Justice McGechan delivered judgment. It was a very long judgment, reminding us of a quote attributed to Mark Twain: 'I am sorry this letter is so long — I didn't have time to write a short one.'[6] The case never went on appeal and the issue was concluded.

Coming back to the law after a parliamentary sojourn of more than twelve years, I cannot understand why the system seems to be so bogged down with delays and paper. In my early years in the law, it was not unusual for judges to give oral judgments both in the High Court and the Court of Appeal. At the Court of Appeal, it was always nerve-wracking when, at the end of argument, the then president, Sir Robin Cooke, conferred with his fellow judges and then said to counsel that judgment would be delivered immediately. I worry about the state of our civil justice system. It has become increasingly bureaucratic and slow. Some years ago, the Supreme Court took more than eighteen months to deliver a judgment on an issue related to the extradition of Kim Dotcom. This is far too long to wait for a judgment, and it does not serve the interests of justice.

In 1990, after four years as a partner in Brandons, I had my first sabbatical. I was very much looking forward to it and had a farewell drink with my fellow partners in the partners' lounge on the Friday before I departed. I remember one of my partners, David Howman, coming into the lounge to say that an Auckland partner had defected to Simpson Grierson. There was a look of horror on the faces of my fellow partners, as this person had been the Auckland liaison partner for Westpac. I made my farewells and left immediately, and was in St Petersburg (then called Leningrad) when the trouble started. About ten days later, Brandons suspended all sabbaticals and made some major changes as the firm was in meltdown. As for me, I had a very pleasant sabbatical, although I was most concerned the first night I arrived in Leningrad, when I had a call from a strange person who said he wanted to come and talk to me. Some months later, I spoke about the incident to my parish priest, who had a PhD in Russian from the University of London and had spent some years in the country. He told me that even in 1989 the caller would have been a KGB operative wanting to 'monster' a tourist. After Leningrad I went to Moscow, where I had the pleasure of telling the mummified remains of Lenin that socialism had lost out to capitalism (although I am not so sure about that now), and then Berlin, where I witnessed the removal of Checkpoint Charlie. From there I had an opportunity to appear at the Privy Council for a second time, on this occasion with my friend John Upton QC in a case called *Holt v Holt*, which concerned matrimonial property.[7] I then joined Bell Gully, where I had twelve happy years as a partner before going to the Bar in early 2003.

I had many interesting commercial and public law cases in my time at Bell Gully. In one particularly intriguing case in the mid-1990s I acted for the governor of Pitcairn in an employment dispute. The governor's office was situated within the British Consulate in Auckland. The governor, who was also the British high commissioner in Wellington, dismissed his typist. She brought a proceeding under the New Zealand Employment Contracts Act 1991, claiming wrongful dismissal. The governor objected to the jurisdiction of the court of New Zealand, but the Employment Court dismissed his protest. He then appealed, arguing that a New Zealand court did not have jurisdiction to deliberate on these matters because he was entitled to claim sovereign immunity. The Court of Appeal accepted that argument, saying that the doctrine applied in New Zealand unless it was expressly excluded by relevant New Zealand legislation. As the Employment Contracts Act did not explicitly exclude the doctrine of sovereign immunity, the objection to jurisdiction was successful. Some weeks after the decision of the Court of Appeal was released, I received a note from the deputy governor of Pitcairn saying that the case had aroused some interest in London, including an article from the *Daily Telegraph* entitled 'Tiny island fights for the right to be British'.[8]

Sovereign immunity is a very interesting but arcane area of the law, and questions around it very rarely arise in New Zealand. I thought that would be the only time I would ever deal with such a case, but in 2021 I found myself acting for Hungary in a case in the High Court. A French company tried to have an arbitration award recognised in New Zealand and Hungary objected on the ground of sovereign immunity. Relying on the finding of the Court of Appeal in my Pitcairn case, the High Court said that the legislation had waived immunity by necessary implication.[9] As attorney-general, I had earlier tried to persuade the minister of foreign affairs, Murray McCully, that this country needs carefully drafted state immunity legislation, but I never received a reply to the letter I sent him. No surprises there.

I hoped to visit Pitcairn Island, and so the deputy governor arranged for me to go in early 1998. Sadly, however, a senior official of the Foreign and Commonwealth Office in London decided that he also wanted to visit Pitcairn. On the basis that I was the last person on the French frigate travelling to the remote island, I was the first person off, and I had to content myself with going to judge a mooting competition in Vienna. I had another opportunity to visit Pitcairn in 1996, shortly after I returned from a sabbatical. The governor wanted a lawyer to accompany two Kent constables to interview a person who had been accused of sexually assaulting a visitor to the island. I felt I could not go, so despatched one of my staff, David Laurenson, who had a lot of experience in criminal law. He had to sail from Wellington for eight days on a container ship and stayed on Pitcairn for about a week, and then the Brits had to send a yacht from Tahiti to collect him and the two constables to take them back to Tahiti so they could fly home. That visit was the forerunner of the sexual abuse cases that have bedevilled Pitcairn Island for many years. I still hope one day to visit, but I must confess that my chances are not good.

Over the years at Bell Gully, I was lucky to work with Bill Wilson, who was probably one of the leading lawyers of his generation. I worked with him on a number of cases, including the very long *Dairy Containers v NZI Bank Ltd* case in the mid-1990s, which arose because of the fraudulent actions of three employees in a company called Dairy Containers Ltd. The trial, before Justice Ted Thomas, went for many weeks in the High Court at Auckland.[10]

Justice Thomas was an interesting man who in 1993 had been involved in a highly amusing incident when I was a member of the *Victoria University of Wellington Law Review* committee. Thomas submitted an article to the journal on the issue of precedent.[11] It was published as a monograph and attracted a lot of criticism. Perhaps the most withering response came from an Auckland practitioner called Don Dugdale. He wrote an article about the monograph and it was published in the journal under the title 'A polite response to Mr Justice Thomas'. It is fair to say that it was anything but polite, as the final two paragraphs indicate:

> Had E W Thomas entered the church he would no doubt have wanted to write his own Bible. One can see him as a great actor-manager, ruthlessly and without compunction eviscerating the Shakespearean canon in order to do it his way.
>
> But in fact Mr Justice Thomas is to be found not in the pulpit or on the boards, but on the bench, where he must learn that what he calls judicial autonomy the rest of us call indiscipline, and that the bold self-confidence that brought him such merited success at the bar needs to be subjugated to the judicial oath he swore on 23 February 1990. Be it for better or worse, there is in that oath nothing permitting judges to make up the law as they go along in reliance on what they divine to be the sense of justice immanent in the community.[12]

Justice Thomas was not amused by Dugdale's effort. He wrote to the *Victoria University of Wellington Law Review* outlining what he saw as serious flaws in the article. He said it was virulent, that it had badly misrepresented his thesis and that the item itself was without any redeeming scholastic merit, and that its publication reflected very poorly on the journal. The committee sent a copy of this letter to Dugdale, who was unrepentant. He responded:

> I am sorry that my innocent wish to answer a monograph whose author must have known that his intentions would stink in the nostrils of at least some of his readers should have involved the Review in what is no doubt an unwelcome brouhaha. It is disappointing that an author who in the work under discussion proclaims the importance of professional opinion in keeping judges on the straight and narrow should react so badly to an expression of professional opinion that happens to advance a view opposed to his own . . . It would be presumptuous of me to suggest how the Review should respond to his correspondence but I would be saddened if suggestions by your correspondent of defamation and contempt of court and his use of terms like 'virulent', 'calumny' and 'tabloid journalism' were to lead the Review to approach the matter on the premise that His Honour has been in some way wronged. Anyone who embarks on the business of authorship risks an adverse review and this is no less so when the author happens to be one of her Majesty's judges.

You may think that the matter ended there. It didn't. The exchange of correspondence became more and more inflammatory, with Justice Thomas telling the *Victoria University of Wellington Law Review* that, 'other than as an after-dinner speaker, many in the profession today do not take Mr Dugdale seriously, and I am among their number'. He reiterated that the article amounted to a virulent personal attack and demanded an apology from the journal.

What was the committee to do about this unfortunate matter? In the end, the dean of the Auckland Law Faculty was asked to take Justice Thomas to lunch to try to resolve the matter, which he successfully did.

I have kept this correspondence for years. Whenever a letter arrived, I phoned my good friend George Barton QC, who responded: 'See you in Parsons in ten minutes.' I have a feeling that George copied the letters and distributed them to his friends on and off the bench.

I have mentioned George Barton QC on a number of occasions. Along with Peter McKenzie, he was the most outstanding lawyer I met in my time in the law. I was so sad when he died in 2010, and was pleased that the former chief justice arranged a special commemorative sitting so that George could be honoured for his contribution to the law. That contribution was massive. George had been a professor and dean in the Law Faculty at Victoria University, then practised for many years at the Bar. I think he holds the record for New Zealanders appearing in the Privy Council. There are two stories about George that he told me himself and are worth recording. The first is about the rank of Queen's Counsel (QC).

George was walking along Lambton Quay one day, he told me, and former Chief Justice Sir Richard Wild said to him, 'Barton, you should apply to take silk.' George applied but was rejected because he was a professor of law and not a full-time barrister, so he decided he would never apply again. When Sir Thomas Eichelbaum was chief justice, George received a call asking to go and see him. The chief justice simply said to George that he would be taking silk. George asked if he could speak to his wife, and this was refused. He wondered how long he would have to make the decision, and Eichelbaum replied, 'As long as it takes to walk from that chair to my door.' George should have been a QC many years before his appointment, and it was a credit to Chief Justice Eichelbaum that he forced the issue.

My second story about George concerns the way he taught at Victoria University. The students loved him. One year he was teaching civil procedure and the Government Printer refused to publish the Code of Civil Procedure (which was the forerunner of the High Court Rules). So George said to his students, 'What do you do when the Government Printer acts in this way? You sue him.' So the first part of the course was all about the procedure for suing the Government Printer. The students went down to court with George when the case was heard and, when the application for judicial review was dismissed, George said to his class, 'What do you do if you lose? You appeal.' So the second part of the course was all about how to appeal judgments. Unfortunately, the case was lost in the Court of Appeal as well.[13] But that was the brilliance of George. He was an outstanding teacher, an outstanding lawyer and an outstanding human being — as well as being one of the world's best gossips. He is much missed, even though he has been gone from us for more than ten years.

The legal profession is rightly criticised these days for some of its behaviour, which has not always reflected well on us. It is fair to say, however, that there are some outstanding people in the profession who have given a lot to their clients over the years. I always recall the death of an old friend of mine, Peter Martyn, a senior partner in Macalister Mazengarb (and illustrious chair of the Wellington Shakespeare Society). I attended his funeral at the Khandallah Presbyterian Church. A person stood up to give what I consider to be one of the best eulogies I've ever heard. He simply said 'In the course of my career I have had ten accountants and one lawyer', and then, pointing to the casket, he said 'him.' There are rogues in the profession, but there are also some very good people.

One of my partners called me one day in 1993 to asked me to come up to his office as his client had a problem. I went upstairs and was introduced to Tipene O'Regan. Thus began my association with Ngāi Tahu, which has been one of the most interesting and rewarding experiences of my life. I have done a lot of work for the iwi over the years and, now that I have left Parliament, I have started to work for them again. One of the first cases I dealt with involved Whale Watch Kaikōura. Ngāi Tahu sought judicial review of the decision of the director-general of conservation to issue whale-watching licences for Kaikōura. The Court of Appeal held that the director-general had a positive duty to act in good faith reasonably and honourably towards Ngāi Tahu, and that merely consulting the iwi before issuing a permit was not enough to satisfy treaty principles — Ngāi Tahu were entitled to a reasonable degree of preference. This was a major judicial review decision, which has been applied on a number of occasions since that time.[14] I also acted for Ngāi Tahu in litigation leading up to their settlement with the Crown in 1997. It was a very challenging and interesting period. Post-settlement, I did a lot of work with such issues as the valuation of high-country sheep stations and forests. I greatly value my association with Ngāi Tahu and have learnt a lot from them.

In the late 1990s I was involved in two cases that were great training for someone who in later years would serve as minister responsible for the Government Communications Security Bureau (GCSB) and minister in charge of the New Zealand Security Intelligence Service (NZSIS). The first concerned an errant New Zealand-born, former MI6 agent called Richard Tomlinson. He had spent some time in a UK prison for breaching the Official Secrets Act 1989 (UK) and had then decided to come back to New Zealand. The British High Commission instructed Bell Gully to obtain an injunction to prevent Tomlinson from publishing a book in New Zealand. He arrived from Tokyo in the early hours of the morning and was met by one of my staff, who served the injunction on him. Tomlinson's account of the events surrounding the service of the injunction, referred to in a book he subsequently published, was fictional.[15] As described to me by my staff solicitor, David Laurenson, nothing that he alleged had in fact happened; he was a fantasist. Tomlinson then decided to leave New Zealand and subsequently published his book in Russia. He has been unable to return to New Zealand because he was in contempt of a court order, and the last I heard of him he was living on a yacht in Antibes in southern France.[16] That was an exciting and interesting case, if only because we needed to obtain the injunction at about 5 a.m. Justice Lowell Goddard was very understanding in the circumstances.

One would have thought that this would be a one-off case. It wasn't. In 1990, Iraq invaded Kuwait and this resulted in the First Gulf War. British Special Air Service (SAS) soldiers served in that war, including a patrol called Bravo Two Zero. They were captured and subsequently released. The first of their number, under the pseudonym Andy McNab, decided to write a book called *Bravo Two Zero* (1993). That encouraged another of the group, under the pseudonym Chris Ryan, to write his account, called *The One that Got Away* (1995). The SAS and Ministry of Defence became concerned about books published about confidential operations, and the SAS therefore decided to introduce confidentiality contracts. These were all signed by SAS soldiers in Hereford, including another soldier who had served in the Bravo Two Zero operation. He was a New Zealander who subsequently decided to head home, where, in contravention of the clear terms of his confidentiality contract, he decided to write a book. Bell Gully received instructions to stop him. We were unable to prevent a documentary on this person being broadcast on TVNZ, and the case proceeded to trial in late 1999 before Justice Peter Salmon in the High Court at Auckland. The defendant was successful in the High Court, whereupon we appealed to the Court of Appeal. This held that he could publish the book but would have to account to the British government for the proceeds.[17] He appealed to the Privy Council, where he was unsuccessful.[18] It was a great honour to appear for the attorney-general for England and Wales in the Privy Council in London. The soldier did subsequently publish the book, after I left Bell Gully, and there was a dispute about the payment of royalties.[19]

One of the highlights of my time as counsel in that case was to be asked to go to Hereford at short notice to brief some of the soldiers. That involved leaving New Zealand on a Tuesday and flying straight through to London. After a helicopter ride from Chelsea to Hereford, the legal team briefed witnesses for a couple of days, flew back to London and then flew home the following morning, arriving back in New Zealand on the Monday morning. It was an unreal experience but really interesting to go to the home of the SAS. As I say, the experience of acting for MI6 and the SAS held me in good stead for my subsequent career as spymaster in New Zealand.

In 2005 I decided to stand for Parliament. By that time, I was acting for the Sisters of Mercy, where a woman alleged she had been abused at St Joseph's Orphanage in Upper Hutt. She commenced a proceeding against the Sisters of Mercy for negligence and breach of fiduciary duty. She alleged that the nuns had failed to protect her from physical and emotional harm, and had failed to promote her educational opportunities. She also said that she had suffered sexual abuse from carers during holiday placements. This was always going to be a long and difficult case, and it was set down for a trial commencing in mid-2005. By that stage I had been selected as the candidate for Mana and there was a lot of talk about a possible early election. I explained my predicament to the leader of the opposition, Don Brash, who very generously told me that I should concentrate on finishing the case for the nuns and that I could come into Parliament after that. I was going to be in Parliament after the 2005 election because I was at 27 on the National party list.

The case went on for many weeks. I had to call numerous witnesses, including nuns who were in their nineties. I will never forget the evidence given by one nun about the mother of the plaintiff contacting the orphanage to say that she would be able to take the child and her two sisters for the Easter break. The children were so excited at the prospect of being reunited with their mother. The nuns dressed them and organised presents for the mother, and then the children sat at the entrance to the orphanage all Easter because the mother failed to show up. The plaintiff was indeed very damaged, but it was not the nuns' fault. The Sisters of Mercy 'succeeded' in both the High Court and the Court of Appeal, although of course, no one ever succeeds in this sort of litigation. It was a very sad case.[20]

I know that the Catholic Church is copping a lot of flak at the moment over child abuse. Church representatives have appeared before the Abuse in Care Royal Commission of Inquiry. These are very sad and difficult issues, which I am sure the commission is anxious to address in a just and sensitive manner. There was abuse in Church institutions and such abuse can never be tolerated or condoned. But equally — and this was my experience as a student of Catholic institutions at primary and secondary school level — there was a great deal of love and care. Not every nun or priest is a monster; the vast majority of them are dedicated to God's service and the Church. While the plaintiff made very serious allegations in this case, and the nuns were required to defend the case, she was cared for appropriately and the nuns could not be held to account for the failings of her parents or the carers in the holiday placements.

For 25 years I had been very fortunate to have worked in two excellent law firms — Brandons and Bell Gully — and then to have a couple of years at the Bar. I had been involved in a number of fascinating cases and will always be grateful to people like Colin Beyer and Bill Wilson who gave me the opportunities that came my way. During this period, I was also actively involved in the New Zealand Law Society, being its nominee for bodies such as the New Zealand Council of Legal Education (where we introduced compulsory ethics), the New Zealand Council of Law Reporting, and the Rules Committee (which governs the practice and procedure of the courts of New Zealand). I also taught civil procedure and other subjects part-time at Victoria University.

I felt in 2005 that I was ready to contribute to public life. Having been very active as a lawyer in private practice, and having spent many years serving in the back rooms of the National party, I was prepared to put my name forward. It was not a comfortable transition, but it was one I was willing to make.

Also in 2005, the solicitor-general phoned me to say that I should put my name forward to be a QC. I applied, but in due course I received a letter telling me that my application had been unsuccessful. I was annoyed at the time because I had not intended to apply at that stage. Michael Cullen was the attorney-general and his office made it clear to a journalist there was no way I could be appointed as I was a member of the National party standing for Parliament. I would probably have made the same decision. What was pathetic, however, was the constant petty reference to me as a failed QC after I entered Parliament. When I became attorney-general in 2008 I was quite happy to leave the matter there, as I did not think it would be appropriate for me to appoint myself a QC. Before I went to the International Court of Justice, John Key called me over to his office in late 2012 and told me he had the power to make me a QC and was going to do so. I remonstrated with him, saying I would have preferred to go to the International Court of Justice as an ordinary barrister, but he refused to countenance this. Thus, I was made a QC, along with the new solicitor-general, Michael Heron. Since then, some people have said I appointed myself a QC, which is simply untrue. Other attorneys-general have been made QCs while in office — including Martyn Finlay and Paul East, before they represented New Zealand in the International Court of Justice in the French nuclear test cases.

I have tried here to outline some of the interesting cases I have been involved in over the years to illustrate how well they prepared me for a career in public life. Little did I know that I would one day be attorney-general, minister for Treaty of Waitangi negotiations and minister in charge of the New Zealand Security Intelligence Service. I had had a number of cases in the area of treaty negotiations and intelligence, and was grateful for that experience. Looking back now, I was very nervous about abandoning a comfortable life at the Bar and going into politics. I had always thought that I would remain a backroom person in the National party, and it never really occurred to me that I would enter Parliament. But having made my decision in early 2005, it was time for me to prepare for a life in active politics.

CHAPTER 3 In opposition

ON THE MONDAY after the 2005 general election, I completed closing submissions in my High Court trial and then hung up my gown, not expecting to use it again for some years. The following day I went into Parliament and was allocated an office opposite Wayne Mapp, MP for North Shore. Over the years Wayne had become a good friend and source of advice. It was disappointing for him that, after such a long apprenticeship, he served only three years as a minister, from 2008 to 2011. He then left politics and joined the Law Commission. Wayne is a good example of a person who did not have much luck in the world of politics. He entered Parliament towards the end of the National government in the 1990s and had to endure nine long years in opposition before he became a minister.

Life as an opposition MP in the third term of a government is a very positive experience. The Clark government was looking increasingly tired and out of touch in its third term. The best example of this was the foolish decision in 2007 to introduce the electoral finance legislation. While there were certainly areas of campaign financing that needed to be tidied up, the Clark government erred by imposing a solution rather than adopting a consensual approach. It is very important in many areas of administration that National and Labour agree, or else the solution will not be enduring. As minister of justice between 2008 and 2011, Simon Power had to tidy up the mess.

Shortly after I arrived in Parliament, Don Brash, leader of the opposition, asked me to be the shadow attorney-general, associate minister for Treaty of Waitangi negotiations, and associate minister for arts, culture and heritage. Tim Groser was appointed spokesperson on arts, culture and heritage, and he and I worked well together, visiting arts organisations and talking about ways in which National could try to appeal to this community, which was traditionally hostile towards the party. I also became deputy chair of the Justice Committee, which played to my strengths as a lawyer, and was appointed to the Māori Affairs Select Committee.

Soon after I joined the Justice Committee in 2005, the Evidence Bill had to be considered. This was a once-in-a-generation overhaul of the law of evidence and raised issues that were both difficult and technical. The chair of the committee, Lynne Pillay, said she thought that, rather than the full committee dealing with the subject, a subcommittee should be appointed. She suggested Russell Fairbrother MP as the chair, assisted by the Green MP Nándor Tánczos, list MP Richard Worth and me. This was my first experience of detailed committee work and it was a positive one. Russell was an excellent chair and had a good knowledge of the law of evidence based on his many years as a criminal barrister. When I heard Nándor was coming on the subcommittee I was a little sceptical, but his contributions were excellent. I liked him and felt that the Greens could have used him better. After Nándor left Parliament and I became minister for arts, culture and heritage, I appointed him to the board of Creative New Zealand because I thought he could make a real contribution, as indeed he did. Richard, a former senior partner of Simpson Grierson and an experienced litigator, also made a good contribution to the discussions. Owing to the technical nature of the bill, the subcommittee appointed former High Court Judge Robert Fisher QC as adviser. Robert said there were a number of key changes that needed to be made, but that we should not get bogged down in the detail. He was an astute adviser and we greatly appreciated his advice.

There were many submissions on the Evidence Bill, and I recall very well the day a number of judges were presenting to the subcommittee in private. Audrey Young of the *New Zealand Herald* sat outside the committee room and was infuriated because she was not permitted to enter, although it was generally understood that when judges make submissions, this is done in private. A number of judges turned up, led by the then chief justice. They were generally dismissive of the proposed reforms and suggested that developing this area of the law be left to them. They were wrong, and the bill that emerged has stood the test of time very well. Before the judges came into the meeting room, Russell was adamant that they were on our patch and that we should not stand up for them when they entered.

Every year, select committees were invited to bid for an overseas trip, generally to Australia. In 2007, the Justice Committee was successful in its bid and a trip was arranged to Victoria in Australia. When I saw the proposed itinerary prepared by Lynne, I was unimpressed. I thought it looked to be a complete waste of time, and I, for one, was not interested in going on some kind of junket to meet with Victorian Labour MPs. I spoke to Gerry Brownlee, then shadow leader of the House, and asked whether it would be possible to pull the National MPs out of the trip, and he was quite happy for us to do so. However, we were roundly criticised by some elements in the media for pulling out of what we considered to be a wasteful and useless trip. If on the other hand, we had gone on the excursion, we would all have been criticised for going on a wasteful and pointless trip. I learnt an important lesson from this: with some sections of the media, it is impossible for MPs to do the right thing; whatever we do will be wrong. This was particularly the case, in my opinion, with the Stuff newspapers, which were invariably anti-National.

Early on, I received some excellent advice from Labour's Marian Hobbs, MP for Wellington Central. She used to laugh at Tim Groser and me as we sat together in the chamber during question time, reading either *The Spectator* or *The Economist.* She suggested that we put the magazines away and try to show some interest in proceedings. She also said to me that opposition can be a fruitful time, and that it was important to do the thinking and the reading before we became ministers, as we simply wouldn't have the time once we had assumed ministerial responsibilities. She was correct. Opposition can be a waste of time for those who are not prepared to think, read and consult. For those who are keen for higher office, however, it gives the opportunity to reflect on what they want to achieve once they assume office and refine policies. One of the major failings of the Labour party between 2008 and 2017 is that they did not do the necessary work in opposition. They were consumed with leadership changes and scoring petty points in the chamber. This may make for headline-grabbing politics, but it is no substitute for hard work. Of course, that failing is not limited to the Labour party. Between 2017 and 2020, National MPs fell into the same trap. They were consumed with in-fighting and quick headlines rather than thinking through, for example, the role of the state, which grew rapidly following the outset of the Covid-19 crisis.

One of the most important contributions made to policy development between 2005 and 2008 was the work done by Maurice Williamson on the broadband roll-out. Maurice, who had been MP for Pakuranga since 1987, had fallen out of favour with elements in the leadership, but I always regarded him as a very fine MP and minister. As a former minister of communications, he had a real interest in the broadband initiative and could see the future better than many people. We spent quite some time in 2007–08 talking about his policy proposals, and they were eventually adopted and became a key part of the National party's campaign in 2008. Steven Joyce was subsequently appointed minister for communications and information technology, and was responsible for developing the policy in government, but a lot of the hard work and thinking had been done by Maurice in opposition. Because of his work, the broadband roll-out was a great success and has subsequently had a profound impact on New Zealand, particularly during the lockdowns occasioned as a result of Covid-19. One can say in a very real sense that, because of Maurice's work, people were able to work from home during the lockdowns and continue to contribute to the economy. Without his efforts, I do not believe the roll-out would have been as successful as it was, and there would have been consequent devastating results for the economy. So, work done in opposition can and does matter.

The 2005 National party intake was generally impressive. Large parts of New Zealand swung in our direction, bringing in some fine new MPs who would make a significant contribution to politics over the next decade. In Hawke's Bay, for example, Chris Tremain and Craig Foss won the seats of Napier and Tukituki, respectively. Tukituki had always been a marginal seat, but winning Napier was a real coup — it hadn't been in National hands since the 1950s. The indefatigable and loyal campaigner Chester Borrows won back

Whanganui on his third try, and Anne Tolley picked up East Coast. Anne had been a list MP between 1999 and 2002, when she lost her seat during the Labour landslide. It was great to have her back, and she went on to make a significant contribution to politics. In the following years she would be junior whip, chief whip, minister of education, minister of police, minister of corrections and minister of social development. She finished her career in 2020, having been deputy speaker.

In the South Island, Jo Goodhew beat Labour's minister for trade negotiations, Jim Sutton, in Aoraki, and Jacqui Dean won the Otago seat from David Parker. Jacqui's win was no surprise, as the Otago seat generally went Labour every 30 or 40 years for a term and then was regained by the National party. Nicky Wagner also came into Parliament, having stood for the second time in Christchurch Central. She had had a great career in business and subsequently went on to regain (unbelievably) the Christchurch Central seat in 2011. Someone from this time who became a good friend was Chris Auchinvole, who was elected as a list MP, having done well as our candidate in the West Coast-Tasman seat. Chris had had a career in business, before moving to the West Coast and deciding to stand for Parliament. Michael Cullen once said of Chris that, when he won the West Coast-Tasman seat for a term in 2008, it was unbelievable that the region's working-class voters had elected a toff as its MP. Chris may have given the impression of being a toff, but in fact he was anything but. His father had been a Royal Air Force serviceman who was killed during the Second World War and Chris grew up in penury in Scotland. He and his family came out to New Zealand in the 1960s and he built his career here. A lay preacher in the Presbyterian Church, he was always generous with his time in voluntary organisations. Chris never attained ministerial office but was greatly loved in our caucus.

Another National candidate who came into Parliament in 2005 and made a very good contribution to politics over the next decade was Jonathan Coleman. He won Northcote, having been unsuccessful as a nominee for the Tamaki electorate. Jonathan went on to hold the immigration, defence and health portfolios between 2008 and 2017. Sadly, he left politics shortly after the change of government in 2017. He rang me after John Key resigned and asked if I would support him for the leadership. I think he would have made an excellent leader or deputy leader, but not at the end of 2016 — he needed more experience, and I told him so. That in no way detracts from the high opinion I have always had of Jonathan. The other person who came in at this time for whom I have great respect is Nathan Guy. Nathan's family had farmed in Horowhenua for well over a century, and his father had been chair of the Horowhenua County Council, which Nathan himself served on. Nathan lowered the majority for Labour in Ōtaki from 7000 to a few hundred in 2005, and then won the seat in 2008. He went on to serve as junior whip, chief whip, and then minister of immigration and minister for primary industries. It was a great shame when he, too, decided to retire from politics in 2020.

The MPs I have mentioned generally stayed in Parliament for between nine and fifteen years. I do not think that term limits will ever be imposed in New Zealand, but I do see that there is a very good argument for compulsory three-year sabbaticals for anyone who has served in Parliament for fifteen years, during which they should re-enter the real world. If they subsequently wish to stand for Parliament again, then that should not be prohibited. I do not think in today's world it is possible for a person to make a contribution to politics if they are a professional politician; they need time out. I always enjoyed my sabbaticals from the law firms at which I was a partner. They gave me a chance to refresh, and they also gave the other partners an opportunity to look at my files to make sure I was acting in a professional and competent manner. I think the same argument applies to sabbaticals in politics. If a person goes back into the real world, they are not only refreshed by the experience, but they can also reflect on whether they want to go back into politics or do something different.

It was pointed out to all the new MPs that we had to disclose our assets and interests in an annual Register of Pecuniary Interests of Members of Parliament. I did so at the time, not knowing that some years later my declaration would come under attack. For some years I had been a trustee of a number of family trusts set up by friends. As a result, my name appeared on the title of their properties as an owner and, shortly after I became a minister, Trevor Mallard started to make all sorts of accusations about my failure to properly complete my declaration under the register. It all seemed nonsense to me, so I made enquiries of the then registrar, who lamely said, 'If in doubt, declare.' I always find that kind of approach unsatisfactory. In no way were the interests pecuniary, because I was acting as a trustee, but I duly complied and amended my declaration. My major contribution to this area of politics is that the register is now called the Register of Pecuniary and Other Interests of Members of Parliament. Its purpose is to promote the highest standards of conduct, thereby strengthening public trust in parliamentary processes. I still fail to see how this noble objective is achieved by listing friends' family trusts for which I am a trustee.

I enjoyed the years from 2005 to 2008. The work was interesting, National had been reinvigorated by the arrival of many new MPs, and it was looking increasingly likely that there would be a change of government in 2008. About nine months after I went into Parliament, Don Brash phoned me to say that he had decided to retire from politics. I was personally fond of Don and acknowledged his great contribution to New Zealand. He had been an effective governor of the Reserve Bank of New Zealand and had come into Parliament as an opposition MP when the National party suffered its worst-ever defeat. He reunited the centre right in 2005 and came within a whisker of being prime minister that year. Unfortunately, after he left Parliament, instead of choosing to accept a diplomatic post and serve on a number of boards, he decided to stay in politics and become leader of the ACT party. In my opinion, that was a serious mistake, and he harmed his reputation as a result. That said, I think Don made a significant contribution and I was sorry when he decided to leave politics.

Following Don's resignation, John Key offered himself as the leader of the party and was unanimously elected. His deputy was Bill English. Gerry Brownlee, who had been Don's deputy from 2003 to 2006, acted with class and dignity in agreeing to step back as deputy leader to enable Bill to take that position. Gerry was deputy leader during some very difficult years and did an excellent job, and he has continued to be a very loyal and hard-working member of the party for many years. He was doubtless devastated about losing Ilam in 2020. If it had been me, I would not have returned to politics after that defeat, but Gerry did stay on, and at the time of writing is National's spokesperson for foreign affairs. Many people in Christchurch criticise him for his work after the earthquakes of 2010 and 2011, but I witnessed first-hand his commitment to his city and his desire to rebuild as quickly as possible. Gerry was a decision maker who got things done. Some people want simply to debate incessantly, but Gerry was determined that his city had to be rebuilt after the earthquakes and he got on with the job. He has made a lasting contribution to New Zealand politics and, as I say, provided yeoman service between 2003 and 2006.

The legislative programme between 2005 and 2008 gave me many opportunities to speak in the House. I have already mentioned the Evidence Bill, but others included the Lawyers and Conveyancers Bill, the Property Law Bill and the Real Estate Agents Bill, among many others. These are all good examples of technical legislation I was involved with during the committee stages in the Justice Committee and made a contribution to in the House during the second and third readings. I learnt early on that you give your best speeches in Parliament when you have no notes. When I gave my maiden speech, I must have written about fifteen drafts, but by the time I finished in Parliament, I hardly ever wrote anything. It is much better to know what you want to talk about and then simply speak — notes can actually be an impediment to making an impact.

Through this period I also began to learn something about my community other than as a lawyer. As the list MP based in Mana, I had to work in that electorate as best I could. It wasn't a particularly easy fit for me. I had had a somewhat traumatic introduction to standing in Mana when I was required to attend a forum in Cannons Creek. Someone asked me what I thought about the National party policy on the Māori seats and I stated the policy. The man then asked me for my opinion, and I said that my opinion was irrelevant because I was standing for the National party, and the party's policy was as I had stated. The man then responded by saying that he didn't like my 'f***ing' tie, and I agreed with him. Unfortunately, he thought I was being flippant, and leapt up on stage prepared to attack me. This attempted assault was deflected by my Labour opponent, Winnie Laban, with whom I have always had a good relationship.

During my campaign, I had been approached by members of the Exclusive Brethren to see if I wanted any help in the electorate. They were offering their services to National candidates throughout the country. I was one of those who politely declined the offer, but after the election I did get to know a few of them. They came under sustained attack after the election, with Labour members calling them a strange cult, weirdos and so on. I felt that some of the attacks went beyond the pale, and defended the group in the House, for which I was roundly criticised by the Labour party. I was once asked to go and speak at the Exclusive Brethren school in Wellington, which was then situated next to Malvina Major Retirement Home in Burma Road, Johnsonville. A few days later, I received a phone call from a journalist at Radio New Zealand, who told me there was a rumour I had been visiting the school and asked me to confirm whether it was correct. I said it wasn't a rumour but a fact, and that I had indeed visited the school to talk about growing up in Khandallah, studying languages and so on. It was all innocent stuff, but material that proved to be potentially very exciting for this rather dreary journalist. Such was the nature of the relationship between the Exclusive Brethren and the National party that one needed to be careful.

As I said, the election of John Key and Bill English heralded imminent change, and I very much looked forward to the 2008 election campaign. I had no particular desire to stand again in Mana. Fortunately, my friend Hekia Parata was running for Parliament and was keen to stand in Mana, where there were many Ngāti Porou voters whom she knew and would enlist to help her fight the campaign. Where was I to go? Ōhāriu was out, as Katrina Shanks had come into Parliament after Don's departure. Wellington Central was a possibility because one-term list MP Mark Blumsky was leaving politics, having decided that it was not for him. That party organisation, however, was looking to former ACT MP Stephen Franks as the candidate in that electorate. Franks was excellent on technical commercial issues, but had some interesting views on criminal and public law. Rongotai did not have a candidate, and so I decided to nominate for that seat. The electorate would have to be one of the most Labour areas in New Zealand, particularly the southern part around Newtown and Berhampore (it was the only place where I was assaulted during an election campaign — unbelievably by an Anglican minister who was obsessed with the National party).

I had a number of interesting interactions with church groups and the clergy during my time in Parliament. Unfortunately, I disagreed with most of what they said. In 2013, for example, the Justice and Peace Commission of the Catholic Diocese of Auckland wrote to me complaining about the Minimum Wage (Starting-out Wage) Amendment Bill. They said the legislation breached Catholic social teaching on just wages and the treatment of vulnerable workers. I thought this was nonsense and replied to say that I disagreed with everything they said:

> How a measure which will allow employers to take a chance on a young employee (who might otherwise have no work at all) can be 'unjust' treatment of that person is beyond me. Hyperbole is never a substitute for rational and coherent argument . . . the Church is not served well by those of its organs which engage in partisan politics. It is quite wrong to use the Church as a mouthpiece for extreme left-wing views. I neither want nor need a lecture from you on Catholic social justice.

A year or so later I received a letter from Cardinal John Dew, the Archbishop of Wellington, inviting me to a picnic on Parliament grounds. The picnic was said to be a chance to celebrate New Zealand, with the sharing of food demonstrating that collectively we have sufficient resources for all New Zealanders to enjoy a moderate standard of living. Once again I was reminded that we are guided by Catholic social teaching, which promotes the principle that everyone has a fundamental right to these things. I declined the Cardinal's invitation, 'which some unkind people may regard as gimmicky, albeit not so gimmicky as your Anglican neighbour's performance where he locked himself in a container for seven days'. I said that I thought the Church would be more influential in our increasingly secular society if it concentrated on spreading the word of God instead of engaging in politics. 'Too often these days the language of "Catholic social justice" is used as a cover for extreme left wing, redistributionist views no longer relevant to modern New Zealand.' I thought Cardinal Dew would benefit from the words of Margaret Thatcher, who gave an excellent speech to the General Assembly of the Church of Scotland in 1988 in which she reminded the clerics present: 'You recall that Timothy was warned by St Paul that anyone who neglects to provide for his own house (meaning his own family) has disowned the faith and is "worse than an infidel".'[1]

I don't know that the cardinal appreciated receiving Thatcher's speech, however, because he wrote back to me providing me with a number of quotes from Pope Francis that indicated how engaging in politics is one way of spreading the word of God. I responded by saying that I didn't regard Catholic social justice itself as a cover for extreme left-wing views, adding, 'Rather, it is the view of Catholic social justice held by the sorts of people who hold picnics to advocate for increased State support and decreased individual responsibility which I regard as a cover for such views.' I tried to clarify my position for the cardinal:

> The point I was trying to make in my letter was that there is a worrying trend and opinion among some in the Church that

> the only legitimate approach to seeking Catholic social justice involves advocating a more powerful State with more control over people's lives. I recall reading in the memoirs of Lord Hurd, the former British Foreign Secretary, that he thought the Anglican Church was rendered less influential in public debate through its blind advocacy for bureaucracy as the solution to social problems. Unfortunately, it seems that approach is ecumenical.

Thus ended my exchange with Cardinal Dew. These interactions remind me of what Prime Minister Jim Hacker once said to Sir Humphrey Appleby in the British sitcom *Yes, Prime Minister*: 'These days, politicians want to talk about God, and the clergy only want to talk about politics.' It would be beneficial for the Church if the clergy concentrated on religious topics rather than politics. My exchanges with the clergy attracted the attention of John Key, who one day said to me that he had had a complaint from some bishops that I had been rude to them. I didn't think I had been rude; rather, I was attempting to tell them how to do their job.

Anyway, I digress. Back to Rongotai. The MP for the electorate was Annette King. I met her for the first time after the 2005 election, and said to her that my mother had told me in no uncertain terms to be pleasant to her as she was a relation. Annette asked me how that was so, and I mentioned my grandmother, whose name she immediately knew. Annette is Mum's second cousin on the Russ side (Chester Borrows also has Russ relations; they were a large Nelson family). She and I were pleasant to one another on the campaign trail and I was always very fond of her husband, Ray, who was thoroughly pleasant and non-confrontational. He would sit in the audience while Annette and I were criticising one another and I was being yelled at by Labour party supporters, particularly in Island Bay, and he always had a delightful grin on his face.

I had no desire to win Rongotai. I once joked, and it was repeated back at me time and time again by Labour MPs, that the first thing I would do if I won is demand a recount. For me, it was and remains totally alien territory. There are a couple of patches that are blue, but most of it is deep red. That said, one of the best aspects of life as a list MP in Rongotai is to do work in the Chatham Islands. The Chathams used to be part of the Lyttelton electorate in the days before MMP, but, since 1996 they have been part of Rongotai. I first went over to the Chathams in 2008 as part of the election campaign, and promised that, win, lose or draw, I would be active in promoting the interests of the islands if I was in government. I was true to my word and spent a lot of time doing my best for the islanders. I got a new barge for Pitt Island (Rangiauria), secured money for the Chatham Islands Museum and established better water reticulation at Kāingaroa in the north, along with other projects. The most important work was a new wharf for the Chathams. I also advocated for improvements to the airport, which are now under way. At one stage, Minister of Finance Bill English said to me that we should simply pay all the islanders around $100,000 and get them to leave the Chathams. He was speaking flippantly, of course, because he understood that if you don't look after communities like the Chathams, why should you look after rural outposts like Dipton in Southland (where he came from), Rakiura / Stewart Island and other such places? The world simply cannot revolve around the metropolitan centres in New Zealand; the regions need to be looked after as well. I put a lot of effort into the Chathams, even though the votes were never there — but that was beside the point. They needed and had a champion while National was in government.

On election night 2008, I succeeded in lowering Annette's majority by a considerable margin, and we did very well in the party vote. My efforts were minimal compared with the hard work of so many other candidates who tasted greater victory, but the critical point was that we were back in government and I was to get my chance as a cabinet minister.

CHAPTER 4

Becoming a minister

A FEW DAYS AFTER THE 2008 ELECTION, John Key phoned me. He was brisk and to the point — not surprisingly given the number of calls he would be making that night. After a few perfunctory comments he simply said: 'Attorney-general, treaty negotiations and arts.' I was elated to be confirmed in those positions and would hold the first two portfolios for the full nine years of the National government, not that I ever imagined this would have been possible the night he called me. Others were not so fortunate. Some MPs were in the ministry but not cabinet, despite their confident expectations to the contrary, while others who hoped for a ministerial position were left out in the cold. Such is political life.

Gerry Brownlee was responsible for allocating offices, and a day or so later he told me that I would be moving to level 5 of the Beehive. Then he called me to say that Paula Bennett, ranked twentieth in cabinet, was keen to work in the Beehive but had been allocated an office on level 6 of Bowen House. He enquired whether I would mind swapping with her, and I replied that I couldn't care less. I spoke too soon, because when I inspected the level 6 office, I found it was a complete dive. I tried to undo the decision but it was too late. I was pretty unhappy with the accommodation I found myself in, and was lamenting that fact to one of my new staff when he mentioned that John Carter, in the ministry but not in cabinet, had a magnificent office on level 19 of Bowen House. It looked down on the parliamentary complex and across to Te Ahumairangi Hill. I went up to level 19 and agreed that the office was indeed fantastic. I phoned the prime minister's new chief of staff, Wayne Eagleson, and suggested that everything would be fine if I could get the level 19 office. He agreed and the change was made without any reference to John Carter. I never told John, who will probably learn of this if and when he reads this book, and I apologise to him if he takes offence. But for me, I think I had the best office for cabinet ministers and I stayed there for many years. I moved across to the Beehive only when instructed to do so by my staff after Gerry offered me Murray McCully's suite when Murray announced that he would be leaving politics at the 2017 election. I shared the nineteenth floor initially with Peter Dunne, who was a minister outside cabinet as minister of revenue and associate minister of health, and more latterly with Todd McClay, who came into cabinet in 2015 as minister of trade.

After the administration was sworn in, one of the first things we all had to do was declare conflicts of interest. The *Cabinet Manual*[1] has specific guidance on ministers' conflicts of interest and states:

> Ministers are responsible for ensuring that no conflict exists or appears to exist between their personal interests and their public duty. Ministers must conduct themselves at all times in the knowledge that their role is a public one; appearances and propriety can

> be as important as actual conflicts of interest. Ministers should avoid situations in which they or those close to them gain remuneration or other advantage from information acquired only by reason of their office.[2]

The Cabinet Office, on behalf of the prime minister, provides support to ministers so that they can identify and manage conflicts of interest, and then follows this up with a meeting to discuss any issues that may arise. Each year, ministers need to review their interests in the light of their ministerial responsibilities and to seek advice where necessary. The *Cabinet Manual* sets out the categories of conflicts of interest, including possible associations that can give rise to those interests. There is also detailed guidance on managing interests, which may include, among other things, transferring responsibility for an issue to another minister or even not receiving certain types of papers that would otherwise be provided.

I immediately declared, for example, that I could not be involved in anything concerning Ngāi Tahu because of my acting for that iwi for many years. Occasionally issues would arise that necessitated my stepping back because of that involvement. Another example, which I refer to in detail in the chapter on my time as attorney-general, was my immediate declaration of a conflict of interest when an issue relating to Bill Wilson, a Supreme Court judge, arose. I could not be involved in that issue because Bill had been a partner of mine at Bell Gully for a number of years and we were personal friends. So I had to watch that particular tragedy from the sidelines as Judith Collins was appointed acting attorney-general to deal with the issue.

Both the Standing Orders and the *Cabinet Manual* have guidance on gifts to MPs and ministers, which have to be declared if they have a market value exceeding a prescribed amount. This includes gifts from foreign governments. I used to list whatever gifts I received in my time as a minister. One day I saw the Russian ambassador's wife on a flight to Auckland and asked where she was going. She said she and her husband were going back to Russia for a holiday and that she would bring me back a present. She brought me back a Putin nesting doll (a modern form of matryoshka doll) that contained previous Russian leaders, including Stalin and Ivan the Terrible (which seems appropriate). It used to occupy pride of place in my office alongside my Gorbachev doll, but in recent months I have put it in the cupboard for obvious reasons.

One of the immediate tasks of an incoming minister is to put together a team of office staff. I always recall Hugh Templeton telling me many years before that he found organising his office both time-consuming and stressful. Fortunately, I found the task easy. I asked Richard May, who had worked in the opposition leader's office, to become my chief of staff. Richard was an excellent organiser and helped me put together a good team. John Harbord joined me as my principal policy adviser and over the next few years provided excellent support on a wide range of issues. He had the patience of Job. One needed those qualities when working with various interest groups to devise solutions to the vexed issue of the Foreshore and Seabed Act 2004. My assistant policy adviser was James Christmas, who had worked for me part-time during my stint in opposition. I said in my valedictory address that James was probably the brightest person with whom I had ever worked. I stand by that statement. He is a history and law graduate from the University of Canterbury and Victoria University of Wellington. I always will be grateful to him for the work he did on the intelligence reforms. James was largely responsible for getting the Māori party on board with those reforms and established a good relationship with the Green party, so that even if they opposed the bill in 2016–17, their contributions were positive and respectful.

I had a reputation for having excellent staff. Both John and James were poached by the prime minister to become his principal policy adviser. And in due course Richard went to work for Gerry Brownlee and spent a number of years organising the House schedule. That requires meticulous planning and Richard was the right person to do it.

I had a number of opportunities to hire press secretaries but chose Ben Thomas, who had been a regular columnist for the *National Business Review*. He had a tremendous rapport with the press gallery and got me off the hook on a number of occasions. He is an astute commentator these days and I really value what he did for me as my press secretary.

I also inherited a number of excellent private secretaries from the Ministry for Culture and Heritage (in my role as minister for arts, culture and heritage), Ministry of Justice (as minister for Treaty of Waitangi negotiations) and the Crown Law Office (as attorney-general). All of them were competent and professional. In 2014, I became the first non-prime minister to hold the GCSB and NZSIS portfolios. Those agencies provided a private secretary whose job it was to liaise between them and my office. I was surprised to learn that this was the first time such a private secretary had been appointed. In the years 2008–14, the job was carried out by the prime minister's deputy chief of staff. That arrangement was criticised by the inspector-general of intelligence and security in a report published in 2014. In order to avoid allegations of a conflict of interest or the perception that the agencies are acting in a political manner, it is important that a private secretary is appointed and the work is not left to a political appointee such as the deputy chief of staff. Many ministers' offices underwent large personnel changes depending on the personality of the minister concerned. I don't like to brag, but my ministerial office was probably one of the most stable offices in the parliamentary complex, if not *the* most stable. I enjoyed working alongside my team and we did some good things together.

Guidance was also provided on the subject of ministerial travel. It is inevitable that a minister needs to undertake overseas travel to meet international obligations or to attend specific meetings. Approval for travel has to be provided by cabinet and there are clear rules on reporting at the end of any visit.

One of Richard May's responsibilities was preparing a list of ministerial travel expenses. He forwarded these to the prime minister's office and they were released to the media on a biannual basis. Once, when Richard and I went to a meeting of attorneys-general in London, we decided to try to cut costs. For a start, we did not accept facilitation at Auckland or Heathrow airports. This is a system whereby a minister can go straight to a VIP lounge to relax while others obtain their boarding pass, check in their bags and so on. It all seemed rather pointless to me and I wasn't too grand to stand in a queue. The same thing applies at the other end, where a minister can simply relax while their bags are collected. Richard and I arrived in London and caught a cab into the city, where we stayed at the East India Club, which is affiliated with the Wellington Club. It sounds rather a magnificent place but is in fact a run-down institution in St James's Square. It is also cheap. I was therefore unimpressed a few months later when a nasty article was published by a *Dominion Post* journalist (surprise, surprise) criticising me for staying at a posh London club. I complained to John Key, who said I should stay at the Sofitel London St James whenever I travelled to the city, which is what I did thereafter. There were never any more stories, even though the nightly rate of the Sofitel was about three times that of the East India Club.

At one stage I received an extremely irate email from someone suggesting it was outrageous that I should stay at Claridge's when

I was in London. I made an enquiry and found that there had been a reference in a documentary on Claridge's to the New Zealand attorney-general staying a few days. The doorman at Claridge's had, however, got it completely wrong — he should have said the governor-general. I went back to the angry correspondent and let him have it, telling him he should check his facts before writing abusive emails to me about all my expenses. He was deeply apologetic.

From time to time other expenses would excite the imagination of some of our biased left-wing journalists. Once, the fact that I had ordered spinach in a restaurant in Washington triggered one journalist. It seems that some people just like to create a story out of nothing. Surprisingly, and perhaps related to the fact that there has been much less travel in these Covid times, comments about ministerial expenses do not seem to feature. Pre-Covid, however, journalists always avoided such criticism of Labour ministers.

Following my ministerial appointments, I immediately received a briefing from each of the departments for which I now had responsibility. Very soon after, I arranged for meetings with the senior leadership team of each ministry. I can recall my first meeting with the solicitor-general, David Collins QC, who had actually been my tutor for the law of contract in 1976. I knew David well and had a high regard for his ability. When he had been appointed solicitor-general a few years before and had been criticised, I said some nice things about him in the *New Zealand Herald*. I remember suggesting to David that it would be good if, as attorney-general, I could appear from time to time in a few cases. He and his then deputy, Matthew Palmer QC (a former dean of the Faculty of Law at Victoria University), exchanged knowing smirks. They knew, and I learnt after a few months, that it is practically impossible for an attorney-general to argue the occasional case. As a matter of reality, there wasn't the time to prepare carefully and, in principle, it is a dangerous thing to do. The only time I actually appeared in a case during my nine years as attorney was in the International Court of Justice in the whaling case. I was a regular attender at the swearing-in of judges in both the District Court and the High Court, but was never involved in any substantive litigation, which as I have said is as it should be. I explain the role of the attorney-general as advocate in the chapter 'The attorney-general' on page 142.

I decided it would be a good idea to visit the Ministry for Culture and Heritage and introduce myself to the team. Their previous minister had been Helen Clark, and I knew that many of them would be grieving at her departure. Most of them were polite, although one particularly obnoxious civil servant said to me 'Who are you?' When I responded 'I'm the Minister', she simply grunted. Over time I would like to think that I gained the respect of the team in that ministry. We certainly achieved some great things together.

The first director of the Office of Treaty Settlements with whom I worked was Paul James, who is now the secretary of internal affairs. He is a fine civil servant and his team were among the best people I ever worked with in government. There had been some talk about restructuring the Office of Treaty Settlements, but I decided against change. Restructuring government departments can be time-wasting and futile — as the Ministry of Business, Innovation and Employment (MBIE) experience shows. Sometimes change is required, but I was not going to have it in the ministries for which I was responsible. I thought treaty settlements had been progressing too slowly, notwithstanding the good efforts by my immediate predecessor, Michael Cullen, between 2007 and 2008, and simply wanted to get on with the job. Restructuring could only delay the process.

It is said, and this was certainly my experience, that most of the work done by a cabinet minister is not necessarily in cabinet but in the cabinet committees. These were refashioned after John Key became prime minister and generally met on Wednesday and Thursday mornings. I served on the newly formed Cabinet Committee on Treaty of Waitangi Negotiations, the Cabinet Domestic Policy Committee, the Cabinet Committee on Domestic and External Security Co-ordination, the Cabinet Legislation Committee, the Cabinet Business Committee, and the Cabinet Appointments and Honours Committee.

The Cabinet Appointments and Honours Committee was probably the most enjoyable. It approved all appointments, for example, to SOEs and Crown Research Institutes. Occasionally, my appointments for organisations such as the Arts Council of New Zealand Toi Aotearoa and the board of the New Zealand Symphony Orchestra also went through the committee. The committee met at least twice a year to consider nominations for New Year and Queen's Birthday honours. As is well known, the honours system comprises the Order of New Zealand (ONZ), the New Zealand Order of Merit, the Queen's Service Order (QSO) and its associated Queen's Service Medal (QSM), and various other awards. The more senior honours, such as the ONZ and Knights and Dames Companions of the New Zealand Order of Merit (KNZM and DNZM), did not often attract a lot of debate. Instead, the focus would be on the Members of the New Zealand Order of Merit (MNZM), the QSM and some of the other lower honours. Actually, these were among the most inspiring applications. Many knighthoods were received, for example, by judges because of the positions they held, but those people who received a QSM or a MNZM had often worked for years without recognition or payment for the benefit of their community. I was always inspired by the material that accompanied those nominations because they allowed me to see the extent of the contribution made by New Zealanders to their various communities. The work was always most enjoyable.

National was not a one-party administration: it had a number of confidence and supply partners. Those parties provided ministers outside cabinet. From the beginning, I had a good relationship with the Māori party ministers, Pita Sharples and Tariana Turia. I have always said that Tariana was my favourite politician. It takes a lot of courage to stand up to one's opponents, but it takes even more courage to stand up to one's friends. That is exactly what Tariana did during the controversy over the Foreshore and Seabed Act in 2004. She is a woman of courage and great principle, and I was keen to work with her on the replacement to this legislation. National and the Māori party had signed a memorandum of understanding, one of the key features of which was a commitment by the government to review the foreshore and seabed legislation to try to devise a more just model. John Key could have formed a government without the Māori party but he wanted to involve them. Thus ensued a strong working relationship over nine years.

I always enjoyed working with Peter Dunne, then MP for Ōhāriu, who served as minister of revenue and associate minister of health (he had held these portfolios in the last three years of Helen Clark's government). He resigned from his ministerial positions in 2013, but came back the following year as minister of internal affairs. He and I worked closely together on Chatham Islands issues. Peter was always on top of his brief and easy to get on with, and I would like to think that together we achieved good things for the Chathams, most notably securing funding for the new wharf at Waitangi.

I had expected to have a much closer relationship with the ACT ministers, given that we were philosophically close, but I found Rodney Hide difficult to deal with. He was minister of local government. The ACT party's performance during the foreshore and seabed legislation reforms was particularly disappointing. Rodney and his team were opposed to the proposed reforms and I was always being asked questions in the House by ACT members. I thought that many of the questions were stupid, such as whether children would be able to build sandcastles on the foreshore if the bill became law. At times it was difficult to be polite. At the end of the day, however, one had to acknowledge that in a coalition government one has to deal with people one does not like. Whether you like or dislike people, you have to get on for the greater good. That comment having been made, however, I acknowledge the excellent work that Rodney did (ably assisted by John Carter) in creating the super city of Auckland. There had been much talk about how to implement the 2009 recommendations of the Royal Commission on Auckland Governance and it was Rodney who pushed through those reforms.

It is often said there are three types of ministers. The first category (relatively small) are those ministers who come into office knowing exactly what they want to achieve and get on with it. Then there are those who are perfectly pleasant and capable, but are largely reliant on the advice from their civil servants. Finally, there are the truly hopeless ones who don't know much about anything and are gone in a relatively short space of time. Over the nine-year period, I saw examples of all three. Some people who became ministers were clearly not cut out for it and were moved on quickly.

I understand that John Key returned from his holiday in early 2013 determined to give the place a bit of a shake-up. Phil Heatley and Kate Wilkinson, both of whom were friends of mine, were asked to stand down. They hadn't done anything wrong, but the prime minister wanted to make some changes to refresh the cabinet in the period leading up to the 2014 election. A prime minister has to understand that there are no friends at the top, and that even if they like a particular minister, that minister is expendable if the circumstances warrant it.

There are certain features of the Key government that are worth mentioning. Unlike the Clark administration, John Key's government was highly decentralised. It's fair to say it was organised more in the nature of a corporate business, with the prime minister as chief executive. He trusted his ministers; they were able to get on with their jobs without necessarily being constantly interrupted by him unless they needed help. John was, however, clinical in making change if that change was required. There was a high expectation that ministers perform and consequences if they did not. There were therefore opportunities to climb the ranks and gain more responsibility if you could persuade the prime minister that you were up to it.

The most important person assisting the prime minister is the chief of staff. John Key was lucky to have Wayne Eagleson as his chief of staff. I had known Wayne for many years, having liaised closely with him when he worked for Jim Bolger. He had briefed me when Winston Peters was misbehaving in the early 1990s and the caucus wanted to take action against him. Wayne was an outstanding chief of staff who worked closely with John Key on personnel and policy issues. He would have been a highly effective minister of the Crown but never seemed to want to get into elective politics, preferring instead to remain behind the scenes. There was no doubt in my mind, however, that he was the equivalent of a senior minister and was highly regarded as one of John's closest confidants. When Wayne spoke, there was no doubt he was speaking with the consent and authority of the prime minister.

The new government was sworn in and settled down to its routine. Unfortunately, the Global Financial Crisis (GFC) served as a bit of a 'welcome', and in my opinion characterised the government in general. The prime minister and his staff attended the first Asia-Pacific Economic Cooperation (APEC) meeting in

Peru in 2008. That was the first of John Key's many international meetings. The biggest part of that agenda was the GFC, and the participants agreed to work towards restoring confidence in their countries' economies. Some of those steps included enhancing regional economic cooperation and intensifying work on structural reform.

Times were tough for spending ministers. As minister for Treaty of Waitangi negotiations, I was asked very early on to attend a meeting with the minister of finance. Bill English and I were there to discuss the proposed settlement with Te Tau Ihu iwi at the top of the South Island. Michael Cullen had almost finished negotiating the outlines of an agreement with the iwi, but Bill considered that the quantum being offered was too large. So my first task as the minister was to lower the quantum figure by around 20 per cent. That entailed a number of tense hui with iwi negotiators.

As minister for arts, culture and heritage, I had great ideas for expenditure, most notably a grand building on the Auckland waterfront that would rival the Sydney Opera House. However, in an age of austerity that kind of project was going to go nowhere. Indeed, in the period leading up to the first budget, I had to work hard to secure some extra funding for the Royal New Zealand Ballet. After all my efforts, I managed to obtain an additional $500,000 per annum. It is not that Bill was being Scrooge-like. Far from it; he was supportive of the arts. It is that times were very tough and there needed to be strict controls on spending.

In early 2009, the prime minister convened the Job Summit. This was an important event that helped define the Key administration, because it was a critical meeting during the GFC and also because the government had started on a zero-sum budget. The summit underlined a lot of economic fundamentals and initiatives that proved so valuable later on. I always remember the discussion about cycleways. It was the prime minister's idea to develop cycleways around New Zealand as a means of encouraging regional tourism. The Labour party had a field day with the proposal and scathingly criticised it as trivial. How wrong they were. These cycleways spread everywhere and have been highly successful. The initiative was John Key's idea and he deserves full credit for its great success.

So, early on the government was economically focused. The GFC defined everything. Accordingly, it was necessary to trim the public sector to save money and to focus on spending only where this was necessary. I think it was during this period that the idea of the social investment approach was developed by Bill English. This involved spending money and investing upfront to allow for future improvements. The social investment approach was discarded by the Ardern administration in 2017, which I think was a serious error.

A few weeks after the 2008 election, the House reconvened. The first item of business was to elect the speaker. Lockwood Smith had been a senior minister in the Bolger–Shipley administrations and was the Key government's nominee for the speakership. He proved to be an effective speaker, and was particularly hard on ministers who did not properly address questions. Under his speakership, the standard of question time improved considerably. Ministers could not get away with less than acceptable behaviour simply because the speaker came from their party. In due course, Smith was succeeded by David Carter. Neither Carter nor Smith attended caucus meetings of the National party. As a matter of principle, it is extremely important for speakers to be impartial and to be seen to be impartial, and that necessitates their 'temporary divorce' from their party caucus. They are champions of Parliament, not of a particular party.

I had a short holiday between 2008 and 2009. In mid-January 2009 I flew to Gisborne with my officials from the Office of Treaty Settlements to begin a series of hui with North Island iwi. I was keen to progress settlements in the Tairāwhiti (Gisborne) region and other areas. My work as a minister had begun in earnest.

CHAPTER 5

My cabinet colleagues

COMMENTS ABOUT MINISTERIAL COLLEAGUES can hardly be regarded as objective. I knew and worked with some fine people over a number of years and, even though I have been out of politics for some time now, I still think highly of many of them and the work they did. The purpose of this chapter is to talk about some of the colleagues with whom I worked closely and to record their achievements because, in many instances, their good work has not been chronicled.

Obviously I need to start with John Key. John was a remarkable prime minister from 2008 to 2016. I did not know him very well when I first went into Parliament in 2005, although it was obvious to me that he was going to lead National to victory in 2008. His accession to the leadership towards the end of 2006 was perhaps inevitable. Shortly afterwards, Sue Bradford's bill on smacking children came out of the ballot. This was a subject that, badly handled, could divide the National caucus. John spoke to

Helen Clark and indicated that National would support the legislation. Looking back now, it was a master stroke. John immediately looked mature and prime ministerial, and from then he was on the road to success.

During the years in opposition, I had been a member of a National policy advisory group looking at the issue of nuclear ships in New Zealand. I was in favour of repealing the legislation and trying to rebuild our relationship with our Australia, New Zealand and United States Security Treaty (ANZUS) allies. However, when John became leader, he indicated that the issue was off the table and that National would not be changing the anti-nuclear policy. I was disappointed at the time, but looking back now I recognise that it was the right decision to make because it would have embroiled us in sideshows during the 2008 election. I still maintain that the anti-nuclear policy is immature, and the product of student-body politics imported into government. I have never understood why the policy inspires so much pride among such a large segment of the population. John, however, did. He was a decisive leader who did not cling to policies of the past but was prepared to discard them if he thought it was in the best interests of the party.

The smacking debate also showed me that John was socially liberal. He dealt with difficult social issues in a way that encouraged moderation in caucus. I understand that during the contentious abortion debates in the 1970s relations between Robert Muldoon and George Gair, MP for North Shore, were so bad that they would not speak when sitting next to each other. Muldoon was a conservative and Gair was a liberal. Fast forward to the debate on marriage equality, and John came out in favour of the legislation, whereas his more conservative colleagues in caucus were opposed to it. The way John conducted himself, and encouraged caucus members to behave, was such that liberals and conservatives avoided attacking one another but were respectful of divergent views. Within caucus, things were always civilised.

As an aside, I voted against the marriage equality legislation because I thought that our matrimonial laws were a shambles. We had civil union legislation, marriage legislation and same-sex legislation. I thought the best thing to do was to abolish state-sanctioned marriage. The law relating to marriage was introduced in England only in the eighteenth century, and before that there were common law marriages. In my opinion there was no need for marriage legislation, and anyone who wants to have a civil union should be able to do so and celebrate it however they choose. My libertarian view was regarded as somewhat quirky, but I believe that will be the next reform in this area. Having said that, however, I always had an excellent relationship with Louisa Wall, who came into Parliament shortly after me. She was hugely respected in our party for her principled way of advancing issues such as marriage equality. Her departure was a huge loss to Parliament. In my time in politics, there has never been such a successful member of Parliament.

John Key's approach to dealing with the issues on marriage equality can be contrasted with the way in which the National party in 2021 dealt with legislation on gay conversion therapy. The party seemed to be having a dreadful fight on the issue in caucus, and Judith Collins then imposed an approach on caucus members that caused upset. John would never have done that, and nor would Judith's successor as leader, Christopher Luxon.

While John was regarded as pragmatic and a realist, he was also a visionary — as exemplified by his call for a referendum on the flag in 2015. I was disappointed that this debate was not more civilised. Labour was actually in favour of changing the flag but did not want the National party to be successful and so opposed it. New Zealand First would oppose anything like that, and so their truculent opposition was not a surprise. The process of change was guided by the deputy prime minister, Bill English. A distinguished panel was appointed and they came up with a number of interesting (although in my opinion overly confused) options. The referendum was defeated. I think that New Zealand's flag is out of date and boring, and that we need to make a change but, thanks to the antics of the opposition parties I don't think this will be achieved for many years. I also think simplicity is the answer — everyone, for example, knows the French flag and (because of Russia's invasion) the Ukraine flag. The options that were devised for a new flag here were too complex, however, and I think that could also have been part of the reason why the referendum was defeated.

Changing a flag is never easy. During the debate, I had to look after the Canadian prime minister, Stephen Harper, when he was laying a wreath in Auckland. I mentioned to him that the Canadian flag is one of the great flags of the world and it was a tribute to Canada that they were able to effect a change in the 1960s. They moved from a similarly boring New Zealand-type flag to something that is instantly recognisable and identifiably Canadian. I said to Harper that we were in the process of having a debate about changing our flag, and he patted me on the shoulder and said 'Good luck.'

Another example of John's visionary approach to politics was the mixed ownership model (MOM) programme, which I explain further in this chapter. It was John's brainchild and was highly successful, giving a much-needed and timely jolt to the stock exchange. The net result of the MOM programme was to improve the management of the resulting companies and produce a greater financial return to the Crown than when they were SOEs. John was a brilliant economic manager, and probably the most financially literate prime minister New Zealand has ever had.

John was also decisive when he needed to be. In the chapter 'Minister for arts, culture and heritage', I talk about the 'Hobbit legislation'. New Zealand was on the verge of losing filming for *The Hobbit* and our reputation in the movie world was being destroyed because of the antics of the trade unions and the torment they were putting Peter Jackson through. John immediately indicated to Jackson that he would alter the legislation, and this was done. He also negotiated single-handedly with the Warner Bros. executives to achieve a very good outcome for New Zealanders. Our film industry is flourishing because of his decisiveness at a critical time.

My other impression of John is his humanity. I know how much he worried about the families of the Pike River Mine workers after the 2010 disaster, and that he was personally traumatised by what had happened. On the morning of the second explosion, I had an appointment with John to discuss a treaty settlement issue. I walked into his office and he was ashen-faced, knowing there could be no survivors. He went out of his way to try to help those families and never played politics with the issue. I, too, feel desperately sorry for the families of the Pike River victims and felt that other parties used them for political ends in 2017. What they needed was closure, but what they got from some political parties were offers that could never come to pass.

John also knew that there are no friends at the top, and that, from time to time, he had to be decisive to make sure his ministers were up to the mark. As I mentioned in the previous chapter, he had a cabinet reshuffle in 2013 that resulted in two people leaving and being replaced by younger ministers. One can contrast John's approach of constantly refreshing his ministry with other examples in New Zealand history where people were permitted to stay on in cabinet well beyond their use-by date. So, for example, in the last few years of Keith Holyoake's regime in the early 1970s, some ministers who should have retired continued in their positions. The worst example, however, was during the final stages of the Muldoon years in the early 1980s, when some ministers should have gracefully gone to the backbenches to await their exit from politics at the next election but instead were permitted to stay on in cabinet. In 1962, Prime Minister Harold Macmillan in the UK sacked half his cabinet to revive the government's fortunes. That led to the great quip from the Liberal MP Jeremy Thorpe that, 'Greater love hath no man than this, that he lay down his friends for his life.' John never indulged in a wholesale slaughter of his cabinet, but he did make very effective changes when these were needed.

I always feared my annual meetings with John to discuss my priorities. As it turned out, these were normally very short. On one occasion, my meeting with him lasted for about a minute, as it was tolerably clear what I had to do — get treaty settlements. Not everyone got off so lightly though — I once went to see John after he had had a 45-minute meeting with one of my colleagues.

The prime minister was also a master communicator. I think he may have thought I was too lawyerly on occasion. On one of the few instances he got short with me, over the foreshore and seabed debate, he said to me, 'Don't be so intellectual. Just make a few points clearly and in plain English. Keep it simple.' It was very good advice and thereafter all I ever said at public meetings was that the legislation was about giving an opportunity for people to go to court and restoring uninvestigated customary title if they could prove that they were entitled to it. In politics, it is not necessarily the sophisticated lawyerly speech that gets across; one has to keep the message simple and repeat it over and over again. I cannot speak highly enough of John Key. I know he will go down in history as one of this country's great prime ministers, alongside Peter Fraser, Richard Seddon, Keith Holyoake, Helen Clark and Jim Bolger.

The deputy prime minister, Bill English, was made minister of finance at probably the worst time conceivable. It is hard to overemphasise the effect that the GFC crisis had on all ministers. In other chapters of this book I have tried to explain how I, as attorney-general, minister for Treaty of Waitangi negotiations and minister for arts, culture and heritage, had to do my bit to cut expenditure. There was going to be very little new money in budgets. Bill was determined to bring the books under control and impose discipline on a bloated and inefficient public service. It was not so much a period of austerity as a period of much-needed discipline. Bill was very much the man of the moment. He had entered Parliament in 1990 and was destined to be a senior cabinet minister. In 1993 Jim Bolger made him parliamentary undersecretary to the minister of health and he came into cabinet in early 1996. From 1996 to 1999 he held the difficult health portfolio and, for a brief period towards the end of the Shipley administration, was treasurer. I always remember Bill on election night 1999, saying to reporters after the loss became apparent, 'We will take our medicine.' I don't think he realised at the time how bitter that medicine would be. In the early years of opposition, he was promoted to deputy leader when Wyatt Creech decided to step back from frontline politics, and then a few months later was made leader of the opposition when it became apparent that Jenny Shipley had only limited support. Many MPs made promises to Bill that they would help him after he became leader, but those came to nothing and he was left pretty much on his own to face a strong and unified Labour party at the 2002 election.

When one considers the atrocious performance of National between 2017 and 2020, it's hard to conceive of a worse time in opposition for the party, but I think that in the period leading up to the 2002 election National was in an even poorer shape. The money wasn't coming in and people simply were not interested in helping — even basic things like organising billboard sites and ordering billboards were not happening. It was an omni-shambles. From my office in Featherston Street, I could look down on Thorndon Quay and other parts of Wellington. A few days after Helen Clark called the snap election in 2002, there were Labour billboards in key places around the city. Labour's president, Mike Williams, and his team were great organisers.

Bill was leader when it all fell apart and the 2002 election was a disaster. But he picked himself up from the canvas and, with an outstanding president in Judy Kirk, started to rebuild the party. After Bill was defeated for the leadership by Don Brash, he did not go away into a corner and sulk, but instead became education spokesperson. He did some really good work in that area, laying the foundations for the development of National Standards. When John Key became the leader, Bill stepped into the deputy leadership role and took on responsibility for finance.

I was very fortunate to have a minister of finance like Bill English. One or two stories can explain why I thought he was so good. In the period leading up to the first budget, many of the arts organisations were under pressure, in particular the Royal New Zealand Ballet. In these austere times Bill was prepared to provide a little extra money to the ballet company so that it could survive. Interestingly, on the day of the budget the only comments my office received were complaints that the Royal New Zealand Ballet had received extra funding. Bill was also always extremely supportive of me in the treaty negotiations area. He understood the importance of treaty negotiations and was mostly positive if I needed extra pūtea (funding) to get settlements over the line. I know other ministers felt the same about his careful and methodical approach to the finance portfolio. Bill (and Roger Douglas) will go down in history as our greatest ministers of finance.

Number three in cabinet was Gerry Brownlee, MP for Ilam. Gerry had come into the House in 1996 after Philip Burdon retired from what had once been the key blue-ribbon seat for National in Christchurch. After a brief period as a whip, Gerry was elevated to the deputy leadership when Don Brash was leader between 2003 and 2006, and then gracefully stood down from the role when John Key became leader of the opposition — he essentially gave the deputy leadership to Bill English. I have always regarded Gerry's actions at that critical time as indicative of the class of the guy.

In 2008 Gerry was made minister of economic development and minister of energy and resources, as well as leader of the House, a role in which he excelled. One of the innovations he introduced was the extra sitting time — normally on a Thursday morning — so that generally non-contentious legislation could be progressed. It was used a great deal by me as minister for Treaty of Waitangi negotiations because there was so much treaty legislation going through the House at the time. In the 1960s and 1970s, Parliament used to sit a lot more than it does now. For example, it sat until 10.30 p.m. on a Thursday night, and then met on Friday morning from 9 a.m. to 1 p.m. There was no question time on a Friday. I always felt that the changes made in the mid-1980s to reduce the amount of parliamentary time were a mistake. Members of Parliament are legislators and legislation needs to be progressed. Under Gerry Brownlee this happened, and the order paper was always manageable. I talk more about Gerry's great contribution to New Zealand in the period following the devastating Christchurch earthquakes in the 'Challenges' chapter (page 215).

In 2008, Simon Power was number four in cabinet. He had a very heavy workload as minister of justice, minister of commerce, minister of state-owned enterprises and deputy leader of the House. Simon had come into Parliament as MP for Rangitīkei in 1999.

It cannot have been much fun for a young, energetic MP to face nine long years in opposition, but he used that time well to prepare for what would be a short but highly effective period as a senior minister. I worked closely with Simon as attorney-general and so am in a good position to assess his record as minister of justice. He faced many problems that had been building up over the years, including a legal aid budget that was out of control. Demands for reform of legal aid were becoming more and more insistent, and the regime could not cope. In addition, the Family Court needed urgent reform — cases were going to the court and being buried in procedural and other delays. The whole purpose of going to the Family Court is to try to secure a just and speedy determination of very difficult and emotional issues, and cases simply cannot languish there. There were many critics of the changes to the legal aid regime, criminal procedure and Family Court procedure, but these changes were very necessary. Simon tackled these sorts of issues with enthusiasm and energy. He was also very effective in the commerce portfolio, which is not generally understood. It covers areas of commercial regulatory control, intellectual property and what I call black-letter law. Again, many of those areas needed urgent reform, and again, Simon was the person to get on with the job.

I was amazed when Simon phoned me in mid-2011 to say that he was retiring from politics. I thought he had an excellent career ahead of him, probably as minister of foreign affairs or defence, followed by a period as prime minister. However, he decided for family reasons that he wanted to leave Parliament after twelve years and instead work in the private sector, where he has flourished. I always think of Simon's career with some disappointment. Nine years in opposition was a horrible apprenticeship for public life, and while he was a very effective minister, it is a great shame that he did not have more time in cabinet.

Steven Joyce entered Parliament in 2008 and immediately came into cabinet as minister of transport and minister for communications and information technology. Every cabinet needs a Steven Joyce. Between 1990 and 1999, Bill Birch was Steven's equal in Jim Bolger's government. One could always rely on Birch to do the heavy lifting, and so it was with Steven. After the 2002 debacle, Steven was appointed to conduct a review into the train wreck known as the National party. His report resulted in a special general meeting of the party, where some significant changes were made to the constitution. Steven then became general manager of the party and guided it through the successful 2005 election. He came to Parliament in 2008, having done great work in the election campaign that year.

I thought John Key's decision to give Steven the transport and communications and information technology portfolios was simply inspired. As I mentioned earlier, Maurice Williamson had done great work in opposition on the broadband roll-out, but it was Steven who got the job done as a minister. I think that was probably his greatest achievement.

Having lived as a teenager in the Kāpiti region, Steven had a very good idea of what improvements to roading were needed in the area. He was directly responsible for the Kāpiti Expressway project, which has transformed the district. I can remember the many meetings he attended where he was criticised for moving ahead with it, even though an area had been designated for such a highway for many years. Most of the complaints were irrational, and Steven pushed ahead. During the time of the National government, the expressway from Peka Peka to Ōtaki was started, and planning was under way for it to extend to Levin and from there to Sanson. It is a great shame that nothing is going to be progressed from Ōtaki to Levin until 2025.

Another of Steven's achievements is Transmission Gully. This project had been talked about for more than a hundred years. The famous cry of the Jewish people 'Next year in Jerusalem', and the Antipodean cry 'Next year we will start on Transmission Gully' had a similar ring to it. Down through the ages, people promised that Transmission Gully was a priority. Indeed, when Roger Sowry, MP for Kāpiti and then a list MP on the coast for many years, retired in 2005, he was farewelled at a function in Parliament. Someone produced a list of press releases Roger had made over the years about Transmission Gully — in the course of a fifteen-year career in Parliament, I think he promised during every election campaign that by the end of that parliamentary term Transmission Gully would be under way. It was, however, Steven who ensured that the project started. The March 2022 opening of the motorway reminds me of what John F. Kennedy once said: 'Victory has a thousand fathers and defeat is an orphan.' Everyone is now rejoicing that Transmission Gully has opened and celebrating how it will transform the lower North Island, but it is Steven who mainly deserves credit for that monumental achievement. In fairness, Peter Dunne's advocacy for the project when he was a minister in the Key government was also important, as was the support of Nathan Guy, MP for Ōtaki.

Steven's work on roading was not limited to the Wellington region. When National came to office in 2008, the Waterview Connection in Auckland was an idea but no funding had been set aside for it. Steven got that done. He also was responsible for the Waikato Expressway. It is a tragedy for Auckland that Steven was unable to complete roading projects that are desperately needed to improve traffic flow in our nation's biggest city.

The National party is always criticised for being obsessed with roads. Steven, however, was also responsible for improving railway lines in the Wellington region and for purchasing rolling stock. It is probably fair to say that, as a result, the Greater Wellington region has the best rail infrastructure of any place in the country. Steven did a similar job in Auckland, although that city lags a long way behind Wellington.

As can be seen, Steven got things done. Many of the projects I have mentioned should have been started years before, but in many instances they were too complex and too big and so were put off to another day. It is a tribute to this outstanding minister that, in the depths of the GFC recession, he managed to achieve so much.

Steven was also the go-to person when there were problems. As a result, he was appointed minister for tertiary education in his first term, and in 2013, in his second term, he had to sort out the Novopay debacle when that payment system for teachers went wrong. In 2016 he became the minister for finance and, like Bill English, was great to work with. I found Steven particularly helpful in the intelligence area in that time.

I have made many mistakes in my life, but way up there among the worst was my decision not to support Steven over Simon Bridges for the leadership in 2018. I thought generational change was probably a good thing after such a lengthy period of stable leadership, but I was wrong. I know others feel the same about Steven. He left Parliament shortly thereafter to begin a commercial consulting career. I still think there is a further contribution that Steven could make, but the chances of his actually going back into Parliament are remote.

Tony Ryall came into cabinet in 2008 as minister of health and of state services. In 2011 he handed the latter portfolio to Jonathan Coleman and became minister for state-owned enterprises, with responsibility for developing the MOM programme.

Tony was first elected to Parliament in 1990 as a very young MP for East Cape. Over the years, as MP for Bay of Plenty, his seat became increasingly centred on Tauranga and he built up huge majorities in the electorate and party votes. Tony enjoyed only a short period as a minister in the 1990s, becoming minister of justice after Jenny Shipley became prime minister. He then had to endure nine years of opposition, so it's fair to say he was really keen to get started as a minister in 2008. Tony had been the health spokesperson in the period leading up to the 2008 election and had done good policy work in the areas for which he was made responsible. He was an excellent minister of state services, focusing on an overstaffed and inefficient public service. Soon after he became minister, for example, the government put an immediate cap on public relations staff. His greatest role, however, was as minister of health. Notwithstanding the GFC, the Ministry of Health was always well treated in the budget — I suppose it helped that Bill English had once been minister of health. During Labour's years, there was generally about a 9 per cent per annum increase in health spending, and following the GFC National needed to reduce that to a more manageable 3 per cent. Tony had to find a way of making health more efficient, so he set key targets of improving the performance of hospitals, waiting times, and cancer treatment and child immunisation. He kept in constant contact with the chairs of the various district health boards, and I understand he would spend each Sunday night speaking to a couple of them. He was right on top of his portfolio, and during his time as minister there were relatively few complaints.

Tony was the key person to implement one of the most important pillars in National's 2011 campaign: the MOM programme. This was the biggest privatisation initiative in New Zealand. Leading up to the implementation of the programme, John Key, Bill English and Tony spent a lot of time convincing the public that it was a good thing. Because of botch-ups in the 1980s, the public were accustomed to think about privatisation in a negative way, but National had to take steps to implement this programme to save the New Zealand economy after the GFC and to pay down the enormous debt the country had piled up.

The key SOEs that were chosen for the programme were Air New Zealand, Meridian and Mighty River Power. They would not be completely privatised, but the government's shareholding would be reduced to 50 per cent. The companies would then be floated on the stock exchange and subjected to the market disciplines of private and public companies. Labour was very much against the programme, and during the week the first company was to be floated they announced a new power policy that caused insecurity around the price of electricity and threatened the shares that were about to be offered. In all my time in politics, this announcement by Labour is probably the greatest act of political bastardy I experienced. It was incoherent and unprincipled, which is perhaps why the Green party so strongly supported it. I always admired David Shearer, the Labour leader at the time, but he got that one wrong. Despite the uncertainty, National went ahead with the programme, as we had a mandate to do so after our big win in 2011. Labour then abandoned their policy. The huge interest in the shares became evident when the website crashed during the launch. As it turns out, the MOM companies produce more for the government now than they did as SOEs. I suppose the great exception to that is Air New Zealand, which has made nothing for the Crown in recent years owing to the effects on travel of the Covid-19 pandemic.

What was the success of the MOM programme put down to? I think it was thanks to the time Tony and other senior ministers took to explain the process of privatisation to the public, and also their efforts to ensure that no individual would have too many shares. Another key factor, as the 2011 result showed, is that National was trusted to be a careful steward in tough economic times. In addition, John Key had been an outstanding businessman in his own right, and could explain to people why the MOM programme was going to be economically advantageous to New Zealand.

I need to mention the attempts by certain groups, led by the New Zealand Māori Council, to throw a spanner in the works by complaining to the Waitangi Tribunal about the MOM programme, which they alleged breached the Treaty of Waitangi and its principles. I suppose I shouldn't have been surprised by the fact that the Māori Council complained to the Waitangi Tribunal, and that when the tribunal released its report, it was, in my opinion, a very disappointing piece of work.[1] It proposed a scheme that would have raised questions about compliance with company law. In my opinion, when dealing with many contemporary issues, the Waitangi Tribunal is out of its depth. The time has come for a future government to consider the role of the tribunal. When the historical grievances have been addressed, the jurisdiction of the tribunal to deal with contemporary grievances should really be transferred to the High Court. Either that, or much more thought needs to be given to the appointment of members of the Waitangi Tribunal. When the tribunal was first started, it was much smaller and its membership comprised very senior and wise members of the community. With respect, the same cannot be said now. In my opinion, many of the tribunal members appear to struggle with complex economic issues.

Although Tony's contribution as a minister lasted only six years, they were six excellent years. He went back into the private sector in 2014 knowing he had made a significant contribution to his country.

Following National's election victory in 2008, Anne Tolley became minister of education. She had entered Parliament as a list MP in 1999 but lost after the 2002 disaster. She came back to Parliament in 2005 as MP for East Coast, and shortly thereafter became junior whip and then senior whip when John Key became the leader of the opposition. As minister of education her task was to introduce National Standards. The essential idea behind this initiative was to set certain education standards to ensure that no child was falling behind, and also to ensure that children got the follow-up that they needed. As was to be expected, the role was a baptism of fire for Anne, and the proposals were rejected by the teachers' unions. I never had any responsibility in the education area, but it was apparent to me that the greatest force against any positive change were the teachers' unions, whose loyalty was primarily to the Labour party. Of the many immovable and wholly negative people in the trade union movement, the leadership of the teachers' unions would have to rank up there among the worst. Anne also did great work developing trades academies, which focused on blending tertiary and secondary education to allow young adults to get experience and a feel for the workforce. The programme was very supportive of Māori medium schools, which allowed rural Māori schools to include secondary education at the same site and also a greater Māori curriculum in secondary education.

In 2011 Anne was made minister of police and minister of corrections. I think she may have been disappointed to lose the education portfolio to Hekia Parata, but the police and corrections portfolios are very difficult and sensitive, and Anne made a significant contribution in her stewardship of those over three years. For example, the work she did on education and mental health in prisons was excellent, and she had a huge focus on education in prisons to enhance rehabilitation. A focus on mental health in high-security prisons is needed owing to the background of the prisoners, and Anne was adamant that more work needed to be done in that area. She also led other reforms, including implementing a dementia unit for ageing prisoners. Her final three years were as minister of social development and minister for children, in which she primarily focused on implementing a reform and redesign of the care system for children. She was also responsible for trying new ways of engaging differently with Māori children and communities.

Anne showed how difficult it was to progress matters after the GFC. Implementing change in the sensitive portfolios she held was always going to be hard, and anything she did to cut wasteful spending was going to be viciously criticised. So when she decided to defund some adult education, such as cooking and pottery classes, and redirect the money to youth education (such as trades academies), she was criticised by various interest groups. She had the courage and determination, however, to proceed with those reforms.

Anne held a variety of highly sensitive portfolios with great distinction, and I think she is one of the true heroes of the government between 2008 and 2017. When we went into opposition, she was elected deputy speaker and I hoped that she would have stayed on with the chance of becoming speaker when National won again. She decided, however, to leave Parliament, and has continued to make a significant contribution as a commissioner of the dysfunctional Tauranga City Council.

As I say later in this book, I regret that Anne did not become Bill's deputy in 2016. She had had an impressive ministerial career and had a good understanding of the party, and I think she would have complemented Bill's talents much more effectively than did Paula Bennett. Looking back now, I wonder why that was never seriously considered as an option.

Some ministers were natural fits for their portfolios and simply got on with the work. An obvious example in this category was Tim Groser, who came into Parliament with me in 2005. Tim had begun his working life in the Department of the Prime Minister and Cabinet when Robert Muldoon was prime minister, and then transferred to the Ministry of Foreign Affairs and Trade where, over the next twenty years or so, he worked mainly on trade issues. He had a stint as ambassador to Indonesia in the 1990s, and then served in Geneva as ambassador to the World Trade Organization, before coming back to New Zealand to enter Parliament as a list MP. For some peculiar reason, Tim always stood in the New Lynn electorate, even though he was a born-and-bred Wellingtonian. Like me, he was often worried that he might win the seat. Indeed, at one stage his chances of winning looked reasonably good, whereas I never had any hope whatsoever of winning Labour-dominated Rongotai. In 2015, Tim left Parliament to become ambassador to the United States. At the time of writing, he is back in Wellington conducting consultancies.

Wayne Mapp was MP for North Shore from 1996 to 2011. He is the best example of what happens if a politician enters Parliament at the wrong stage of the cycle. After three years as a backbencher, he had to endure nine years in opposition, during which he held a variety of spokesperson roles. I was very fond of Wayne, and one year asked him if he could speak at the Mana electorate annual dinner. He chose political correctness as his topic. It was an excellent address, but I have always wondered whether he regretted choosing that topic because, some weeks later, Don Brash made Wayne the 'political correctness eradicator'. It was a bizarre appointment and Wayne was embarrassed; I don't think he ever lived it down.

In 2008, Wayne became minister of defence and minister of science, and immediately had to deal with a variety of issues relating to defence procurement. Our defence personnel have done an excellent job over the years, both in defending the country and representing New Zealand in very difficult areas of combat. It is also fair to say that they do not know the first thing about procurement — every plan between 1999 and 2008 seemed to go wrong.

We purchased used Boeing 757s from United Airlines that were constantly on the ground needing repair, the inshore patrol vessels that were acquired for the Navy proved to be lemons, and the Hercules were well overdue for replacement and always breaking down. The equipment was not in good shape. These were the sorts of issues Wayne had to deal with in an era of great financial pressure. He told me in early 2011 that he had decided to retire because he thought fifteen years was enough. However, I think he made a mistake and should have stayed on for at least another three years. He remains a very astute commentator on national security issues.

Others who made significant contributions over the years include Nick Smith, who was minister for the environment and minister of conservation. Nick was always very supportive of treaty negotiations. One of his great fans was the late Archie Taiaroa, the leading rangatira of Whanganui. Archie worked with Nick when he was associate minister for Treaty of Waitangi negotiations in the late 1990s, and he told me that Nick had been very supportive of him. Sometimes I needed to push the boundaries in treaty settlements when dealing with natural resources, but I found Nick both understanding and supportive. I doubt whether there could be a greater zealot for conservation than Nick — he could out-green the Greens any day. He became minister of conservation in 2013 after Kate Wilkinson left Parliament. Again, I found him very supportive when I needed conservation land for treaty settlements.

Nick and I did have a bit of a falling-out in later years over reform of the law of contempt. I had been very enthusiastic about progressing this subject, but Nick, who was an assiduous local MP, had particular views about using the law of contempt to stop criticism of judges. In opposition, he had actually been convicted of scandalising the court because of some intemperate comments he had made about the Family Court on behalf of one of his constituents. I think he would have been best to have stayed away from the debate on reform of the law of contempt but, after I left Parliament at the beginning of 2019, the contempt reforms were still in the Justice Committee. For some reason, Nick persuaded the committee members that the sections dealing with scandalising the court should be removed. I received a tip-off and managed to persuade the attorney-general, David Parker, that they needed to go back in again, and then Nick and the National party voted against what had been my member's bill. Time has somewhat diminished my anger for what, in my opinion, was their perfidy, but I still don't think it was a particularly impressive performance by either Nick or the National party.

I came into Parliament at the same time as Nathan Guy. Nathan came from a very successful family who had farmed in Horowhenua for more than a century. He reduced the majority held by Darren Hughes in Ōtaki from over 7000 to a few hundred, then won the seat in 2008. Nathan spent some time as a junior and then senior whip, and came into ministerial office as a minister outside cabinet holding a number of portfolios. He then became minister of agriculture when David Carter was made speaker in 2013. Nathan was a very solid and dependable minister in this critical portfolio. He had to deal with a number of very serious issues, which I describe more fully in the 'Challenges' chapter. I was terrified after the 1080 scandal broke in 2014. A very serious threat had been made to the CEOs of dairy companies about infant formula being contaminated with 1080, and I thought it could have a very harmful effect on our trade with China. Nathan handled that highly sensitive issue with class. He was a reliable, understated minister who got things done, and I was very sorry when he decided to leave politics in 2020 after fifteen years as an MP. I always thought that, if he had stayed, he would have ended up deputy leader of the party; he was young enough to have another lengthy period as a minister, possibly in the trade or economic development area. As a local MP, he was a tireless champion for Transmission Gully and other developments.

The only other National minister I will mention is Michael Woodhouse, who came into Parliament in 2008 as a list MP based in Dunedin. Like me, he stood in a very safe Labour seat, Dunedin North (as it then was), and was always heavily defeated. He eventually became minister of labour (or workplace relations and safety, as it subsequently became) and had to shepherd through the reforms to the health and safety laws that followed on from the 2010 Pike River Mine disaster. That portfolio was still very much driven by the memory of the disaster, even four years after it had happened, and dealing with the legislation was a very fraught affair. National could generally be considered a party less dominated by rules, and certainly caucus did not want a rule-driven piece of legislation. This was problematic, however, as health and safety law is often dependent on rules. On the one hand, Michael had to work on a bill that kept businesses safe while ensuring there would not be an overkill of regulations on small business. And on the other hand, he had to deal with unions, who thought the bill was not going far enough and who wanted more regulations. I think he did an excellent job of reaching a balance between the different expectations.

One of the difficulties Michael faced is illustrated by what became known as the 'worm saga'. The farming industry was very difficult to classify. Farmers were, of course, used to working by themselves and did not want any regulations and rules around the dangers of the industry because they were typically working on the basis of risk every day. Michael needed to create a system that did not have huge loopholes and that covered all parts of the industry. This was sometimes very challenging, as there could be more than one industry on the same land — for example, pig farming could also have worm farming on the same land, or a farm might also offer high-risk adventure experiences such as bungy jumping. Michael's efforts in dealing with all the varying issues led to him becoming known as the person who was trying to secure worm farms.

I could look at the careers of other ministers but I am conscious that I may appear to be something like a headmaster marking student performances. What I want to do is illustrate the fact that the 2008–17 National cabinet was, in my opinion, the most competent cabinet since the outstanding Labour cabinet of 1984, when the likes of Roger Douglas, Richard Prebble and David Caygill, assisted by Geoffrey Palmer, Michael Bassett and others, transformed the New Zealand economy. Those changes are the most significant changes that New Zealand has ever experienced and it is shameful that the Labour party cannot embrace the reforms with greater pride. Other ministers made contributions, but the ones that I have discussed were, in my opinion, truly outstanding.

Something needs to be said about a few of the ministers outside cabinet and the support ministers. Maurice Williamson was MP for Pakuranga from 1987 to 2017 and is someone I regard as a good friend. He was a minister for nine years in the Bolger–Shipley administrations but had a difficult time in opposition, and at one stage he was suspended from caucus. It occurred in the aftermath of a very difficult period in 2002, when I think Maurice had some problems with the administration of the party at the time, and some of his forthright criticisms were not well received. I never really worked out what happened, but I think the then leader, Bill English, took some of Maurice's criticisms to heart and Maurice was punished accordingly. When John Key selected his cabinet in 2008, Maurice was excluded but was offered the customs and building and construction portfolios outside cabinet. I am sure he was very disappointed, but he did some great work over the next six years in both of those areas. Examples of his achievements include introducing the photo driver licence. Although some opponents said it was a way of tracking people and was inhumane, it did indeed result in a drop in the road toll. Maurice was also responsible for the introduction of SmartGate in our international airports.

As I have said previously, Maurice did a lot of the preparatory work on the broadband roll-out. In 2006, he was adamant that New Zealand needed to do something drastic to improve our technology, and it was his idea that fibre to homes was the way of the future. No other country had thought this way except for South Korea, so Maurice had a huge challenge persuading the leadership that it needed to be done. He went off to San Diego and talked to Verizon, who were trialling and running tubes of fibreglass to properties in the city, and he thereafter wrote a very long paper saying that if roads were the enabler of economies in the industrial age and electricity was vital in the nineteenth and twentieth centuries, then in his view the internet was the future for the twenty-first century. When he first took his paper to the Caucus Policy Committee, he was rebuffed and told he needed to revise it. Some months later, he managed to persuade his colleagues otherwise — Maurice tells me that John Key threw his paper at him, saying 'You can have your f***ing fibre', and it was signed off. As I said earlier, Steven Joyce implemented this game-changing programme, which proved to be an economic saviour for the country during the Covid-19 pandemic.

When the Canterbury Earthquakes Royal Commission produced the first part of its final report in 2012,[2] Maurice and I had to go to Christchurch to explain its contents to the audience of families who had lost loved ones. I basically worked off my briefing notes, but Maurice was a sight to behold. He was so on top of his brief and understood the geotechnical and other issues so well that he departed from his notes and spoke for at least half an hour on these difficult subjects with great authority. I don't know how the families felt, but I was really impressed by his performance that day. He showed just what a good minister he was.

Maurice left Parliament in 2017 to be consul-general in Los Angeles, returning in 2020. He is one of those former ministers with whom I keep in touch quite regularly. I enjoy his company and his irreverent sense of humour. We need more Maurice Williamsons in Parliament.

Another minister outside cabinet, albeit for only three years, was John Carter, who with Rodney Hide was responsible for setting up the super city in Auckland. The previous administration had talked about improving governance in Auckland, but it was the National government that achieved it. The idea was to bring regional and district councils together to make a more efficient council. There were huge protests from the locals because so many people wanted their town back, and John was just the right person to front up to explain what was happening and why.

John was also the minister for Civil Defence. This portfolio was once regarded as relatively light, but John had to deal with the aftermath of the 2010 and 2011 earthquakes. He heard about the 2010 earthquake on the morning of the disaster and spent much of the day trying to get to Christchurch from Auckland, and was then criticised by the media for being unavailable. That is the sort of unfairness ministers can be subjected to by journalists. In the aftermath of the 2011 earthquake, John moved to the Beehive for 72 hours and conducted media interviews every fifteen minutes to inform and reassure the public. He left Parliament in July that year to become high commissioner to the Cook Islands. I think he was probably bored because he came back within a couple of years and, more recently, has been the mayor of Far North district. John was a tremendous local MP and was great to deal with when I was concluding treaty negotiations for Te Hiku iwi.

One day in late 2010 John came to see me. He looked stunned and told me he had been scolded very severely by the police. Apparently, brothers John and Wikatana Popata (nephews of Hone Harawira) were putting on a performance at a beach near Taipā. They were protesting to the proposed reforms I was working on to replace the Foreshore and Seabed Act with the Marine and Coastal (Takutai Moana) Act. John was infuriated at their behaviour and phoned the local police commander, telling him to get the Popata brothers off the beach. The police told him in no uncertain terms that they were responsible for operational matters, not him, and that his request was inappropriate. I reminded him of the very clear requirements of the Policing Act 2008 and suggested he phone the police to apologise. It was a timely reminder to ministers that, although they have responsibility for policy, it is for the police to make decisions on operational matters. So John Key, for example, could not have ordered the police to enter the Pike River Mine any more than Jacinda Ardern could have ordered the police to remove the protesters performing in front of Parliament in early 2022.[3]

Pita Sharples and Tariana Turia were also support ministers. As associate minister of Māori development, I worked with Pita from 2011 until his retirement in 2014. He was easy to get on with and supportive of my ultimately unsuccessful attempts to reform Māori land law. As I have mentioned earlier, however, my real favourite was Tariana, who I always admired for her courage in standing up to the Labour party over the Foreshore and Seabed Act in 2004. She resigned from Parliament and contested her electorate as a member of the new Māori party. She always spoke common sense and I was determined to ensure that, during my time as a minister, the Foreshore and Seabed Act was repealed and replaced by a more just and enduring model. I was also determined to see the Whanganui River claim settled, because I felt that the negotiation had been put on the back burner as a means of punishing Tariana after the foreshore and seabed controversy. She was of immense assistance to me when dealing with the Taranaki negotiations and helped out on the Parihaka negotiations when they were in a difficult patch. I cannot praise her enough for her work during my time as a minister.

I have briefly mentioned Rodney Hide, who was minister of local government from 2008 to 2011. His great achievement was in pushing through the reform of Auckland governance, assisted by John Carter. From time to time in this book I have also mentioned Peter Dunne, who was MP for Ōhāriu from 1984 to 2017. I worked closely with Peter on issues relating to the Chathams, and he was always on top of his brief and good to work with. He briefly resigned from the ministry in 2013 because he did not want to make available his telephone records. This was during a time when there had been a leak and ministers were being questioned as to whether they were the source. At one stage it appeared possible that Peter might even resign from Parliament, thus triggering a by-election in Ōhāriu. John Key mentioned this to me and suggested I stand in the electorate because I had been born there and knew the place so well. I always wanted to be the MP for Ōhāriu, which takes in my home suburb of Khandallah and was where I had my introduction to politics, but the thought of being National's candidate in a by-election horrified me. I immediately went round to Peter's office and told him that there was no way he could leave Parliament; he simply had to stay the course and would no doubt come back into the ministry in time.

I think our team operated extremely effectively between 2008 and 2017. There were some exceptions, but I prefer to concentrate on the positive. I was privileged to be part of that team, and I miss the camaraderie and company of my colleagues.

CHAPTER 6

The attorney-general

IN 2021, SIR ROBERT BUCKLAND, a former solicitor-general for England and Wales, wrote a foreword for a paper published by the Policy Exchange entitled *Crossing the Line? The Attorney-General and the Law/Politics Divide*. He said this about the office of attorney-general:

> David Mallet, in his 1740 'Life of Francis Bacon', memorably described the offices of Attorney and Solicitor-General as 'rocks upon which many aspiring lawyers have made shipwreck of their virtue and human nature.' JP Collier wrote in 1819 that, of all the offices in the gift of the Crown 'that of Attorney-General is perhaps the least to be coveted for . . . the person filling that place can scarcely avoid being the object of general dislike'.[1]

I am unable to comment on whether my time as attorney-general from 2008 to 2017 made me the object of general dislike, but I can say it is the job I most coveted after I entered Parliament. To have been attorney-general from November 2008 to October 2017 has been the highlight of my legal career.

Much has been written about the role of the attorney-general and solicitor-general over the years, but much of it is theoretical and academic. What I want to do here is look at the office of the attorney-general from a practical point of view, providing examples from my time.

The office of attorney-general originated in the appointment — at first informally, and then from the reign of King Edward IV (1461–83) — of counsel to appear on behalf of the sovereign, as sovereigns could not appear in their own courts. In New Zealand, the office of attorney-general was established as one of the three members of the colonial Executive Council in 1841, and then, from self-government in 1852, variously continued as a non-political and, more recently, a political office.

The *Cabinet Manual* (2017) describes the responsibilities of an attorney-general.[2] These are twofold: first, as a minister in cabinet with responsibility for the Parliamentary Counsel Office and Crown Law Office; and second, as the senior law officer of the Crown, providing legal advice to the government and ensuring that the business of government is conducted in accordance with the rule of law.

The attorney-general for England and Wales has similar functions, although unlike the New Zealand attorney-general they are not responsible for the appointment of judges. In England, the complex and varied nature of an attorney-general's responsibilities has given rise to a debate about the role, which is focused on two areas. The first of these is the apparent tension between the various functions of the attorney-general — being a minister and a member of the government, and being an independent guardian of the public interest and performing superintendence functions. And the second area of debate is the tension between being a party politician and a member of the government, and giving independent and impartial legal advice.[3] The tensions are a justifiable cause of concern in England. In 2014, Attorney-General Dominic Grieve was dismissed by Prime Minister David Cameron because he gave legal advice to cabinet, not political advice. This was rationalised by Cameron in his biography *For the Record* when he said of Grieve:

> He was a brilliant lawyer, and had huge respect among the legal profession. But there was a genuine problem. The European Court of Human Rights was finding against the UK for refusing to give prisoners the right to vote. The idea that convicted criminals should have that privilege disgusted me. And to my mind, Parliament was sovereign: this was a matter for MPs to decide, not the courts, particularly not foreign ones. Not according to Dominic: he said our international obligation should override our Parliamentary sovereignty. Linked to that, he cited the Ministerial Code, which said we couldn't break the law. So he ended up arguing it was impossible for us not to propose legislation to allow at least some prisoners to vote, and that as Ministers we would have to back it. I fundamentally disagreed. The right of prisoners to vote was not part of any international charter we had signed up to. It was the view of a foreign court, and if Parliament wanted to disagree, it should feel able to. As a result of this disagreement I could see how impossible it would be for Dominic and me ever to reach a more general agreement about reforming the ECHR, the Human Rights Act and the European Court of Justice. So he had to go.[4]

I had a very successful meeting with Grieve in London a few days before he was dismissed. He was a lawyer's lawyer and an excellent attorney-general, and I was very sorry to see that he had been dismissed. I contacted him to ask what had happened, and he simply said that he was called in to Cameron's office near the House of Commons, where he was told that he had done a wonderful job but that it was time for a change. And that was that.

One can contrast the principled approach of Grieve with that of Peter Goldsmith, another senior English barrister, who was attorney-general for some years under Tony Blair. In 2003 he gave Blair politico-legal advice justifying the prime minister's wish to join the coalition that waged the Iraq War. Blair and others have been condemned for getting involved in that conflict, invading Iraq and causing misery to millions of people. Having looked at the matter closely, I think that the advice Goldsmith gave was more in the nature of political than legal advice. As a consequence, his reputation was diminished.

There are attorneys-general from other jurisdictions who have faced similar conundrums. During my time as attorney-general, I always had a photo of Elliot Richardson in my office. Richardson was a Boston Brahmin who held many senior offices in the Nixon–Ford administrations from 1969 to 1977. He was appointed secretary of defense by Richard Nixon after the president's landslide victory in 1972. Within a few months, however, the Watergate scandal was starting to unravel and Richardson was asked by Nixon to move from the Department of Defense to the Department of Justice as attorney-general. Having dealt with the resignation of Spiro Agnew, the unlamented vice president, he then had to deal with his president's concerns about the activities of the special prosecutor, Archibald Cox. Richardson refused to fire Cox and resigned on a matter of principle in what has subsequently been named the Saturday Night Massacre. While he held other offices after Gerald Ford became president, Richardson never again scaled the heights in American politics. He paid a heavy price for doing the right thing.

Fortunately, my time as attorney-general did not involve clashes with the two prime ministers I served. There were, however, situations where I was obliged to give legal advice. Unlike some of my friends who have held office as attorney-general, I did not pay a political price for this because both prime ministers understood and accepted the importance of obtaining full and frank legal advice from their attorney-general.

The attorney-general as minister

The first of the attorney-general's functions is as a government minister, generally in cabinet, with responsibility for the Parliamentary Counsel Office and Crown Law Office.

The Parliamentary Counsel Office is not well known but is a crucial part of government, responsible for drafting legislation, regulations and tertiary instruments. It is situated in the Reserve Bank building in Wellington, and its staff are among the best of the civil servants with whom I worked for many years. They work under huge pressure, much of it caused by ministers wanting something drafted in five minutes. There were a number of occasions when the chief parliamentary counsel came to see me to say that their office was under great pressure to have a draft bill ready for introduction within an unreasonable period of time and that they could not certify it. What so often happened was that cabinet made a decision on a major policy matter and the department concerned would be instructed to prepare drafting instructions for the Parliamentary Counsel Office. In the meantime, the minister responsible for the particular policy was (justifiably, in many instances) anxious to see a bill introduced so that it could have its first reading and be referred to a select committee. However, bills cannot be drafted overnight; translating complex and difficult policy decisions into legislation takes time. Rush the process and the bill will be flawed and ultimately the subject of litigation. Whenever I was told of the concerns of the Parliamentary Counsel Office, I would raise these with the minister. Generally the minister accepted the reality of the situation, but sometimes they were quite difficult. I will not name names.

One of the key principles of the rule of law is that it has to be accessible. What does that mean in practical terms? After I became attorney-general, I read a book by Tom Bingham, a former senior law lord in the United Kingdom, entitled *The Rule of Law* (2011). He talked about the importance of accessibility of the law, and complained about the amount of legislation pouring out of the House of Commons, so much of which was astonishingly complex. Who is the biggest loser in this process? It is the ordinary person who wants to try to find out, probably with professional help, what the law is. An example Bingham cited is terrifying:

> A defendant was accused of tobacco smuggling and pleaded guilty in 2007. A community sentence was imposed and an application was made for a confiscation order . . .
>
> To show he was liable the prosecution relied on some 1992 regulations. The Trial Judge was satisfied that he was liable, and ordered him to pay £66,120 or serve 20 months in prison if he did not. He appealed. The appeal came before three Senior Judges in the Court of Appeal who heard argument and announced they would give their judgment later in writing. They concluded that the defendant was liable to pay the duty under the 1992 regulations, and circulated a draft judgment upholding the confiscation order. On the eve of formally delivering judgment however, they learned

> that the 1992 regulations no longer applied to tobacco products, as a result of different regulations made in 2001. Neither the Trial Judge, nor the Prosecutor, nor Defending Counsel, nor the Judges in the Court of Appeal knew of these later regulations, and they were not at fault.[5]

Lord Bingham referred to one of the judgments of the senior judges allowing the appeal, who complained at the lack of a comprehensive statute law database with hyperlinks that would enable someone, using a search engine, to find out all the legislation on a particular topic. The lack of such a rudimentary tool meant that the courts were, in many cases, unable to discover what the law was. The judge giving that judgment complained that this very poor state of affairs had been raised by responsible bodies on many occasions.

Is New Zealand any better? Of course not. We are one of the fastest law-makers in the West (as Geoffrey Palmer used to say) and MMP has not improved things. Moreover, vast numbers of regulations are passed each year. This is not a theoretical topic that is of interest only to lawyers and academics — let me illustrate my point by reference to the biggest food safety scare in New Zealand's history. In early August 2013, there was a concern that infant formula and possibly other products were infected with *Clostridium botulinum* bacteria, which cause botulism. The source of the suspected contamination was whey protein concentrate made by Fonterra, the output of which constitutes nearly 90 per cent of this country's dairy production. Alarm bells started ringing at the Ministry for Primary Industries, and very soon cabinet was discussing the issue and its potential for harm to be caused to our exports, particularly to China. In order to alleviate public concern, and the concern of the Chinese government, the New Zealand government appointed Miriam Dean QC to conduct an urgent review into the issue and make recommendations for improvements. In her first report, dated December 2013, she suggested a number of areas for improvement. One of her first recommendations was for clearer and more accessible tertiary instruments:

> The regulatory framework governing the dairy industry is spread across a variety of instruments, including the Animal Products Act 1999 and numerous regulations, specifications, notices and approved criteria . . . These various specifications, notices and so on are known as the tertiary layer of regulation.
>
> This tertiary layer includes numerous instruments of different types and runs to about 12,000 pages, taking up more than three metres of shelf space. Submitters noted this layer was 'difficult to navigate', 'inaccessible', and 'a bit of a nightmare'. The burden of navigating the tertiary layer is particularly felt by small to medium sized businesses.[6]

Both the Ministry for Primary Industries and the Parliamentary Counsel Office supported the inquiry's view that the tertiary instruments for the dairy sector needed to be consolidated into a smaller number of principal instruments, divided into subject matter or sector-specific parts. I recall that when this inquiry was underway, Dean and the other inquirers were concerned because they could not find all of the relevant tertiary instruments. This unsatisfactory state of affairs could not continue in an area as critical to New Zealand's economic well-being as the dairy industry. That is why change was needed.

The Law Commission had been looking at this issue and had produced an excellent report on New Zealand legislation and regulation. It referred to the glut of legislation and to the need for a new approach to be taken to ensure that legislation and regulations were readily accessible, not only to judges and lawyers, but also to the ordinary person. I decided that this report needed to be implemented.

The Legislation Act was passed in 2012. One journalist expressed surprise when it was introduced, commenting that it was highly technical, not politically sexy and the sort of thing one would expect a government to introduce in its third term. That kind of ignorance is understandable but completely wrong. These were very important measures, fundamental to the need for the law to be accessible, and had to be actioned as quickly as possible.

The Legislation Act 2012 was intended to address some of the issues referred to by Lord Bingham in the passage above. In particular, the aim was to make all of New Zealand statutes, regulations and tertiary instruments more accessible. An ambitious project of putting everything online has since begun; it will take some time to be completed, but it is worth the effort. The Legislation Act 2012 was replaced by the Legislation Act 2019, the purpose of which is to promote high-quality legislation for New Zealand that is 'easy to find, use, and understand'. To that end, the Act provides, among other things, for all legislation to be published electronically in one place over time.

A second component of the rule of law is that the law be clear and, so far as possible, easy to understand. Again, what does that mean in practical terms?

The Legislation Act 2012 (and the Legislation Act 2019) provides tools for modernising legislation. A revision bill may revise the whole or part of one or more Acts, and can combine or divide Acts or parts of Acts; omit redundant and spent provisions; and make changes in language, format and punctuation to achieve a clear, consistent, gender-neutral and modern style of expression. What a revision bill cannot do is change the effect of the law, although

ABOVE Me sitting with Ohariu MP, Hugh Templeton (right), and other members of the electorate team, with me barely sneaking into the picture (far right), at the lower North Island conference held in Whanganui in 1978. ©*Whanganui Chronicle*

BELOW LEFT At the Privy Council in 1990 for *Holt v Holt*. ©Chris Finlayson

BELOW RIGHT Speaking at the swearing in of a High Court Judge in Wellington. ©Simon Woolf

ABOVE The legal team in the Court of Appeal in *Green v BCNZ* with the late Hughie Green (centre). ©Chris Finlayson

BELOW Me with two great lawyers, George Barton QC (far right) and Peter McKenzie QC. George Barton's wife, Ailsa, was also present for the dinner. ©Chris Finlayson

LEFT In front of the Peace Palace when appearing on behalf of New Zealand at the International Court of Justice. ©New Zealand Embassy, The Hague

BELOW Me standing with New Zealand's ambassador to the Netherlands, George Troup (next to me, at centre) and members of the legal team at the International Court of Justice. ©New Zealand Embassy, The Hague

ABOVE The 2005 National Party intake. ©New Zealand National Party

ABOVE A special day: meeting Pope Francis shortly after his inauguration. ©*Vatican News*

BELOW Being introduced by Prime Minister John Key to the Governor-General Sir Jerry Mateparae at the swearing in of cabinet in 2011. ©Government House

ABOVE With my mother's second cousin, Annette King. ©Chris Finlayson

BELOW With John Key and Nathan Guy when John returned to the House for valedictory speeches of his colleagues. ©*New Zealand Herald*

LEFT With Parekura Horomia, late MP for Ikaroa-Rāwhiti. Parekura was always very supportive of my Treaty settlement work. ©The Crown

ABOVE A recent cartoon in the *New Zealand Herald* on dealing with my views on co-governance. ©Rod Emmerson, *New Zealand Herald*

ABOVE With the late Koro Wētere and Tiwha Bell, a great leader of Ngāti Maniapoto. ©Crown

BELOW With the late Inge Woolf at a Holocaust Remembrance Day function in the Great Hall, Parliament. ©Chris Finlayson

minor amendments to resolve ambiguity or reconcile inconsistencies between provisions are permitted.

After consulting with the Parliamentary Counsel Office, I decided to start revising the existing legislation by updating the law of contract. Important principles relating to the contract law were scattered across many pieces of legislation and the law was very untidy. Thus, the first revision bill was called the Contract and Commercial Law Bill. It has been a great success, although a certain professor of law has apparently complained to his students about the changes. The pettifogging concerns of professors of law did not worry me. The current revision programme approved by David Parker includes updating civil liability legislation. That is a timely and overdue revision.

In my last term, I was keen to push through a revision of all legislation relating to Parliament. There is a lot of legislation dealing with matters such as the Parliamentary Service Commission and parliamentary privilege, and these are scattered throughout the statute book. I thought they could be more conveniently grouped together in one statute called the Parliament Act. Unfortunately, I could never interest the leader of the House, Gerry Brownlee, in this project. I think he thought it was an academic idea being promoted by me that would be of little practical use. I disagree. I think there is a need for consolidation of all the legislation relating to Parliament, and, as with so many reforms, it really would be quite easy to achieve. I have tried to persuade the current government of the need to move in this direction.

The rule of law is not some esoteric topic, appropriate for a discussion in a Law Society or Bar Association seminar, but a very practical issue affecting everyone. It is undermined if the law itself is inaccessible, outdated and difficult to understand. It cannot be in the interests of justice for either statutes or regulations that could be highly relevant to determining the rights of an individual to be inaccessible. It is therefore very important to ensure that, as technology changes, ways of presenting the law also change, so that all relevant statutes and statutory instruments are readily available to the ordinary person. That is why I spent so much time on this very important and practical issue.

Another area where an attorney-general has ministerial responsibility is for the Crown Law Office. In practice, the office is headed by the junior law officer, the solicitor-general. Over the years, a solicitor-general has been appointed from the Bar, and that person should be a very senior and highly respected QC. The solicitor-general is responsible for the day-to-day administration of the Crown Law Office — the Crown's lawyers, who are generally responsible for conducting the major litigation of the Crown in the Supreme Court. Three solicitors-general held office during my time as attorney-general. The first was David Collins QC, my former contracts tutor. He was a respected medico-legal lawyer and had obtained a Doctor of Laws from Victoria University for a book he published on that subject. My second solicitor-general was Michael Heron QC, who had been a partner in Meredith Connell and, later, Russell McVeagh. He had been at the Bar for only a few years when he was approached by me about the possibility of his becoming solicitor-general. Unlike most solicitors-general, he elected to go back to the Bar rather than to the bench when his term came to an end. During his time in office, Michael was responsible for some major reforms, a few of which I will outline in this chapter. After Michael decided to go back to the Bar in Auckland, Una Jagose was appointed solicitor-general, the first woman to hold the post. Unlike her two predecessors, she had not practised in a law firm or at the Bar, but instead had come up through the ranks of government lawyers and had had a short period as acting director of the GCSB.

One of the first inquiries I had to undertake as attorney-general was to conduct a review of the Public Prosecution Service. When I became attorney-general, concerns were expressed to me about the cost of public prosecutions, which had increased by 52.6 per cent between 2005/06 and 2009/10. In other words, the cost of prosecutions rose from $21 million to $32 million. Over the same period, the cost of Crown solicitors increased by 51 per cent, from $25 million to $39 million. There were a number of reasons for these hikes, including a series of legislative and other reforms that had increased the cost per prosecution, and there had also been an overall rise in the number of cases. The incoming minister of finance, Bill English, told me that he wanted this area closely examined to ensure that the Crown was getting value for money. Accordingly, I asked the businessman John Spencer to undertake an inquiry.

As I have said, the Crown Law Office is essentially the government's law firm. One of its responsibilities is conducting appeals from criminal trials and Crown appeals against sentence that seek to clarify points of law. It is also responsible for supervising and conducting indictable prosecutions. New Zealand is very lucky to have a public–private partnership involving Crown solicitors. These are private-sector lawyers who are appointed to prosecute under warrants held at pleasure and issued by the governor-general. Each warrant relates to a particular geographical area, usually a High Court area. Crown solicitors are personally responsible for filing indictments, conducting indictable prosecutions and appearing on certain appeals. When Spencer reviewed this area, there were fifteen Crown solicitors in New Zealand holding seventeen warrants (the Crown solicitor in Nelson holds the warrants for both Nelson and Marlborough). Each Crown solicitor is a partner within a law firm and the lawyers within their firm assist them in exercising their prosecution-related responsibilities. Obviously, as private-sector lawyers the Crown solicitors bill the Crown Law Office for the work their firm undertakes. An example of a Crown solicitor's office is Meredith Connell in Auckland, which has held the warrant for a hundred years. When I was attorney-general, the Auckland warrant was split. There is now a firm of lawyers in South Auckland who prosecute crime south from Onehunga, while Meredith Connell continue to act for the rest of Auckland.

The Serious Fraud Office also conducts prosecutions. It has a panel comprising very senior lawyers who have experience in criminal and commercial law proceedings. The Police Prosecution Service was established in 1999 as an autonomous nationwide prosecution service within the New Zealand Police. That service is responsible for managing all prosecution processes in the summary jurisdiction after initial charges are laid by police investigators. Finally, there are departmental prosecutors. For example, the Ministry of Social Development will be responsible for certain prosecutions, and for these it will use in-house prosecutors or brief the matter to a Crown solicitor. Generally, such prosecutions are carried out by an in-house prosecutor if they are reasonably straightforward.

There are guidelines for prosecutions, the most recent set of which was published in 2010. The purpose of the guidelines is to assist all those involved in instituting and conducting criminal prosecutions by ensuring that there is consistency, openness and fairness.

This brief overview of the prosecution system in New Zealand shows how it operates and also helps to explain why it is so expensive to maintain. From time to time there have been suggestions that the Crown solicitor network should be abolished in favour of a fully funded public prosecution system. Those arguments have always been rejected. It is generally accepted that the Crown solicitor network provides an excellent service to the Crown and the public on the prosecution of crime in this country.

John Spencer's review endorsed the current structure of the prosecution system in New Zealand. However, it did say that much better monitoring and reporting arrangements are needed, involving the solicitor-general, enforcement agencies and prosecutors, to promote accountability, consistency, transparency and overall efficiency. The review made particular recommendations for improving the operation of the system.[7]

From time to time Crown solicitors contacted me about departmental prosecutions. For example, one Crown solicitor advised me that he had told the Ministry of Social Development he would carry out a prosecution for them for a fixed sum. The department insisted, however, that one of their in-house prosecutors conduct the prosecution to give them some experience. Thus, that prosecutor was to fly from Wellington to a provincial centre and make submissions on sentence to a judge following a guilty plea. The cost of undertaking that task would have greatly exceeded what the Crown solicitor was going to charge. It is that kind of patch protection one often found in government, and as attorney-general with responsibility in the area, I did my best to stop it.

Next, I decided to conduct a review on the scope and focus of the solicitor-general's role and the operating model of the Crown Law Office. Although I had been attorney-general for only a relatively short period, I was unhappy with the performance of the Crown Law Office and felt that the solicitor-general was overworked. At the time, the solicitor-general was the senior barrister for the Crown, arguing difficult cases in the Court of Appeal and Supreme Court. The solicitor-general was also expected to be the principal legal adviser to the Crown on a number of difficult issues, some of which required urgent attention, and in addition was expected to be the chief executive of a large law firm. It was obvious that one person could not adequately discharge all three responsibilities, and that reforms were required. I was also concerned at the quality of legal advice across government and whether the Crown Law Office was keeping a proper eye on that advice. For that reason, I appointed two senior lawyers, Miriam Dean QC and David Cochrane, special counsel with Simpson Grierson, as independent reviewers. Their task was to look at the office of solicitor-general and the role of the Crown Law Office in improving the quality of legal advice and better management of legal risk across government.

They reported some months later, endorsing the office of solicitor-general but making some sensible suggestions about the way in which management of the Crown Law Office could be improved.[8] They also commented on the quality of legal advice across government, which led to my third major reform. This was the introduction of the Government Legal Network.

While the Crown Law Office is the major provider of legal advice to the Crown, it is not the only source. Within government departments, large teams of lawyers provide advice to their departments. If need be, a matter can be referred to the Crown Law Office if their view is required or if litigation eventuates. Generally speaking, the system had worked adequately, but I was keen to develop a Government Legal Network so that recruitment, ongoing training and mentoring could be conducted from the centre. In-house solicitors could often feel isolated if they gave advice on a particular subject that did not meet with favour from the departmental head. Who could they turn to for support? The Government Legal Network is up and running and is modelled on the system in England. As a result of its establishment, I think continuing legal education within the government service has started to improve.

I was very pleased with the quality of the reports produced by the external experts I engaged. They were independent and insightful, and made sensible and practical recommendations. They could be contrasted with the work done by Dame Margaret Bazley on her review of the legal aid system. Clearly, the cost of legal aid was (and remains) a problem in New Zealand and needed to be addressed, and the government appointed Dame Bazley to undertake that review. My suspicions were aroused when she visited me to ask about my expectations for the outcomes of the inquiry. I told her that, as attorney-general, I wanted her to do a good job and provide my fellow ministers and me with a robust report on the burgeoning costs of legal aid and what could be done about it. In my opinion, her report was disappointing.[9] For example, she wrote off an entire cohort of hard-working criminal lawyers in South Auckland who, many years later, still feel very hurt because of the comments made in that report. That said, legal aid and its mounting costs were a very serious problem for the incoming minister of justice, Simon Power, and reform was required. I would have bulk-funded the legal profession to administer the legal aid system because they knew its operation better than government departments. However, the Ministry of Justice was made responsible for administration of the system and the costs have continued to mount.

It is no answer to say, as the New Zealand Law Society always contends, that the legal aid budget is too small and needs to be increased. This is all very well, but there are many competing claims on government funds and the Law Society and lawyers have to recognise that those funds are not inexhaustible. What is also required is greater efficiency on the part of lawyers conducting cases to prevent unnecessary delay and increases in cost.

When National came into power in 2008, the state of the government finances was very poor — we had inherited a mess. The minister of finance, Bill English, was determined to ensure that the taxpayer received value for money across the board. As attorney-general, I was not immune to fiscal pressures. My predecessor,

Michael Cullen, had had a much easier time, being both minister of finance and attorney-general — if he, as attorney-general, found there were cost pressures involving Crown solicitors, then he could have a very brief conversation with himself as minister of finance and make the necessary changes to ensure the funding was increased. I did not have that luxury and was subjected to the rigorous disciplines imposed by Bill.

The lamentable state of government finances in recent times means that any future government will have to undertake similar inquiries. A review of each of the areas I have referred to probably needs to be conducted once every ten years to ensure things are not slipping away again.

The attorney-general as law officer of the Crown

The attorney-general is the senior law officer of the Crown. That means they are responsible for ensuring that the business of government is conducted in accordance with the rule of law. As I said in the introduction, compliance with the rule of law means 'that all persons and authorities within the state, whether public or private should be bound by and entitled to the benefit of laws publicly and prospectively promulgated and publicly administered in the Courts'.[10] Note the reference here to 'public or private', indicating that the Crown is not above the law. Were that so, this country would cease to be a liberal democracy. That is why the attorney-general is responsible for ensuring that everything government does is in accordance with the rule of law. Note also that the rule of law does not mean rule by judges. Geoffrey Palmer once said that the safest and most dependable part of the constitution is the judiciary. In my opinion, judges should not be afforded a super-elevated status. Of course they perform important work in the state, but they are not safer or more dependable than other parts of the constitution. The rule of law does not mean rule by lawyers, a point emphasised by the former chief justice of Australia, Murray Gleeson, in a lecture he gave in Melbourne on 7 November 2001 where he lamented the commercialisation of litigation as a result of the fee imperatives of the legal profession.[11]

An important component of the rule of law is that the law must afford adequate protection of fundamental human rights. That is why the New Zealand Bill of Rights Act 1990 was passed. Since then, there has been much litigation in our courts on the meaning of various provisions of the Bill of Rights.

An attorney-general has an obligation under the Bill of Rights Act 1990 to bring to the attention of the House of Representatives any provision of a bill that may breach the Bill of Rights. This is a non-political legal function by an attorney-general, who should be prepared to report, whether or not doing so is politically embarrassing. In my time, I issued a number of reports — for example, on the changes that were made in 2010 to the Sentencing Act 2002. These changes introduced what are known as the three strikes provisions, and their purpose was to create a three-stage regime of increasing consequences for the worst repeat violent offenders. I prepared a report to the House under the Bill of Rights Act, concluding that the Sentencing and Parole Reform Bill appeared to be inconsistent with the Bill of Rights and saying:

> I consider that the differential treatment of offenders, and in particular the imposition of a life sentence for offences that would otherwise be subject to a penalty of as little as five years, based on whether they have been previously convicted of listed offences and warned in terms of cl 5 may result in disparities between offenders that are not rationally based. The regime may also result in gross

> disproportionality in sentencing. For these reasons I consider that the proposed regime raises an apparent inconsistency with the Bill of Rights Act.[12]

The legislation passed and has since been the subject of a lot of public comment. It has even been referred to in various cases that have come before the Court of Appeal and Supreme Court, one of which made reference to the provision I have quoted.

As I said, the attorney-general has an obligation to bring these matters to the attention of the House, whether or not they are politically acceptable. Generally speaking, I think that attorneys-general have been faithful to their responsibilities. However, I was concerned that there was no report under the Bill of Rights Act 1990 when the notorious Foreshore and Seabed Bill was introduced in 2004 when Margaret Wilson was attorney-general, and that no report was prepared when the Electoral Finance Bill was introduced in 2007. Regardless of the substantive merits of the legislation, both bills raised important human rights issues. More recently, the changes to the abortion legislation, which raised important issues of freedom of conscience for medical practitioners and nurses, did not attract a Bill of Rights report. This surprised me because, putting aside the merits of the legislation and whatever one thinks of abortion or otherwise, there were questions of freedom of conscience which should have been properly canvassed. Indeed, it was all the more important to have a report as this was to be a conscience vote in the House.

Drafts of Bill of Rights reports are prepared by a specialist section of the Ministry of Justice or Crown Law Office if the bill being examined is the responsibility of the ministry. This ensures there is no conflict of interest between the department promoting a bill and another section of the same department vetting the bill.

However, the report is that of the attorney-general. There were many instances where I rewrote reports to make them more intelligible, or because I disagreed with what was being said and had a debate with the officials concerned. Once I rewrote a report three or four times, largely because earlier versions were simply unintelligible, and the solicitor-general scolded me for being such an enthusiastic editor. I regarded it as bad luck for the solicitor-general. Whatever civil servants wanted or expected, I was not and would never be a nodding automaton in this area.

The attorney-general and the judges

The relationship between the attorney-general and judges is a very important one. The *Cabinet Manual* says that the attorney-general is responsible for being the liaison between the executive and the judiciary.[13] A fundamental aspect of our constitution is the separation of powers. It may seem a statement of the obvious to many, but the judiciary is a separate branch of government; it is not part of the Ministry of Justice. Unfortunately, during my time as attorney-general this somewhat obvious statement needed to be emphasised and re-emphasised to civil servants, particularly in the Ministry of Justice, who simply either did not or could not accept that the judiciary is in fact a separate branch of government. In a variety of practical ways, the Ministry of Justice has a tendency to treat judges as civil servants. They are not, and it is offensive to the constitution to regard them in that way. For that reason, I was very keen to develop a protocol detailing in clear terms the proper constitutional relationship between the judiciary and the executive. I think that protocol was finalised after I left office.

This confusion was not always the fault of the Ministry of Justice (although they were the prime offenders). Sometimes judges became too involved in the operations of the executive. On one occasion a judge wrote to me to let me know of meetings he had scheduled with ministers who had portfolios that impinged on his area, including the associate minister of justice, the minister of education, the minister of corrections, the minister of police and others. I was concerned about the way in which judges were becoming overly involved in the administration of the executive. Judges should not be press-ganged into working for the executive on policy matters because it potentially exposes them to political controversy and criticism. I emphasised to that particular judge and to the head of bench that this kind of involvement was both unfair to judges and constitutionally improper.

It is also important to emphasise that the first point of contact between members of the judiciary and the executive is through the office of the attorney-general. I emphasised to my ministerial colleagues that judges should not contact them except through the attorney-general and I reminded them that it was undesirable for judges to become involved in policy formulation. I asked judges to stop the practice of approaching ministers without my knowledge. It was not a question of control freakery on my part, but a measure to ensure that there was adherence to the fundamental constitutional principle that the attorney-general is the liaison between the executive and the judiciary.

The *Cabinet Manual* has this to say about the relationship between the attorney-general and the judiciary: 'The Attorney-General is the link between the judiciary and executive Government. The Attorney-General recommends the appointment of judges and has an important role in defending the judiciary by answering improper or unfair public criticism, and discouraging Ministerial colleagues from criticising judges and their decisions.'[14] This is a very important role of an attorney-general. During my time, I had regular meetings with the chief justice (on behalf of the High Court, Court of Appeal and Supreme Court) and the chief District Court judge. I would also meet from time to time with the principal judges of the Family Court and the Environment Court, and occasionally with the chief coroner.

As outlined in the quote above, the attorney-general is responsible for the appointment of judges. I once explained to the then United States attorney-general, Eric Holder, how we appoint judges in New Zealand. He almost wept because it seemed so non-partisan and straightforward in comparison with the highly political, contentious and unpleasant hearings that are conducted in the United States Senate whenever a person is nominated to sit on the United States Supreme Court.

The Senior Courts Act 2016 provides that the attorney-general is required to publish information explaining the process for:

> (a) seeking expressions of interest for the appointment of Judges and Associate Judges; and
> (b) recommending persons for appointment as a Judge or an Associate Judge.

The correct constitutional provision on the appointment of senior court judges is set out in section 100 of the Senior Courts Act 2016:

> (1) A Judge is appointed by the Governor-General in the name and on behalf of Her Majesty.
> (2) The Chief Justice is appointed on the recommendation of the Prime Minister.
> (3) Every other Judge, and every Associate Judge, is appointed on the recommendation of the Attorney-General.

It is important to note, and this is not necessarily always understood by judges, that judges are appointed by the governor-general. Sometimes I gained the impression that some heads of bench thought they would be responsible for the appointment of judges — in other words, that it would be some kind of self-appointing priesthood. That is wrong and constitutionally objectionable. Of course judges need to be consulted on proposed appointments, but they do not do the appointing themselves. The procedure for appointment of judges in the District Court is the same as for the senior courts — it is the governor-general who, on the advice of the attorney-general, makes the appointment. As with the senior courts, the attorney-general is required to publish information concerning the process, including seeking expressions of interest for the appointment of judges and nominating persons for appointment as a judge.

These days, the great clarion call is for diversity and transparency in judicial appointments. I was always keen on diversity and actively promoted the appointment of judges who would reflect the make-up of New Zealand society. However, my primary consideration was competence. While it is desirable and indeed necessary to have diversity on the bench, the prime requirement is to ensure that those who serve are competent to do so and will transact the business of the courts in a just and timely fashion. While steps have been taken over the years to persuade judges to give timely judgments, it is not unknown in some courts to have a wait of twelve or eighteen months for a decision. That is contrary to the interests of justice.

It is often said that the process for appointing judges in New Zealand is not transparent. That is wrong. The system is not particularly well known, but that does not mean it is not transparent. Let me outline a few examples from the District Court and the High Court during my time as attorney-general. If a vacancy arose for a judicial appointment in, say, Christchurch, an advertisement would be published inviting candidates to apply. The chief District Court judge would give me a long list of potential candidates and make comments about their application and qualities. From the long list, I would choose three or four candidates. These would then be interviewed by the chief District Court judge, sometimes another judge, and representatives of the Ministry of Justice. I would then receive a memorandum outlining comments on the various applicants and recommendations on whether they were appointable now, appointable at some time in the future or not appointable. I cannot recall any instance when I acted contrary to the recommendations of the chief District Court judge and the panel; it would have been foolish to do so. For me to have appointed a non-appointable person to a District Court position — for political reasons, for example — would have been inappropriate and risky. There were several people I knew who applied for judicial positions but did not interview well. They were not appointed. Often I was given warnings about candidates from sources I will not outline here.

I used to try to attend the swearing-in of District Court judges as often as I could, although in recent years these ceremonies have become longer and more elaborate, often lasting more than two hours. They should be a swearing-in, not a coronation. An attorney-general who appears at such an event is undertaking an important public duty in introducing the judge to the community. As I always used to say at the swearings-in of District Court judges, without a top-quality District Court judiciary, the justice system would collapse. Those judges have to undertake huge amounts of work in a timely manner. I was conscious of the need to ensure that all regions of New Zealand were adequately staffed with judges of the District Court, which is why during my term as attorney-general I placed additional judicial resource in places like Manukau and Gisborne. At the time I was appointed, there was no resident judge in Gisborne and judges had to travel there from Auckland. I regarded that as unsatisfactory, and as a result there are now three judges in Gisborne.

I worked with the chief justice to establish a protocol for the appointment of High Court judges. At the beginning of a year we would have a number of informal discussions about impending retirements and vacancies. On occasion, advertisements would be placed in newspapers inviting lawyers to express an interest in becoming a High Court judge. The Law Society and the Bar Association were regularly consulted, although I was always concerned that if I spoke to some members of the profession they would talk — lawyers can be notorious gossips. The chief justice and I would then draw up a short list. We had to agree on three appointable applicants and then I, as attorney-general, would make the decision.

The appointment of a High Court judge is an important occasion and I used to try to attend as many swearings-in as possible, missing very few in my nine years. I was always very formal in my address to the court because, as I said in relation to the District Court judges, I was performing a public function in introducing the judge to the legal profession and the community. It is not a time for flippancy or humour. From time to time, I would give a relatively serious speech and was then followed by members of the legal profession who would try to be funny in their speeches, telling stories about the judge's past. I always looked on those speeches with contempt. The swearing-in of a judge is not a stag do or an after-dinner speech when people have had too much to drink. While one does not have to be straight-laced, references to aspects of a judge's past that may amuse the speaker are not amusing to the judge or anyone else. On one occasion, a lawyer stood up, addressed the newly appointed judge and told a story about an escapade that was incorrect, and on another, a representative of the Bar Association used a swearing-in as an opportunity to attack the government on aspects of legal aid funding. I thought that was inappropriate and despatched the solicitor-general to have a quiet chat with them to point out that a swearing-in is not an occasion for those sorts of comments.

The procedure for appointment of Court of Appeal and Supreme Court judges was slightly different again, and I was generally guided in this by the recommendations of the chief justice. The role of a Court of Appeal judge is to identify any errors in a High Court judgment and produce (hopefully) a succinct and timely judgment. The Court of Appeal has a very heavy workload — in excess of 300 appeals a year — and so judges appointed to that court must have a lot of experience in trial work and a good understanding of the law so that they can identify a critical issue quickly, deal with any apparent error and publish a judgment. Occasionally, there will be direct appointments to the Court of Appeal but, in my view, these should be a rarity. There is no substitute for having at least some experience as a High Court judge.

Appointments to the Supreme Court have generally been conservative since the court was created in 2003. This has been particularly so following the very sad resignation of Justice Bill Wilson, about whom I will say something shortly. In my time as attorney-general, the most senior judge in the Court of Appeal was generally appointed to fill a vacancy in the Supreme Court. I made a number of appointments, one of the saddest being when I replaced the late Sir Robert Chambers as a judge of the Supreme Court. Justice Chambers, a very fine academic, barrister and judge of the High Court and Court of Appeal, was appointed to the Supreme Court in 2012 and everyone was hopeful that he would be able to serve at least twelve years on the bench. However, after only about eighteen months on the bench, he died very suddenly.

His loss is still keenly felt within the profession and on the bench. He was a wonderful judge and I was devastated when I learnt of his untimely death.

It was always a delight to appear before Justice Chambers. Once I had instructions to appear in the Court of Appeal to oppose an application for leave to appeal out of time. The judge was very courteous, telling me that, generally speaking, the Court of Appeal allowed an applicant to appeal out of time, although the court would impose costs and ensure that the case was timetabled for an early hearing. After I had finished, the lawyer for the applicant stood up and wanted to answer some of my points about the hopelessness of the appeal. Justice Chambers said he didn't need to go into that because the appeal could proceed on the basis he had put to me. The lawyer, however, insisted on making submissions, at the end of which Justice Chambers said, 'Oh, I see now what Mr Finlayson was saying. Your appeal is hopeless.' The application for leave to appeal out of time was dismissed. It was a classic example of a lawyer talking too much. It happens a lot.

By convention, an attorney-general will consult the shadow attorney-general in the opposition to advise of an impending appointment and to invite any comments they may feel are appropriate. This normally occurs a day or so before the appointment is announced.

After I entered Parliament, Don Brash made me the shadow attorney-general. One afternoon I received a phone call from Michael Cullen, Helen Clark's attorney-general, to tell me that Bill Wilson QC was shortly to be announced as a judge of the Court of Appeal. It was a rare case of a direct appointment to that court. I had known Bill for many years, and he was an outstanding lawyer as well as a good friend. He had been a partner of mine at Bell Gully for a number of years and we worked together on several interesting cases. Shortly after he went to the Bar, he was made a QC — I don't think anyone else has taken silk more quickly. I also think he conducted more appeals to the Privy Council than any other New Zealand lawyer, with the possible exception of George Barton QC. Bill was a very public-spirited man. He served with distinction on the Law Society for many years (including on its board) and on bodies such as the Waitangi Tribunal, where he wrote a very important report on Napier Harbour. In my opinion, there was no better person to be appointed to the Court of Appeal than him. I thought it was one of those rare situations where a direct appointment was justified and to be applauded, and I said as much to Cullen. What subsequently happened to Bill was the most distressing thing that occurred during my nine years as attorney-general. Let me outline this very sad story.

A company called Saxmere marketed merino wool, and it sued the Wool Board Disestablishment Company Limited (the successor to the New Zealand Wool Board) for refusing to provide it with market subsidies. I need not outline the detail of the case. The High Court found that the Wool Board had breached its statutory duty and had been negligent. The Wool Board appealed to the Court of Appeal, which unanimously overturned the High Court decision. One of the judges in the Court of Appeal was Justice Wilson. Saxmere applied for leave to appeal to the Supreme Court on the basis that the Wool Board's lead counsel in the Court of Appeal, Alan Galbraith QC (a senior and highly respected member of the Bar), was a longstanding friend of Justice Wilson, with whom he was in a financial relationship. The Supreme Court rejected the appeal, failing to find a case of apparent bias.[15] After the first judgment, there were allegations that the nature of this financial relationship was more extensive than the judge had previously stated. So Saxmere applied for a recall of the first judgment, and the Supreme Court found that there was an imbalance between the contributions of the two investors, which was well above the level of an indebtedness that could be regarded as minimal or immaterial. As a result, the judgment was recalled.

Attention then turned to the investigation of Justice Wilson's conduct by the judicial conduct commissioner, who recommended the appointment of a judicial conduct panel to investigate the various complaints that had been made by Saxmere and another from a former Court of Appeal judge, Ted Thomas. The commissioner decided a full inquiry into Justice Wilson's conduct was justified. The panel began its hearing in late 2010, but then Justice Wilson chose to resign after a negotiation with the acting attorney-general. I could not be involved in this matter because of my previous association and friendship with Bill, and so I declared a conflict of interest and the prime minister asked Judith Collins to deal with the issue as acting attorney-general. I therefore had to watch the tragedy developing from the sidelines.

It seems to me that at the time of the hearing in the Court of Appeal, Justice Wilson did not owe any money to Galbraith, and nor did he owe anything to the jointly owned company. At the same time, the company owed both Justice Wilson and Galbraith substantial sums because both men had advanced money to it, and the assets of the company exceeded its liabilities, including any current account advances by the shareholders. The company owed Galbraith about $75,000 more than it owed Justice Wilson. In the overall scheme of things, that was a very small, immaterial amount that should not have concerned the Supreme Court.

I have always thought the first Supreme Court judgment was correct, but I continued to be concerned about the second judgment. In particular, I have never been able to understand why it was said that Justice Wilson was either directly or indirectly indebted to counsel appearing before him. I fail to see how the difference in the shareholder accounts of both shareholders could be said to create indebtedness from him to Galbraith. Indeed, I have difficulty understanding what 'indirect indebtedness' is. All that was apparent to me was that the company owed one shareholder more than it owed the other. The other point I would make is that the difference in question was around $75,000. If that created some kind of 'indirect indebtedness' to the lawyer who was appearing before the judge, then there was a question of materiality. In other words, the sum was so small as to not be of concern.

This question of the alleged indebtedness has been the subject of a lot of discussion throughout the legal profession over the years. There are a number of very senior lawyers who have questioned the correctness of the second judgment and think that Bill Wilson was treated very unfairly.

I was also concerned at the intervention of the former Court of Appeal judge, Ted Thomas. For reasons best known to himself, he entered the fray and laid a complaint. I thought it was inappropriate for a former judge to involve himself in such a controversial matter. In my opinion, sitting judges should speak through their judgments and retired judges should shut up. I disdain the notion of the celebrity judge.

From time to time judges have been appointed to Royal Commissions. This can be fraught with danger. In 1980, Robert Muldoon appointed the Christchurch-based Supreme Court judge Peter Mahon to investigate the tragic Air New Zealand plane crash on Mt Erebus the previous year. His report was the subject of a lot of criticism, and the phrase 'orchestrated litany of lies' he used is well known to most lawyers. As a result of the criticism, he resigned his position and his career was destroyed. There is also the case of Dame Lowell Goddard, who was appointed to the High Court of New Zealand in 1995. She also served on the Independent Police Conduct Authority, and in 2015 was appointed by United Kingdom

Home Secretary Theresa May to chair the Independent Inquiry into Sexual Abuse in England and Wales. The inquiry panel had become very toxic and had lost a number of chairs, and the government was anxious to find an independent chair, preferably from within the Commonwealth. Following her appointment, Justice Goddard resigned from the New Zealand High Court. Sometime later, however, she wrote to me advising that she had decided to resign from the inquiry because of very intense personal attacks on her. I fear that when Justice Goddard indicated that she was going to investigate certain matters, the establishment was not at all happy. Her career as chair of that body came to a sudden end.

Fortunately, my appointments of judges as chairs of two Royal Commissions were highly successful. After the 2010 Pike River Mine tragedy, the government needed an experienced person to chair the Royal Commission into it. The chief justice suggested Graham Panckhurst, who had been born in Reefton. He was an experienced High Court judge held in great esteem by the profession and by his fellow judges. He and his fellow members of the Royal Commission did an outstanding job. After Kate Wilkinson resigned as the minister of labour, I was charged with reporting to the families in Greymouth about the contents of the Royal Commission report. It is a tribute to Justice Panckhurst and the team that every one of their proposals was accepted by the government and given effect in what is now the health and safety at work law, shepherded through Parliament by Michael Woodhouse as minister of labour. The other appointment I made, again at the urging of the chief justice, was of Justice Mark Cooper as the chair of the Canterbury Earthquakes Royal Commission in 2011. He and his fellow commissioners undertook an extraordinary inquiry on behalf of the people of Christchurch, and their recommendations were, as I understand it from various sources, world class. Justice Cooper is now president of the Court of Appeal. We are indeed very fortunate to have in this country people of the calibre of those judges, who undertook sensitive and difficult inquiries and did such a good job.

I was also responsible for the inquiry that looked into the problems associated with the Havelock North drinking water system. On that occasion, I approached Judge Lyn Stevens (then ten days retired) of the Court of Appeal and asked him if he could undertake the inquiry. Justice Stevens, ably assisted by Nathan Gedye QC as counsel assisting, produced an excellent report that laid the foundations for many of the water reforms being advanced by the Labour minister of local government, Nanaia Mahuta.

Defending the judiciary

It is a well-established convention that ministers should exercise judgement before commenting on decisions, whether generally or in relation to the specifics of an individual case. They must not comment adversely on a judge. From time to time, I would need to remind my colleagues of this important principle. I can recall one time where a judgment was given in a somewhat contentious matter involving land that had been zoned in Christchurch following the 2011 earthquake. Gerry Brownlee, as the minister responsible, made a comment about Justice Panckhurst. To Gerry's credit, he sent me a note in the House apologising for the comment as soon as he made it, and I phoned the chief justice after question time to advise her of what had happened. Gerry knew he had overstepped the line and was deeply apologetic. Given the pressure he was under as the minister, I fully understood and took the matter no further.

On occasion, people — including members of the legal profession — make unfair comments about a judge. I can recall that, when one judge retired, I appeared on behalf of the Crown to acknowledge his public service and thank him for his contribution.

In his speech he spent quite some time talking about an attack on him following a judgment he had given in a contentious criminal matter. I was very angry that the matter had not been brought to my attention because I would have said something on behalf of him. The criticism of him was very unfair and he was clearly hurt by it. The Crown Law Office failed to advise me of what was happening and they made a serious error in so doing.

Sometimes I was required to explain the rationale for a decision. On one occasion, the Crown decided to prosecute two people in Rotorua for the manslaughter of their child rather than prosecuting them for murder. There was a great public outcry about the matter, and I felt that after the sentencing had been pronounced in the High Court in Rotorua I should make a statement. John Key was concerned about my making public comments and in particular what I was going to say because it was a matter of great public interest. He feared a backlash if I got it wrong. After the sentencing that afternoon, I appeared on the tiles in Parliament and explained the rationale for the decision, which was that the Crown did not have enough evidence to be sure it could succeed in securing a conviction of murder. The defendants were prepared to plead guilty to manslaughter, and that was regarded as acceptable in the circumstances given the evidential hurdles that the Crown faced in prosecuting them for murder. As it turned out, the trial judge sentenced the defendants to a very long time in prison. I felt it was one of those occasions where an attorney-general's explanation of what had happened was in the public interest and was helpful. The media understood exactly what I was saying and the criticism and questioning ceased.

Mentioning appointment of judges in cabinet

By convention, once a decision has been made to appoint a person to a judicial position, the attorney-general informs cabinet. This takes place in oral items towards the end of a cabinet meeting. The prime minister would say to me 'Mr Attorney, judicial appointments, please', and I would then proceed to outline the appointments and the persons concerned. Very rarely there would be some discussion about the appointments, but it was generally accepted that these were simply mentioned in cabinet and were not brought to cabinet for approval. I have been told that, since the Second World War, there has been only one occasion when a judicial appointment was rebuffed by cabinet. I will not go into the detail of this matter because it is sensitive, even after all these years, but I will say that the attorney-general was told by another senior member of cabinet (who outranked him) that the appointment was unacceptable because of the appointee's political affiliations and tendencies. The attorney-general was asked to reconsider the matter. As it turned out, the nominee was not appointed.

Had my judgement been questioned in that way, I would have felt no alternative but to resign immediately. I appointed a number of people who I knew were left wing, but in my opinion a person's political affiliations were secondary to their ability to do a good job on the bench. In his autobiography, Michael Cullen made the same point, and he commented that I appointed his brother-in-law as a judge — as indeed I did.[16] It never occurred to me to waste one minute on thinking whether or not his brother-in-law was a Labour party supporter or voter; I neither knew nor cared. All I knew is that he had been an excellent Crown solicitor in Napier and would be an excellent judge. The politics of an appointee are irrelevant.

The attorney-general and law reform

The attorney-general is not the minister of justice. That may seem to be blindingly obvious, but some explanation is required. Until the

Bill of Rights Act 1990 was passed, it was generally the case (with some exceptions) that the attorney-general would also be minister of justice. For example, Ralph Hanan held both positions from 1960 to 1969, as did Jim McLay from 1978 to 1984 and Geoffrey Palmer 1984 to 1989, at which point the roles were split. One of the major reasons why an attorney-general is not now the minister of justice is related to the attorney's Bill of Rights responsibilities. Specifically, it is not desirable for an attorney-general to vet his or her own legislation. On certain occasions, some of my legislation was vetted for Bill of Rights compliance and an acting attorney-general was appointed for the purpose, such as when Simon Power was made acting attorney-general in 2010 to vet the Marine and Coastal Area (Takutai Moana) Bill for which I was responsible.

That does not mean to say that an attorney-general is not involved in law reform. As someone responsible for ensuring that the business of government is conducted in accordance with the rule of law, and as the link between the judiciary and the executive, it follows that on a number of occasions issues are raised with the attorney-general that involve law reform. The attorney-general then raises these issues with other ministers, principally the minister of justice.

Occasionally, the minister of justice would let me take the lead on substantive areas. I had always had an interest in the law of limitation and, as an opposition MP, I had drafted a bill to repeal the Limitation Act 1950, which was badly out of date, and replace it with modern limitation legislation. I raised the matter with the then president of the Law Commission, Geoffrey Palmer, when it was justifiably felt by the National caucus that the issue was too large for a member's bill, and Geoffrey convened a committee to look at reform of the law. Having consulted the then minister of justice, Annette King, Geoffrey asked me to serve on that committee and I was very pleased to do so. The Law Commission did some excellent work on reform of the law, and after I became attorney-general they published a report recommending legislative change.[17] I asked the minister of justice, Simon Power, if I could be responsible for pushing that legislation through, and he was supportive of my so doing. So I actually was the minister responsible for reform of the law of limitation thanks to Simon.

I also had an interest in reform of the law of contempt. Many people think it is about protecting judges from justified criticism, but that is unfair and wrong. In fact, it is about protecting the administration of justice. Sometimes judges will have to deal with those who breach suppression orders or who scandalise the court. Personal and vicious attacks on judges because of decisions they have made cannot be allowed to continue. One can always criticise a judgment, but sometimes the criticism of a judge goes so far that the law must intervene to protect the administration of justice. It is a complex and difficult area, and that is why I thought there needed to be some work done on it. However, I could not persuade the ministers of justice with whom I worked to give this priority over other areas. Accordingly, I asked the Crown Law Office to do some preliminary work on the subject. They engaged a professor of law of Victoria University, Tony Smith, who had published a leading text on this subject. He reported, and in due course it was referred to the Law Commission by Judith Collins for further work. In 2017 the Law Commission published a report recommending reform and annexed to their report was a draft bill.[18] Unfortunately, I could not persuade Amy Adams as minister of justice that this legislation deserved priority, and so the project languished. After I became an opposition MP again, I took the draft bill and put it in the ballot as a member's bill. Amazingly, after I had spent so many years trying to advance the project as a minister, the bill was pulled out of the ballot in 2018. I told the minister of justice, Andrew Little, that this reform was too big for an individual MP and the government should take the bill over, and he did so. I will not traverse the interesting procedural tale of the contempt bill here, as that has been described extremely well by Sir Douglas White, a former president of the Law Commission, in a very interesting article.[19] Suffice it to say that the law of contempt has now been reformed and the Act seems to be working well.

So, a positive working relationship between the attorney-general and minister of justice is essential if there is to be reform in important areas of the law. I always had a good relationship with Judith Collins, who was minister of justice from 2011 to 2014. I told her that the legislation relating to the courts and judicial review needed to be reformed, and she was enthusiastic about the project. The result was the first major reform of courts legislation since the Judicature Act 1908, and she deserves credit for that excellent work. I did not share a similarly close working relationship with Amy Adams, and law reform suffered as a result. For example, I was disappointed that we did not reform Part 5 of the Crimes Act 1961 (dealing with public order offences) or the Terrorism Suppression Act 2002, which I considered to be ineffective. The latter had been used initially at the time of the raids on Rūātoki in the rohe (territory) of Ngāi Tūhoe in 2007. That particular raid was a disaster, but it did expose the inadequacies of the Act.

Legal proceedings involving the Crown

The *Cabinet Manual* states the principle that the conduct of legal proceedings involving the Crown is the responsibility of the attorney-general.[20] In practice, however, the solicitor-general, the Crown Law Office or departmental legal teams generally provide legal services to the minister or department involved in proceedings.

The attorney-general is responsible for monitoring litigation or prosecutions in which the Crown is involved and will inform cabinet of progress.

What does that mean in practice? It would be contrary to the public interest for an attorney-general to be actively involved in prosecutions. As the *Cabinet Manual* says, an attorney-general will be intensely interested in the course of a prosecution but will not take an active role in it, instead delegating to the solicitor-general responsibility for such matters. A good example is the prosecutions that followed the Pike River Mine disaster. As attorney-general, I had no involvement in the decision to prosecute Peter Whittall or the subsequent arrangement that was entered into and that resulted in an appeal to the Supreme Court. As mentioned by Rebecca Macfie in her biography of Helen Kelly, I had doubts about the wisdom of entering into any agreement with Whittall.[21] Sometimes it is in the public interest that a prosecution proceed, but in the case of the Pike River tragedy I felt that a decision had been made that was not in the public interest. When the case was going to the Supreme Court, I expressed my hope to the solicitor-general that the Crown would lose, because I thought Whittall should have been prosecuted through to trial.

Another example is extradition cases, in which I had no involvement. Take the Dotcom case. Kim Dotcom was brought to my attention in the middle of the 2011 election campaign. The solicitor-general asked to see me and briefed me in my capacity as a law officer about inquiries being made about Dotcom and his associates. I was specifically asked not to talk to my colleagues about this matter. Given that I was in the middle of an election campaign, I received the information but was far too busy to reflect on it or indeed talk to anyone. The next I heard about the affair was shortly before the raid on Dotcom's Coatesville mansion in 2012. As it turned out, I was in San Francisco on holiday at the time and so joined a telephone conference where the solicitor-general briefed the prime minister and me about the impending raid. Contrary to what Dotcom may think, the prime minister knew nothing about him. When his name was first mentioned, John Key's first question was 'Is he Korean?' And then after some discussion he said, 'Oh, is that who's living in that mansion in Coatesville?' (Coatesville was in his Helensville electorate.) He and I were briefed and the raid took place a day or so later. Then began the extradition saga. I received regular reports on how the litigation was going, but I had nothing to do with it at all. The suggestion that I was some kind of *éminence grise* conducting the litigation on behalf of Warner Bros., with whom I had met when their representatives were in New Zealand, is laughable. As I said, I could take no active part in the litigation. The same principle applied when John Banks was subsequently prosecuted over an alleged breach of the rules relating to donations.

This is as it should be. Politicians should not actively involve themselves in any issue affecting the liberty of a subject. It would be contrary to the rule of law and to our liberal democracy for an attorney-general to be seeking to make decisions about whether a person should be prosecuted, whether an appeal should be filed against a decision and so on. That should always be left to the non-political law officer and their team. It is simply wrong to suggest that I played any role in either the prosecution of a citizen or New Zealand resident, or the conduct of any civil litigation, during my nine years as attorney-general.

The attorney-general as advocate

In England and Wales, the responsibility of an attorney-general appearing as counsel has been increasingly devolved on the solicitor-general over the years, although certain serious crimes against the state such as treason and sedition, as well as cases involving serious constitutional considerations or public order, were prosecuted personally by the attorney-general as advocate, as were poisonings. The latter practice — understood to reflect either public abhorrence or historical forensic difficulty in such cases — lapsed in the course of the twentieth century, with one solicitor-general, Sir Stafford Cripps, describing it as 'the most ridiculous thing imaginable' and a constitutional expert, John Edwards, criticising the practice as weakening the 'cardinal principle' of separation between the attorney-general as political law officer and the conduct of prosecutions.[22]

English attorneys-general have continued to appear from time to time in cases of particular moment. For example, Dominic Grieve QC appeared in the Supreme Court (in the first appearance by an attorney-general in that court since its establishment in 2009) in a Human Rights Act case concerning prisoner voting rights. While no reason for that appearance was given, the particular issue was not only politically contentious but also the subject of judicial conflict, with senior United Kingdom judges expressing criticisms of the European Court of Human Rights, and vice versa.

An attorney-general may sometimes act personally, such as in stays of proceedings in matters affecting the public interest. In New Zealand, the most prominent example of this was in 1991, in respect of charges against the alleged French agents who bombed the *Rainbow Warrior*.[23] Apart from that there has not been much comment about an attorney-general being involved as an advocate and appearing in court. During Geoffrey Palmer's term as attorney-general, he stated publicly that he would not appear before the New Zealand courts at all, referring to variable results and concern that it might suggest political interference.

There are records of appearances by the attorney-general as the Crown's representative and — in the nineteenth century — as a practitioner for a private party,[24] but the practice was very uneven. There are regular reported appearances in the late 1880s by Sir Robert Stout, and from the early 1900s to 1925 by Sir John Findlay, KC, Sir Francis Bell, KC and others, but only occasional reported cases since then:

- Rex Mason QC appeared in *Godwin v Walker* [1938] NZLR 712 (CA), an extradition case, and in *R v Morison* [1950] NZLR 247, concerning the jurisdiction of the Māori Land Court to inquire into certain titles — the latter issue having recently arisen again in *Paki v Attorney-General* [2012] 3 NZLR 277 (SC).
- John Marshall appeared in *R v Freeman* [1955] NZLR 718 (CA), concerning preventive detention.
- Martyn Finlay QC appeared in *Green & McCahill Contractors Ltd v Minister of Works* [1974] 1 NZLR 661 (CA), a Public Works Act case.
- Jim McLay appeared at first instance in *R v Bryant & Ors*, a high-profile prosecution of assaults on two police constables, although not on appeal (*R v Bryant* [1980] 1 NZLR 264 (CA)), where the attorney-general was found to have been an unwitting party to a procedural error. To the best of my knowledge, no attorney-general has since appeared in the criminal jurisdiction of the High Court or the Court of Appeal.
- Paul East QC appeared as *amicus curiae* and on behalf of the House of Representatives in *Prebble v Television New Zealand Ltd* [1994] 3 NZLR 1 (PC), concerning parliamentary privilege, and in the two courts mentioned below.

There is a more consistent practice of appearances by attorneys-general as counsel in international proceedings. In addition to the

Whaling in the Antarctic (Australia v Japan: New Zealand intervening) case in 2013, in which the Australian attorney-general and I appeared, Martyn Finlay QC represented New Zealand in the country's first appearance before the International Court of Justice in *Nuclear Tests (New Zealand v France)* (1974), while Paul East QC appeared in New Zealand's request for re-examination of that claim following the resumption of French underground nuclear testing in 1995. Paul East QC also appeared in the International Court of Justice's advisory case *Advisory Opinion on the Legality of the Threat or Use of Nuclear Weapons* (1996).

Much of what I have written here on the varied tasks of the attorney-general may appear to be very lawyerly and dry; that is because much of it is. But what I have endeavoured to show is that New Zealand is a country governed by the rule of law. This means that everyone, including the greatest and most powerful, are the servants of the law and have to comply with it. There can be no exceptions, which is particularly the case insofar as the Crown, the most powerful body in the land, is concerned. It is important that the Crown and its servants understand that, in everything they do, they are subject to the law. The person responsible for ensuring both compliance with, and understanding of, those fundamental principles is the attorney-general.

CHAPTER 7 Minister for arts, culture and heritage

WHEN TONY ABBOTT WON THE ELECTION in Australia in 2013 and became prime minister, he appointed George Brandis QC of Queensland as attorney-general and also minister for the arts. I immediately wrote to George congratulating him and welcoming him to my exclusive club. To the best of my knowledge, he and I were the only attorneys-general who also held the culture portfolio. Whenever we had a meeting of the quintet of attorneys-general, we both received comments from our United States, Canadian and English colleagues about how strange it was that an attorney-general should also be in charge of culture.

Actually, it's not all that strange. In my opinion, the arts run best when they are administered by lawyers. Our best arts administrators over the last half-century were lawyers, not least Bill Sheat, who was a partner in the respected Lower Hutt firm Gibson Sheat. His primary love, however, was the arts. During the course of an outstanding career, Bill was responsible for creating the New Zealand Film Commission in 1978, he served as a long-time trustee of the now defunct Downstage Theatre in Wellington, and he also served on the board of the Royal New Zealand Ballet for years and on the Queen Elizabeth II Arts Council (the forerunner of Creative New Zealand). Bill told me many stories about his time as deputy chair of the Arts Council when Bill Sutch was the chair, especially around the drama in the early 1970s when Sutch was being prosecuted for treason. Someone who shall remain nameless told me recently that Sutch had not really wanted to be chair of the QEII Arts Council; he wanted to be the head of the NZSIS! Another giant of the arts in New Zealand is David Gascoigne, a former partner of Watts and Patterson (now known as MinterEllison). He was responsible for creating the New Zealand International Festival of the Arts (now the Aotearoa New Zealand Festival of the Arts) and served with distinction on the QEII Arts Council, the board of Te Papa and many other arts organisations.

Out of loyalty to Bell Gully, I should also mention Dick Simpson, who was a foundation member, then subsequently chair, of the QEII Arts Council, as well as president of the Katherine Mansfield Menton Fellowship, the Wellington Youth Orchestra, the National Art Gallery, the Dominion Museum and many other organisations.[1] The first chair of the QEII Arts Council was Gordon Watson, a senior partner of Chapman Tripp.

I, too, had had a long career in arts administration before becoming minister, although my first involvement was rather strange. One day in the mid-1990s, I received a phone call from the late Michael Hirschfeld, subsequently president of the Labour party and a leading light in Circa Theatre. He wanted me to sue the QEII Arts Council on behalf of Circa because it had made some silly decisions about the theatre's funding. Traditionally, the QEII Arts Council favoured Downstage Theatre and regarded Circa as an upstart, and the inequality around funding continued for many years and irritated Circa. We commenced a proceeding seeking judicial review of the council's decisions, but it was settled after a couple of rounds.

Shortly after that, I was approached about being a member of the Arts Board of Creative New Zealand. When he was minister of cultural affairs, Doug Graham reformed the old QEII Arts Council and it subsequently became known as Creative New Zealand. The organisation is run by the Arts Council, which has overall responsibility for governance and policy, and for two boards, including the Arts Board, which was responsible for funding decisions. With respect, this 1990s obsession about the funder–provider split did not make a lot of sense in the arts, and when I became the minister, I reversed it so that there is now one council.

My involvement in the Arts Board was very satisfying, and I thought we achieved a great deal with very little funding. After Claudia Scott resigned as chair, I was appointed to the position by Simon Upton, who was then minister of cultural affairs. During my time as chair, we established the Berlin Writer's Residency and finally decided to attend the Venice Biennale, known as the Olympic Games of the visual arts. I discussed with David Gascoigne why we had not participated in Venice before the late 1990s, and he said it was always a question of money. I thought it was time we went, so after the council staff carried out some research we made the decision to attend. As chair of the Arts Board, I had to report to the Arts Council and secure the agreement of its members. Peter Biggs, now chief executive of the New Zealand Symphony Orchestra (NZSO) but then chair of the Arts Council, was very supportive, but some of his council members were opposed to the idea. When

I addressed council members about New Zealand's participation at the Biennale, the leading opponent was the former MP Marilyn Waring, who was sceptical about the merits of attending. Marilyn and I had an interesting exchange of views. Eventually, she backed down and approval was granted. New Zealand's contributions at the Venice Biennale since the late 1990s have always been very well received. There was some controversy in the early 2000s when the person selected to attend (who went by the name of Et Al) refused all interviews. Moreover, there was more than a little concern about her proposed installation, which involved a donkey braying in a toilet. Helen Clark was minister for arts, culture and heritage at the time and was not all that happy with the proposal — and nor would I have been. Poor Peter had to front up to Paul Holmes and other aggressive journalists and respond on behalf of the Arts Council.

As minister for arts, culture and heritage, I was responsible for, among other things, the New Zealand Film Commission, which has done much to develop and nurture the film industry in New Zealand. The chair at the time of my appointment in 2008, David Cullwick, had been excellent, but I decided that it was time to refresh the commission and appointed Patsy Reddy, an outstanding Wellington commercial lawyer, to the role. Patsy was a former tutor of mine when I was a law student at Victoria University (she always hated my referring to that fact), and had a great interest in, and experience of, the film industry. She made an outstanding chair.

One of the most important arts issues in my time as minister concerned filming of *The Hobbit*. One night in 2010, Richard Taylor of Weta Workshop contacted me. He said that Peter Jackson and his partner, Fran Walsh, were beside themselves with worry because of militant union action, which they feared would result in Warner Bros. deciding to exit New Zealand and relocating filming to somewhere more congenial. Richard asked me whether it would be possible for the prime minister to meet with Peter over the coming weeks to discuss the issue. I checked with the prime minister's office as to his availability, and John phoned me back to say he would see Peter immediately. An hour or so later, Peter and Fran came down to Parliament and met with John and me. Peter explained the situation and the activities of the union representatives, which were undermining the interests of the film industry in New Zealand. The prime minister was very straightforward, saying that the government could change the legislation to clarify the position of contractors so that production could proceed in New Zealand. The decision to legislate in urgency infuriated Helen Kelly and the union movement, but I think the unions had only themselves to blame.

After the Employment Relations (Film Production Work) Amendment Bill was passed in the House in October 2010, Peter and Fran wrote to me thanking the government for its support and for advocating on behalf of the thousands of people who work in the film industry, especially those who were facing the loss of their jobs on *The Hobbit*. They said: 'You have given film workers, producers, and local and overseas investors, the clarity they need to keep building film investment in New Zealand and perhaps more importantly you have protected the New Zealand film community from ill-conceived and pernicious attack from an off-shore organisation which has no regard for the welfare of our industry.'

As a result of the legislation, the producers of *Avatar* indicated they were giving very serious consideration to filming the two sequels in New Zealand, which is exactly what happened. While the union movement may have complained about the legislation, it was necessary to protect the film industry, and I was pleased we were able to help two great New Zealanders and their company at a critical time. Had we not done so, the film industry in New Zealand would have been very severely harmed.

In her biography of Helen Kelly, Rebecca Macfie referred to the good political connections held by Peter Jackson and the fact that he had recently completed a review of the New Zealand Film Commission for me.[2] It is true that Peter had undertaken a review of the Film Commission; his report was excellent and well received by the film industry.[3] It is also true that he had good political connections, not simply with the centre right but across politics — everyone knew the contribution he had made. The problem was that the Australian representative of the Media, Entertainment and Arts Alliance, of which the New Zealand Actors Equity was a branch, was putting undue pressure on the film industry in New Zealand. Simon Whipp, the Australian representative, was in New Zealand, and it was said he was keen to unionise the entire film industry. If that had happened, then there would be no international productions in New Zealand and we would have become a backwater. Urgent action was required to change the law to protect and promote such an important part of the economy.

The next issue was what incentives would be required to persuade Warner Bros. to stay in New Zealand. Their directors and lawyers were invited to New Zealand to speak to the government. A number of officials arrived a few weeks later, and Gerry Brownlee, then minister of economic development, and I met with those officials in Premier House in Tinakori Road. After a few hours, I was concerned that their demands were excessive and reported as such to the prime minister. John said that he would speak to them, and then went to a meeting and sorted out a deal in no time at all. What amazed me was that he did so without any briefing notes or officials; he was well seized of the issues and negotiated with authority. It was a superlative performance by John, and I know that the Warner Bros. officials were amazed that New Zealand had as its prime minister a man who was so on top of the detail and could address issues without the need for extensive briefing papers or armies of civil servants.

During my time as minister I was determined to restructure the Arts Council to remove the funder–provider split distinction, which had been embedded in the Arts Council of New Zealand Toi Aotearoa Act 1994. I wanted to simplify the structure and felt that those at the top table had to be conversant with funding decisions as well as policy. The reformed legislation provided for the appointment of thirteen members of a council, which is too large but was the result of negotiations with, among others, Georgina te Heuheu, who was then associate minister of Māori affairs.

Another major reform concerned updating the historic places legislation. The National Historic Places Trust had been established by a previous National government in the 1950s, but the legislation governing it was overdue for reform. What resulted was the Heritage New Zealand Pouhere Taonga Act 2014 and the establishment of Heritage New Zealand, which is a more appropriate organisation to preserve historic buildings in New Zealand.

Heritage issues were, of course, extremely important after the earthquakes in Christchurch in 2010 and 2011. The reality, however, is that many of the buildings that collapsed should have been demolished years before. Some years ago I was talking to Sir Michael Fowler, who was mayor of Wellington from 1974 to 1983. He told me that he had received some horrifying reports about Wellington's buildings shortly after he was elected, and had to make some tough decisions about heritage buildings in, for example, Manners Street. Many of them simply had to be demolished because they did not comply with the then earthquake requirements and were not in a good state, even though they looked great on the outside. Unfortunately, in Christchurch many equally unsafe buildings were not demolished and their destruction during the 2011 earthquake contributed to the loss of life.

As minister, I was very concerned about the two finest buildings in Christchurch: the Roman Catholic Cathedral of the Blessed Sacrament in Barbadoes Street and the Anglican Christ Church Cathedral in Cathedral Square. Of these two buildings, there was really no debate that the Catholic cathedral was superior. Many people know the story about the Irish playwright George Bernard Shaw upsetting the snobs of Christchurch when he referred to their outstanding cathedral and then clarified that he was talking about the Catholic cathedral. Tough decisions needed to be made about that cathedral after the February 2011 earthquake, and it has now been demolished. That is a tragedy, but the Catholic Church simply did not have the resources required to restore it.

The Anglican cathedral is now being repaired, but this should have been done years ago. One day in 2014 I was in Christchurch and saw the state of it, and so phoned Gerry Brownlee and suggested that we really should try to do something about having it repaired. He arranged for a meeting with the Anglican bishop of Christchurch, Victoria Matthews, and a subsequent meeting with Jim Anderton and Philip Burdon, who were leading the campaign to restore the cathedral. I always felt sorry for the bishop, who was concerned about her flock. About 40 per cent of the population of Christchurch was once Anglican, but that has dwindled to about 10 per cent. Bishop Matthews was responsible for a number of heritage buildings that the Anglican Church could not afford to restore, and she was more concerned with getting people to church than protecting museums. I said to her that we could help, but she had a real concern about spending more than $100 million on repairing a cathedral. That was a legitimate way of looking at the issue. Her principal antagonists at the time were Anderton and Burdon. When Gerry and I met with them, Anderton (who was actually a Roman Catholic) said that he had a couple of points he wanted to make. Forty minutes later, the monologue was continuing and I endeavoured to ask a couple of questions. He effectively told me to shut up because he still had more to say. His was a somewhat bullying performance. I felt that if he had shown some courtesy and understanding to the bishop, there may have been a more positive outcome.

The reality of the matter is, however, that Christchurch does not need two cathedrals. I note that the Catholics have now decided to build their own cathedral not far from the Anglican cathedral. Why they cannot join forces and use the same cathedral simply escapes me. I had an idea that the church could be rededicated by the archbishop of Canterbury and the Pope, and that people could learn to pray together. Sadly, that common-sense approach has not prevailed, and the Catholics are now going to spend huge resources on building their own cathedral — a waste of money in my opinion.

In 2008, when I was an opposition MP, the then deputy mayor of Wellington, Ian McKinnon, asked me if I could visit Mt Cook School with him. This school, situated on the corner of Tory and Buckle streets in Te Aro, is a well-established primary school in the capital and at the time was led by an outstanding principal called Sandy McCallum. It was a richly diverse school, with children from many nationalities and backgrounds. I established a good relationship with Sandy and wanted to help the school in any way possible. The school was particularly concerned that the redevelopment of the National War Memorial precinct would involve moving State Highway 1 closer to it, with attendant pollution and noise problems.

Nothing happened for a few years, and then one day John Key mentioned to me that if we won the 2011 election we should do something special at the precinct and that it should be ready before the events in 2014 commemorating the start of the First World War. After we won the election, cabinet made the decision to have a 'cut and cover', whereby a tunnel would be created so that the traffic would not bisect what was regarded as sacred ground. I asked one of my staff to phone Sandy and invite her to my office. She turned up looking extremely apprehensive, as though she were expecting to be told the bad news about the motorway development. I have never seen such delight and relief as when I told her that government had decided to create a tunnel and that I would be very grateful if her children could act as kaitiaki of the project. I was determined that the children of Mt Cook School should have a very special role to play. I had always been disgusted when, just after I became the minister, I attended a wreath-laying at the National War Memorial and children from a private school, St Mark's, were given a special place at the ceremony while the children from Mt Cook School looked on as bystanders. I told the officials I never wanted that to happen again. Mt Cook School was the very close neighbour of the National War Memorial precinct and in my view should be given priority.

We needed urgent legislation to get the project ready. The Labour party spokesperson at the time was Charles Chauvel, with whom it is fair to say I did not enjoy a close and pleasant relationship. Gerry Brownlee was accordingly despatched to negotiate with the Labour opposition to ensure that we obtained their support, because if I had done so there probably would have been problems. That having been achieved, the legislation progressed very quickly and work got under way. The tunnel was ready in October 2014 and opened just after the general election that year. I think it was my last official act as minister, and I was very proud to attend the ceremony. It had been my idea, after a visit to the battlefields in France, to call the tunnel the Arras Tunnel, in honour of the miners who had worked in France in the tunnels underneath Arras. I was told by my officials that there were many reasons why it would not be possible for the tunnel to be named by a minister, but as it turned out, that is exactly what it was called. When the name was announced, the miners' descendants were immensely proud because they felt that the contribution of their ancestors had not received enough publicity over the years.

It had been my ambition to create a 'war museum' in the precinct, based in the old Dominion Museum building, which is owned by Massey University. Wellington's mayor at the time, Celia Wade-Brown, did not like the term 'war museum' and instead preferred 'war and peace museum'. As I said to her, a war museum does not glorify war; it is the antithesis of glorifying war. I wanted a museum that could trace conflict from pre-European times, covering the New Zealand Wars and other conflicts in which New Zealand had been involved over the years, but also include a place that honoured conscientious objectors such as Archibald Baxter, who stood up against the madness of the First World War. I hope that one day New Zealand does have a national war museum to tell the history of conflict. I still believe the old Dominion Museum building would be ideal, but Massey University seems to want too much for that building.

During this period, I was also very involved in the events held in remembrance of the First World War. One major project, thanks to the publication division of the Ministry of Culture and Heritage, was Damian Fenton's splendid history of the war.[4] However, the book greatly upset the former Turkish ambassador, who asked for an appointment to see me one day to complain about references to the 'Armenian massacre'. I said that I, as minister, was not in a position to censor official publications and had no power to excise references to the genocide.

One of my responsibilities as minister was to supervise the Regional Museums Fund, which had been established some years prior by Helen Clark. The idea of such a fund was a very good one. During my time as minister, assistance was provided to Napier so that it could complete its art gallery, and to New Plymouth so that the beautiful Len Lye Centre could be completed. This building, designed by renowned architect Andrew Patterson, is probably one of the finest public buildings in New Zealand. Even the Chatham Islands benefited from the fund, when I granted them $1 million so they could redevelop their museum. The former Chatham Islands mayor, Alfred Preece, phoned me one day after the announcement was made to tell me that mayors of much larger towns and cities around New Zealand had been contacting him to ask how on earth the Chatham Islands managed to secure funding for their museum. Alfred responded that it helped when the minister was also a list MP with responsibility for Rongotai, which takes in the Chathams.

Over the years, my primary love has been classical music. I am a great fan of the NZSO and I am honoured that the Ardern government appointed me to its board. It is a labour of love. Early in my time as minister, the former chief executive of the orchestra, Peter Walls, came to see me about obtaining some additional funding so that the NZSO could tour Europe in 2010. I was very supportive of the project and managed to obtain about $500,000 from the Cultural Diplomacy International Programme for the NZSO tour. I happened to be in Vienna the night the NZSO performed at the Wiener Musikverein before a packed audience. I was incredibly nervous because I knew how difficult and discerning a Viennese audience could be, given that its home orchestra, the Vienna Philharmonic, is one of the best (if not *the* best) orchestras in the world. However, my worries were unfounded, and I was so proud of the NZSO that night. I still recall the first notes of Douglas Lilburn's *Aotearoa* overture, and the outstanding performance by Hilary Hahn of Sibelius's *Violin Concerto*.

New Zealand has a great national orchestra and it needs to be protected. When I became minister, there was much agitation around funding, particularly by the Auckland Philharmonia Orchestra (APO), which wanted to be on an equal financial footing with the NZSO. There are some in Auckland who think that the NZSO should be Wellington's orchestra and the APO should be Auckland's orchestra, with the NZSO never performing in Auckland. That is a fundamentally flawed proposition. Peter Fraser established the NZSO as New Zealand's national orchestra, rightly thinking that people in every corner of the country should be able to experience classical music of the highest quality. But pressure for change was growing. What was to be done? I established a review of the orchestral sector. Peter Biggs was one of those I appointed to examine the issue, along with the secretary-general of the Israel Philharmonic. The review recommended that the NZSO remain New Zealand's national touring orchestra, but also recognised that the APO is very fine and should be regarded as a metropolitan orchestra, entitled to additional funding through the Arts Council.[5] In my opinion, this arrangement works well, and any future government faced with the same sort of agitation needs to be very firm that the NZSO is the primary orchestra of New Zealand and has a remit to bring world-quality classical music to all cities and towns in our land. It cannot and must not be excluded from Auckland.

Another important initiative of mine was to try to increase the level of cultural philanthropy in New Zealand. I set up the Cultural Philanthropy Taskforce, again chaired by Peter Biggs, which produced an excellent report in 2010.[6] This made a number of recommendations to improve private-sector giving, noting that the government had done its bit, directly through grants and indirectly by establishing a favourable tax environment for charitable giving.

After I became the minister in charge of the NZSIS and GCSB, I mentioned to John Key that it was probably time for a change in the culture sector. I knew that many people thought I was the minister for high arts (they were probably right) and that the time had come for an Aucklander to hold the portfolio. I suggested Maggie Barry, who I knew was going to enter cabinet as minister of conservation and minister for senior citizens. The primary responsibility of a National minister for arts, culture and heritage is to keep the luvvies at bay and stop them complaining. By the end of 2014 I felt I had done that reasonably well and, in many respects, I could out-luvvie the luvvies in terms of my love of culture, particularly classical music. Unfortunately, Maggie seemed to alienate most, if not all, of the cultural sector within months of her appointment. By then, however, I had moved on to other jobs.

I look back at my time as minister for arts, culture and heritage with gratitude. When I was in opposition, I used to enjoy winding up the Labour party by saying that the greatest minister for the arts in New Zealand's history was Allan Highet, who held the job during the Muldoon years. They thought I was insulting Helen Clark, who held the portfolio between 1999 and 2008. (The left can be humourless at times.) The reality of the matter is, however, that she was an excellent minister for arts, culture and heritage, and I felt I had big shoes to step into when I followed her in the job. She had a genuine interest in the arts and had provided good support for the sector over many years, ably assisted by Judith Tizard as the associate minister. The arts really should not be a matter of partisan rancour. We are all very fortunate to have a vibrant arts sector, and the role of government is to ensure that it is successful and contributes to the well-being of New Zealanders.

I was fortunate also to work alongside some excellent officials when I was minister. Soon after I stepped into the role, Lewis Holden was made the chief executive of the Ministry for Culture and Heritage. Lewis was a film-maker but also an economist, having spent some years in the Treasury. I had great respect for his ability. One day, the chair of one of the arts organisations came to see me, to report that he had been at a meeting where Lewis said, 'The minister doesn't know anything about the financial side of things.' He expected me to be horrified, but I was not. Lewis was right — I was the arts person and he was the numbers person. I think we made a good team and achieved a lot in our time.

Lewis did an outstanding job when the wonderful opportunity for New Zealand to be the country of honour at the Frankfurt Book Fair in 2012 came our way. This is one of the most important intellectual events in Germany and has been around since Shakespeare's time, and such is its prestige that it is opened by either the chancellor or vice-chancellor of Germany. Lewis and his team developed the theme 'While you were sleeping' for New Zealand's presence, and it proved to be a great success. It was opened by Deputy Prime Minister Bill English and the German vice-chancellor and foreign minister. It attracted more publicity for New Zealand in Germany than I believe we have ever had. It was one of the ministry's finest moments and its success was due to Lewis's hard work and dedication.

Aside from the Frankfurt Book Fair, a number of other events stay with me from my time as minister. In 2014, I was invited by the former Polish ambassador to visit Poland. During the course of my visit, I went to Auschwitz concentration camp, near Kraków. It was the most horrifying experience of my life, and I believe it is one every human being should face to understand what happens when hatred wins. A few months before my visit, I had been approached by the Auschwitz-Birkenau Foundation enquiring whether New Zealand would be prepared to contribute to a fund that was being established so that Auschwitz could be maintained as a memorial. Many of the buildings were starting to collapse in the harsh winter environment in Poland. We contributed $50,000 from the Cultural Diplomacy International Programme, but after my visit I said to Murray McCully, the minister of foreign affairs, that we really should contribute another $50,000, and he was supportive. That donation registered greatly with the authorities in Poland. When Wendy Hinton was presenting her credentials to the Polish president as New Zealand's ambassador to Poland, he referred to the contribution. The Cultural Diplomacy International Programme has been used to great effect over the years.

Probably the most amusing incident during my time as minister came towards the end of 2012, when *New Zealand Herald* journalist Claire Trevett invited me to go on a tour of Parliament with her to comment on the various artworks. She took me to a corner of the main building and pointed out a woven woollen work with an agricultural theme. She asked me my views about it and I said I thought it was awful (my exact words are unprintable). She said it had been a donation to Parliament by the National Spouses' Group in the late 1970s. More blunders were to follow. She asked me what I thought of a piece by Ralph Hotcrc, and I complained that it was very dark and gloomy. When her article was published, I was castigated by the luvvies for my comments on Hotere. Sadly, the artist passed away some months later. I was asked to give a eulogy at his requiem at St Joseph's Cathedral in Dunedin and approached the undertaking with some trepidation, given my recent foot-in-the-mouth performance. However, thanks to the outstanding work of one of the ministry's speech writers, the eulogy was widely praised — even the prime minister contacted me to say he had heard it had been well received. I was much relieved and rang the speech writer to tell her how grateful I was for her efforts.

My only real disappointment in the arts was not being able to do more to grow the El Sistema music programme in New Zealand. This initiative was started in 1975 by José Antonio Abreu, a Venezuelan musician and economist, who understood that music has the ability to transform the lives of children in poverty. Beginning in an abandoned garage with only a few students, he created a nationwide movement that involved putting instruments into the hands of hundreds of thousands of poor children and bringing them hope and meaning. In her 2012 book on the programme, Tricia Tunstall says, 'El Sistema's over arching goal is "to rescue the children" from the multiple dangers of poverty, and most importantly, from the sense of hopelessness and low self esteem that can lead to gang membership, drugs and violence.'[7]

The star of the El Sistema movement is Gustavo Dudamel, who is the music director of the Los Angeles Philharmonic. He continues to conduct the Simón Bolívar Symphony Orchestra, a youth orchestra in Venezuela, and he is a tireless ambassador for El Sistema's vision of improving the lives of children and young people by giving them musical training and orchestral community. Dudamel has claimed that music saved his life and the lives of thousands of children in Venezuela.

The concept of El Sistema has since spread throughout the world. Sistema-like programmes run in cities from Los Angeles to Glasgow, and the idea reached New Zealand some years ago. A Sistema programme began in South Auckland, supported, to their great credit, by musicians from the APO. Other programmes that do not include the Sistema name but essentially use the same methodology operate in Wellington and the Hutt Valley.

The promoters of Sistema in South Auckland approached me in 2013 for my support and I visited them on a number of occasions to see the students perform. It was inspiring to see young people from Ōtara and Māngere learning how to perform classical music in an orchestra. I was sold on the idea and sought to ensure that funding was available so that the programme could grow and the idea could spread to other parts of the country. The Ministry for Culture and Heritage supported me in my efforts, but I regret to say that the cross-government response was disappointing. Indeed, many of the responses from civil servants reminded me of the British sitcom *Yes Minister*: the Ministry for Youth Development said it was an excellent idea but really one that should be funded by the Ministry of Education, who said it was an excellent idea but really one that should be supported by the Ministry of Social Development, while the Arts Council of Creative New Zealand said it wasn't really their line of work. I eventually managed to get some funding, but was disappointed I could not secure more for such a worthwhile project. The difficulties I faced showed me that without the support of civil servants, initiatives such as this can fail to achieve their potential.

More recently, a number of people associated with the Wellington project have been lobbying to secure extra funding, and I am very supportive of their efforts. The government spends millions of dollars supporting sports initiatives — rightly so, because physical health is obviously extremely important — but a project like Sistema, which has been shown to achieve amazing results worldwide, should also receive support. I hope that the idea continues to spread in New Zealand and that those who run such worthwhile projects do not have to spend too much time seeking funding from various sources.

Since leaving politics I have resumed my deep involvement in the arts. I am back on the Adam Foundation, which was established by Denis and Verna Adam to promote the arts, and in particular to support young artists. Denis was a great New Zealander. He was born in Berlin but had to escape in the 1930s because he was Jewish. He went to England, where he served with distinction in the Royal Air Force, and then he came out to New Zealand almost penniless and made his money in insurance. He and his wife decided to establish the foundation many years ago, and since that time it has made a significant contribution to the arts in New Zealand. In 2021, the foundation made a significant contribution to what will be the National Music Centre in Wellington, with the main auditorium set to be called the Adam Auditorium. I have also been asked to serve on the Sarjeant Gallery Trust, the NZSO board and several other organisations, all of which I respect enormously and am delighted to be involved with. I love the arts.

CHAPTER 8

Minister for the spies

A FEW DAYS AFTER THE 2014 ELECTION, John Key asked to see me in his office. He explained that he was going to create a new portfolio for himself — minister of national security and intelligence, with overall responsibility for this area of government — but asked me to look after the management of the Government Communications Security Bureau (GCSB) and the New Zealand Security Intelligence Service (NZSIS). So, I became the first non-prime minister to hold those two portfolios. The change attracted a reasonable degree of attention when the new cabinet was announced, with predictable criticism from Winston Peters. A few years later, when Andrew Little succeeded me as minister, Peters made no comment — the change had by then become part of the usual operation of government.

National security is a very important area of government. All citizens expect their government to ensure that the country has safe borders, and that they live in a free and democratic society and are safeguarded against terror. My appointment took place against the backdrop of the then recent hostage crisis at Martin Place in Sydney and the shooting at Parliament Hill in Ottawa. As we know from the 2019 Christchurch mosque tragedy, terrorism can strike anywhere at any time. That is why there are two state agencies in New Zealand to provide intelligence on threats so that law enforcement agencies can protect citizens. The agencies carry out a range of vital functions, from gathering intelligence about individuals or organisations and collecting foreign intelligence, to helping prevent organised crime and protecting our borders from undesirable people and biosecurity threats.

The NZSIS is a civilian intelligence and security organisation that was founded in 1956. It is New Zealand's human intelligence organisation and has three functions: to investigate threats to security and to work with other agencies within government, so that the intelligence it collects is actioned and any threats that have been identified can be disrupted; to collect intelligence; and to provide a range of protective security advice and services to government.

The GCSB is our signals intelligence organisation. It ensures the integrity and confidentiality of government information, and investigates and analyses cyber incidents against New Zealand's critical infrastructure.

In the chapter covering my role as attorney-general, I talked about the Dotcom case. During one of the hearings involving Kim Dotcom, his lawyer obtained under cross-examination an admission that the GCSB had been assisting the NZSIS in surveilling both Dotcom and his associates, in apparent breach of the Government Communications Security Bureau Act 2003. I thought there were arguments either way as to whether there had really been a breach of the law, but in any case the legislation needed to be urgently clarified. Hence, I introduced amendments in 2013 and was responsible for the parliamentary passage of that legislation. There was a great deal of public debate about it at the time, much of it malignant and ignorant.

A group of the great and good, led by prominent New Zealanders like Dame Anne Salmond, engaged in a campaign against the proposed amendments. They made allegations along the lines that the National government was creating a surveillance state. New Zealanders, they said, would abhor living in a surveillance state. Others joined the fray, and there were predictable contributions from people like Nicky Hager. I had hoped we could at least rely on a rational black-letter approach to the law from the New Zealand Law Society, but unfortunately that was not to be. The Law Society delegated responsibility for its response to a small group of lawyers. Rodney Harrison QC presented submissions to the select committee that greatly disappointed me.

In July 2013, the Stop the GCSB Coalition announced it would hold a public meeting in the Mt Albert War Memorial Hall to address the nefarious amendments. The sponsors went so far as to say that the bill would legalise mass surveillance of New Zealanders. Indeed, it was regarded as so important that people attend the meeting that it was streamed live on the internet across New Zealand and the world. The speakers at the meeting were — no surprises here — Dame Anne Salmond, Kim Dotcom, Thomas Beagle from Tech Liberty NZ and Rodney Harrison. Sir Edmund (Ted) Thomas, a retired Court of Appeal judge, agreed to chair the meeting.

Over the years, I have become increasingly disappointed with the submissions made to select committees by the Law Society. The role of the society is to make careful non-partisan submissions on a bill. In recent years, this trend towards making political submissions rather than legal submissions has diminished the authority of the Law Society. I can recall, during the course of the debate on the Evidence Bill in 2006, quoting a famous United States judge, Learned Hand, that 'it is the Bar that makes the statutes'.[1] In the case of the Evidence Bill, the Law Society made a very valuable contribution to public debate by making careful legal and technical submissions. Sadly, its approach has changed and that is unfortunate.

The damage done by the partisan hyperbole was serious. It prevented the government from taking a close look at other laws relating to terrorism, such as the Terrorism Suppression Act 2007, which is not, and has never been, fit for purpose. Hyperbole has consequences and in this case it was not in the public interest.

Despite all the brouhaha, the legislation was passed and at the same time the government announced that there would be a complete review of the intelligence legislation in the next three-year period. It was important to emphasise that the intelligence agencies are governed by, and operate under, the rule of law. The exact nature of what they do operationally cannot be detailed, but the rules under which they operate must be clearly set out and available for all to see.

The government appointed Sir Michael Cullen and Dame Patsy Reddy to undertake the review. We could not have chosen better people thanks to their ability and experience. In addition to the Government Communications Security Bureau Act 2003, they reviewed the New Zealand Security Intelligence Service Act 1969 (which had not been comprehensively reviewed since its enactment), the Inspector-General of Intelligence and Security Act 1996 (which had been amended in 2013 at the time of the amendments to the Government Communications Security Bureau Act), and the Intelligence and Security Committee Act 1996, which provides for parliamentary oversight. Once Michael and Patsy had delivered their report in 2016,[2] I recall John Key meeting with the then leader of the opposition, Andrew Little, and saying to him that the government wanted to progress with the comprehensive reform but would not do so unless there was a guarantee that the Labour opposition would support the reforms. Legislation of this kind should never pass with a majority of only one or two votes; it is essential that the two big beasts of politics cooperate on these issues. Andrew adopted a very responsible approach to the reform, and I found him good to work with, despite the significant pressure the Labour party came under from commentators on its side of the political aisle. I remember saying to Andrew that one day Labour would be in government again and he would have to deal with this legislation. It was a very prophetic remark, as he was my successor in 2017 and had to deal with a number of hugely important issues, particularly following the Christchurch mosque tragedy.

The new legislation was a complete rewrite, and it has stood the test of time. In particular, the Royal Commission of Inquiry into the Terrorist Attack on Christchurch Mosques on 15 March 2019 had no criticisms of the updated legislation. We included an ongoing review clause stipulating that the legislation needs to be re-examined every five to seven years. At the time, we needed to assure critics that the legislation could keep being amended as any problems emerged. In my experience as minister, the legislation operated as intended, barring a few minor issues.

It is very important to emphasise that while the intelligence agencies have enormous powers, they are held to account by other means. New Zealand's answer to the question of 'Who will watch the watch people?' includes four key levels of scrutiny.

The first level is the inspector-general of intelligence and security. This role was significantly strengthened by the government in 2013. Prior to those changes, the inspector-general was a part-time position normally filled by a retired judge of the High Court. Following the reforms, the inspector-general became a full-time position with an office of around seven staff. The inspector-general now has unrestricted entry and access powers, can review whatever material they like and can inquire into any matter they wish. The powers associated with the role are some of the broadest available to any independent officer in New Zealand.

The second is parliamentary oversight through the Intelligence and Security Committee (ISC) of Parliament, which includes the leader of the opposition and other senior MPs. Each year, the heads of the NZSIS and the GCSB are called to appear before the ISC in public session. The heads of both intelligence agencies provide information and context to their work, which prior to the reforms had not been in the public domain. The British equivalent of our ISC, the Intelligence Security Committee of Parliament, is a very powerful independent body that exercises considerable control over the British intelligence agencies.[3] The New Zealand ISC does not have the powers of the British committee, although that may change in years to come.

I support making our ISC a stronger and more influential parliamentary committee. This could be achieved in a number of ways. First, I don't think it should be chaired by the prime minister and have a membership comprising the leader of the opposition, senior ministers and senior opposition MPs. Instead, I think it would be better if it was chaired by a former minister or senior MP with an interest in, and some expertise of, the topic. In the United Kingdom, for example, Dominic Grieve, the former attorney-general for England and Wales, was elected chair of the House of Commons ISC after he left government. Even though the New Zealand Parliament comprises only 120 members, I think there is a case for structural reform of membership of the ISC along these lines. At the moment it receives reports from the GCSB and the NZSIS, and holds both public and private sessions, many of which have been essentially meaningless. I believe the ISC should instead have the capacity to undertake its own inquiries.

It will be interesting to see what the 2022 review of the Intelligence and Security Act 2017 comes up with, but I hope there is a move to make the ISC more powerful. It would also be very useful if membership of the committee could reflect the more diverse nature of Parliament — it shouldn't simply be a committee of National and Labour MPs. That is the approach taken in the United Kingdom, where the Liberal Democrats and the Scottish National party have at times both been represented alongside Conservative and Labour members.

The next level of scrutiny is the commissioner of security warrants. This is a statutory provision that must be filled by a retired High Court judge. The commissioner provides a level of scrutiny in issuing interception warrants relating to persons who are either New Zealand citizens or residents. The warrants are issued jointly by the commissioner and the minister responsible for the intelligence agencies.

The final level of scrutiny is ministerial oversight. Obviously, the intelligence agencies do not operate autonomously. Their work is carried out under the oversight of the minister and under warrants and authorisation signed by the minister. As minister, I scrutinised every warrant and asked questions in order to satisfy myself of the need for, and the proportionality of, any action taken. As minister, I was responsible to Parliament for my actions.

The suggestion that the intelligence agencies can run amok and spy on people without proper authorisation is wrong. Under both the former legislation and the current Act, there are very strict controls on the agencies. From the earliest days of the NZSIS, there have been accusations that ministers can authorise the agency to spy on individuals of their choosing. This is false. Were I to have suggested that the NZSIS spy on a political opponent, for example, I would have lost my job within days. The minister does not get involved in operational activities, other than to consider warrants and maintain ministerial responsibility for the agencies and their performance. They have to act in accordance with the law, which I have set out above. It would be contrary to the basic rules of our democratic society, governed by the rule of law, for me as the minister in charge of the NZSIS to involve myself in operational matters.

During the 2013 review and, shortly after the 2014 election when some urgent amendments were required to the NZSIS legislation, David Shearer, former leader of the opposition and the MP for Mt Albert, mentioned to me his interaction with the Auckland Muslim communities at the time of the amendments and that they were very worried. He also said that the government had not kept in touch with the communities as well as it should have. I took his criticisms on board and gave an undertaking to the House that, when the review resulted in new legislation, I would keep in close contact with the Muslim community. I kept my word.

When the Intelligence and Security Act was introduced in 2017, I visited a number of Islamic centres throughout the country, including Christchurch, to explain the role of the intelligence agencies and the general nature of the work they undertook. I emphasised that it was not communities that were the subject of attention, but behaviours. I particularly recall my visit to the Al Noor Mosque. The members were very welcoming, and we had a really good discussion on a wide variety of topics. I even mentioned the increasing problem of ransomware and the need for the GCSB to combat it, and several community members said they had been victims of ransomware. I really enjoyed those visits and, like every

New Zealander, was distraught about the actions of the Australian terrorist in Christchurch in 2019.

On one occasion, I was due to speak in Hamilton to a meeting of Muslim community leaders and was asked to talk with representatives of the Islamic Women's Council New Zealand. I said I would be pleased to do so, and attended the meeting with the MP for Hamilton West, Tim Macindoe. Several of the council's representatives raised examples of Islamophobic behaviour and said how much it concerned them. I recall in particular one woman telling me about an incident in a supermarket car park in Hamilton, where someone had told her she should go back to where she came from and objected to her wearing the veil. She commented, however, that another stranger had approached her and apologised for the behaviour of the abuser. These and other incidents were described to me, and I reported them to the director-general of the NZSIS, saying that she and her agency should keep in touch with the council because they needed a lot of care and attention. I met with the council on at least one other occasion after the intelligence and security legislation was passed in early 2017.

It has been suggested that the intelligence agencies have been too concerned with Islamic terrorism. That is unfair. In February 2015, soon after I was appointed as minister, I was asked to attend the White House Summit on Countering Violent Extremism, hosted by United States Secretary of State John Kerry. This was an opportunity for government officials and members of civic society from various countries to meet to discuss violent extremism. The topic was not confined to Islamic violent extremism. Throughout my time as a minister, violent extremism in all its forms was considered, but the reality is that most of the global area of concern at the time related to Islamic extremism, heightened by the existence of the Islamic State of Iraq and the Levant. It was only after the attack in Charlottesville in Virginia in August 2017 that the issue of white supremacy came very much to the forefront, but it was never ignored. New Zealand has always had citizens who hold a range of extremist views.

The events of recent years, both here and overseas, have illustrated why it is important for liberal democracies to have well-functioning and well-funded intelligence agencies like the GCSB and the NZSIS. If amendments are made to the Intelligence and Security Act 2017 following the 2022 review, I hope the debate will be more elevated than it was in 2013. Those who behaved as they did then did not encourage sensible and rational debate.

In April 2022 the government announced that it was contemplating a law change to deport potential terrorists. This is a serious and difficult issue and needs a mature debate. If it occurred on National's watch, I imagine the great and good would be appalled, accusing us of being fascists and so on. I suspect they will be more respectful of the decisions of a Labour government.

CHAPTER 9 Māori affairs and Treaty of Waitangi negotiations

IN MY BOOK *HE KUPU TAURANGI* (2021), I explained the background to, and rationale for, Treaty of Waitangi settlements, and I also covered topics such as the foreshore and seabed controversy.[1] I will not repeat that material here and instead will consider developments since 2017. First, however, I will say something about Māori land reform.

Reform of Māori land law

As part of National's confidence in supply agreement with the Māori party in 2008, Pita Sharples became minister for Māori affairs, with Georgina te Heuheu of the National party acting as his associate minister. Georgina retired in 2011 and I was asked by John Key to take on the role. It hadn't occurred to me that I would ever be asked to do that job, but when invited to do so I was very enthusiastic. I asked the prime minister if I could reform Māori land law, and he replied that I could certainly pursue that aim.

Reforming Te Ture Whenua Maori Act 1993 was not a spur-of-the-moment idea. Many iwi leaders had told me about their concerns with the Act, which they felt was flawed. The former minister of Māori affairs, the late John Luxton, had felt the same way, and commented to me towards the end of 2011 that he had his doubts about whether the Act had been successful. So I was not the only one concerned about the Act and the inability of landowners to achieve an economic return for their investment in Māori land. In February 2013, PricewaterhouseCoopers prepared a report for the Ministry for Primary Industries (MPI) entitled *Growing the Productive Base of Māori Freehold Land*. The executive summary says this:

> There are positive economic consequences associated with facilitating Māori freehold land into the productive sector:
>
> 1. This study explored the potential 'size of the prize' in economic terms around MPI applying new governance and management models to facilitate the introduction of currently under-utilised and unproductive freehold Māori land into production.
> 2. The tangible benefits from introducing more Māori freehold land into production include realising an additional nominal \$8 billion in gross output and \$3.7 billion in value added above MPI baseline pastoral sector forecasts between 2013 and 2022.
> 3. The potential barriers to introducing the land include requirements for additional investment in the land of just under \$3 billion and time required to bring the land into production — the benefits are tangible but likely to be incremental.[2]

It was a very good report and it influenced me as I embarked on this reform. While the potential was great, the reality was very bad indeed. A 2011 Ministry of Agriculture and Forestry report had identified 1.5 million hectares of Māori freehold land, of which only 20 per cent was considered to be operating productively at or above relevant industry benchmarks. The balance was considered to be either underperforming (40 per cent) or underutilised (40 per cent).[3] The registration system was also hopelessly out of date. One day in 2015 I was in Tairāwhiti (Gisborne) and paid a brief visit to the Māori Land Court. It was like going back in time 50 years — it was antiquated, slow and unimpressive. I felt that Māori were entitled to a quality land registration system like the world-class land registration system for general land. The Māori Land Court procedures were also out of date. There had been a number of reforms to the practice and procedure of the general court system, starting with reforms to the High Court in 1985. The idea of a judge supervising every aspect of a case was considered out of date and parties were encouraged to get on with matters themselves, calling on a judge only where necessary. I felt these reforms could be extended to the Māori Land Court. I also thought greater use could be made of alternative dispute resolution to encourage parties to try to sort out differences between themselves using mediation, for example, rather than get caught up in the often lengthy and bureaucratic processes of the Māori Land Court.

I prepared a paper for cabinet on the appointment of a review panel. Tony Ryall, the minister of health, sat next to me in cabinet. He was like a parrot on my shoulder, constantly whispering in my ear: 'You will fail; everyone fails to reform Māori land.' I tried to put a positive spin on the project and told him he was too negative. As it turns out, he was right. The other warning I received was from a leading kaumātua in Wellington. When I was initiating the reform, he said to me: 'If you give the impression you're Moses coming down from the mountain with tablets that contain the answer, you are going to fail. It is imperative that you not only consult but are seen to consult throughout the rohe, otherwise it will not succeed.'

In June 2012, I appointed an independent panel of experts to review the 1993 Act and to recommend changes, which I hoped would assist Māori landowners achieve their aspirations. It was a distinguished panel, made up of Dame Patsy Reddy, who subsequently became governor-general; Matanuku Mahuika, who had worked extensively on the subject and whose father was one of those instrumental in getting me to conduct the reform; and Toko Kapea and Dion Tuuta, both young Māori leaders with great experience in their iwi and also in matters relating to Māori economic development. Some months later, the panel published a discussion document containing five key propositions for reform:

1. Utilisation of Māori land should be able to be determined by a majority of engaged owners
2. All Māori land should be capable of utilisation and effective administration
3. Māori land should have effective, fit for purpose, governance
4. There should be an enabling institutional framework to support owners of Māori land to make decisions and resolve any disputes
5. Excessive fragmentation of Māori land should be discouraged.[4]

In the course of its work, the panel met with many people throughout the country, including the judges of the Māori Land Court, many landowners, the representatives of financial institutions and the Māori trustee. As one would expect from such a competent and distinguished panel, both the way in which they conducted the review and the review itself were very comprehensive and of high quality.

Once the review panel released its discussion document, it then undertook a further series of consultation hui across the country. Written submissions were invited, and many were received. The panel's final report was released in April 2014. One major recommendation they made was that the current Act should be repealed and replaced by new legislation rather than have a series of amendments to the existing Act.

Because Te Ture Whenua Maori Act 1993 was administered by Te Puni Kōkiri Ministry of Māori Development (TPK), that department was responsible for these reforms. Unfortunately, TPK was simply not up to it as they had very little quality policy support. Much of the material I received from the department during my time as associate minister was of very low quality. For that reason, John Grant, a senior public official who worked in the Office of Treaty Settlements and had a lot of experience in Māori land law, was seconded to TPK to lead the policy team. I was greatly relieved when I heard this news as I had, and have, great respect for John's ability and knew that, with him in charge, things would get done.

Cabinet agreed in principle to a comprehensive reform to implement the recommendations of the review panel, and I then issued drafting instructions to the Parliamentary Counsel Office. I went to a number of hui to outline the intentions of the government and ways in which administration of Māori land could be improved. I went because I was so interested in the subject and in the potential for real economic benefits to result from the reforms. Many people attended and the response was generally favourable.

After the 2014 election, I retained the associate minister's role but Pita Sharples retired and was replaced by Te Ururoa Flavell. Te Ururoa was great to work with and involved himself in the reform. He announced the appointment of a ministerial advisory group to provide independent advice on the development of an exposure draft of Te Ture Whenua Maori Reform Bill, and that group conducted a whole series of pre-consultation hui with a range of leadership groups. In May 2015, the exposure draft of the new bill was released, along with a consultation document that set out the rationale for the proposed reforms. The exposure draft was comprehensive and provided details on what the government was proposing so that submitters could address key points. Te Ururoa announced that there would be a number of regional consultation hui and landowners were given an opportunity to make written and oral submissions. These hui extended for some while, and so Te Ururoa extended the deadline for submissions so that landowners had sufficient time to respond.

The purpose of the law reform was to recognise the significance of Māori land and to create a more workable set of rules and practical supports. Specifically, it was hoped that it would result in four outcomes for Māori landowners: more autonomy over their whenua; greater ability to use their whenua; greater simplicity and efficiency when working with Māori land; and safeguarding whenua for current and future generations. Some people had suggested that the whole purpose of the reform was to complete the alienation of Māori land. In other words, that it was some kind of twenty-first-century land grab by the Crown. That was mischievous rubbish. Its purpose was to safeguard the land and to give owners an opportunity to develop their land for their own economic benefit. The suggestion that a minister, who had done more than any other in history to return whenua to iwi, would somehow be at the centre of a scheme to cause Māori to lose the remainder of their land was insulting.

After the consultation hui, further changes were made to the exposure draft of the bill. I think it is fair to say that, in my time as a minister, there was never greater consultation than there was over the reforms to the Te Ture Whenua Maori Act. Moreover, there was not a single consultation draft but numerous drafts, the latter versions resulting from ideas that were picked up at the consultation hui.

One would have thought that such a reform would have been welcomed, but the reality was far from it. In mid-2014, the Waitangi Tribunal received a number of claims relating to the Crown's proposed reform of the Act. A panel was appointed, although the presiding officer subsequently stood down because his term on the tribunal had come to an end. After a number of hearings, the tribunal, unsurprisingly, found against the Crown.[5]

The first recommendation of the Waitangi Tribunal was that there be further engagement nationally with Māori landowners. This was an incredible recommendation given the amount and quality of the consultation that had been held to date. As I said, it was the most consulted piece of legislation in my time as a minister. The tribunal also recommended that the Crown continue to take advice from independent Māori experts. Why would they recommend a continuation of what was already happening?

In addition, the tribunal recommended that work continue urgently on such matters of importance as rating, valuation, landlocked land and paper roads. Again, urgent attention had been and was being given to these very issues. I was aware of the problem of landlocked land. Much Māori land was landlocked in the nineteenth century in what was a form of de facto confiscation of the land. The best example given to me came from a landowner in the Rangitīkei district. His whānau land was surrounded by general land. He approached the farmer who owned the surrounding land, asking if he could gain access to his land. The farmer said he could walk through his farm any time he wanted, but when he said he needed vehicular access, the farmer said that was not possible and would see him in court. These kinds of issues could also be seen around Wairarapa and in the Rotorua region, and a lot of work was being done to resolve them.

The final set of recommendations made by the tribunal basically sought to restore all of the Māori Land Court's jurisdiction that the reforms had proposed be altered. Given the strong objections of the Māori Land Court judges to any changes, this recommendation was also unsurprising but wrong.

The bill was introduced and referred to the Māori Affairs Select Committee in 2016, where there were many submissions. The process was not rushed and all submitters had an opportunity to appear if that was their wish. The bill was back in the House for further consideration when Parliament rose in August 2017, but when the new government was formed after the 2017 election it was discharged. This was a real tragedy for Māori and for the Māori economy.

I was very disappointed at the mindless objections of the Labour party because, having represented the Māori seats for so long, they should have known that this was a significant reform that would benefit Māori landowners. Their objections were unprincipled and unreasonable. I was neither disappointed nor surprised by the objections of New Zealand First — as usual, they simply wanted to throw a spanner in the works. Indeed, one of their number, who had served on the Māori Affairs Select Committee, told an official that it was a good piece of legislation but they were opposing it for political reasons.

So what is the moral of this story? Perhaps Tony Ryall was right at the outset, and the answer is that it is impossible to reform Māori land law because of the vested interests and ignorant opposition of so many groups. The kaumātua who told me not to act like Moses was quite right, and that is why I made a valiant effort not to be seen to have all the answers, but to work carefully and cooperatively with people to explore options for reform. I think it is a tragedy that so much land remains undeveloped or underdeveloped, and believe that these reforms could have gone a long way to addressing those problems.

I hope this reform is picked up as soon as possible by a future National government. The proposals will greatly benefit Māori landowners and improve the service provided to them. The current regime is ill-suited to the needs of the twenty-first century.

Treaty negotiations

During my time as minister, I engaged extensively with Ngāpuhi to try to advance their treaty settlement but was unsuccessful in this. I agreed a mandate process with a group of Ngāpuhi, and that was criticised by the Waitangi Tribunal (again, unsurprising). By early 2017, my patience was exhausted and I decided to concentrate my efforts on negotiations that were more likely to be successful. When Bill English was prime minister, he also visited Ngāpuhi leadership and reached the same conclusion.

There is a lot of talk about the Ngāpuhi settlement having the potential to be the biggest treaty settlement. However, that is wrong. When historical treaty settlement work began, $1 billion in 1992 dollars was allocated for settlements. The amount set aside for Ngāpuhi was in the region of $40 million, which in 2022 dollars is probably worth about $150 million. It is important when dealing with treaty settlements that relativity between settling iwi is maintained, and if Ngāpuhi receive more than $200 million, there is a grave risk that this relativity will be harmed. The Crown cannot play favourites and must settle with iwi in a principled manner. Quantum is determined by the nature of the treaty grievance — for example, whether the settling iwi was forced off their land by raupatu (confiscation) or lost their land in other ways, such as through a contract entered into under duress. Population is another factor that must be considered — how many people are affected? Finally, the extent of the land lost must also be considered. While it is true that Ngāpuhi is the largest iwi in the country, it did not suffer raupatu and did not lose a lot of land. Therefore, applying a principled approach to the Ngāpuhi settlement, this should not amount to more than about $150–200 million. My work to progress a settlement was challenged in the Waitangi Tribunal which, unsurprisingly, found against the Crown.[6]

In 2017 Andrew Little began his term as minister for Treaty of Waitangi negotiations determined to resolve the Ngāpuhi matter. Several commentators in the press emphasised that I had failed and that Andrew stood a much better chance of success. Large sections of Ngāpuhi are loyal to the Labour party — indeed, a former chair of the Labour party's Māori Council, the late Rudy Taylor, was active in promoting a Ngāpuhi settlement for one faction. However, despite all corners of Ngāpuhi being represented in the coalition government, no settlement has yet been reached.

I think the time has come to recognise that it will not be possible to settle with Ngāpuhi as one iwi and that perhaps a number of settlements are needed instead — for example, with Ngāti Hine, the Hokianga hapū and the central area. Whatever approaches are taken, it will not be easy to achieve a settlement, and in my opinion Andrew would be better to concentrate on some of the other settlements that are reasonably well advanced.

Co-governance

Co-governance is a means by which iwi can have greater participation in the management of the environment. So, for example, an iwi may seek to have co-governance over a river within their rohe. In the past, iwi have often objected to the Crown taking unilateral steps to regulate or govern a natural resource without recognising legitimate Māori rights and interests in those resources. It is important to note here that Māori are treaty partners; they are not just stakeholders who need to be consulted by local or central government prior to a decision being taken. I said this on the subject in *He Kupu Taurangi:*

> Involving iwi in the management of natural resources brings with it a number of benefits. Iwi often have unique knowledge of particular resources and can help local authorities better manage them. There is a growing consensus that the utilisation of traditional knowledge can lead to better environmental decision making. More generally, ensuring Māori have an appropriate level of input into natural resource management is just a matter of good Government, consistent with contemporary Treaty rights.[7]

In my time as minister, I negotiated many co-governance arrangements. Sometimes, however, the local authority decided to introduce a co-governance arrangement without any involvement of central government, such as when the Greater Wellington Regional Council entered into a co-governance arrangement with the iwi within its region in 2013.

The first co-governance arrangement I had to consider as a minister was the one entered into by Michael Cullen with Waikato Tainui in respect of the Waikato River. While a settlement had been achieved with Tainui, there were other iwi who had an interest in the river, namely Ngāti Tūwharetoa, Raukawa and Te Arawa. Over the next few years, I was heavily engaged in negotiations with those iwi and it was necessary to streamline the arrangements so that there would be one, not multiple, co-governance regimes for the river. In due course, as a result of negotiations with Ngāti Maniapoto, the Waipā River was also brought into the co-governance arrangements.

In 2010, Fran Wilde, one of my negotiators, contacted me to say that she thought there could be a better and more streamlined way of dealing with co-governance issues in Hawke's Bay. Fran had a lot of experience in local and regional government — she had left Parliament in 1992 to become mayor of Wellington and had also been involved in the Greater Wellington Regional Council. She knew what she was talking about and I was very happy to accept her recommendations about an appropriate co-governance regime in Hawke's Bay. Fran considered it would be unduly burdensome on regional government if co-governance regimes were developed for all the rivers of the region, and thought it would be more sensible to develop a regional planning committee.

It was about this time that the minister of local government, Rodney Hide, who was also leader of the ACT party, raised some concerns about the various proposals. As a consequence, he and I had a number of discussions, which resulted in the development of co-governance guidelines. An important feature of those guidelines — and Rodney was adamant that this needed to be included — was the principle that, being democratically elected, local and regional government would be the final arbiters if the co-governance body (with equal numbers of local body representatives and iwi representatives) could not reach agreement on a particular issue. The guidelines also stated that any co-governance arrangement involving iwi needs to: provide an effective role for iwi in natural resource management; lead to good environmental outcomes for iwi and other New Zealanders; address issues giving rise to the treaty claim; be well designed, simple, transparent and affordable; and result in a durable settlement. The guidelines were adopted by government and were applied in future settlements.

There were some variations, such as the Whanganui River settlement and the Ngāi Tūhoe settlement in relation to Te Urewera, which was very much a one-off arrangement.

The issue of co-governance is now becoming very topical, and the current government appears to be applying the principle of co-governance to areas other than natural resources in treaty settlements. There is a concern in the community, most recently expressed by the ACT leader, David Seymour, that there are too many co-governance arrangements and that race-based advantage is wrong. Personally, I think there is an opportunity for a principled debate on co-governance and whether the guidelines Rodney and I negotiated could or should be applied to other areas. For example, should it be appropriate for Crown Research Institutes, as a matter of principle, to have co-governance arrangements such that 50 per cent of all directors are Māori? Should the principle extend to SOEs and other Crown bodies? Or should appointments to these bodies be made on the basis of who has the best qualifications, regardless of ethnicity? While I hope it will be possible to have such a debate, I don't think that demanding a referendum on the subject is a wise thing to do. That will simply encourage argument by epithet and produce more heat than light. It will also encourage groups like New Zealand First to enter the fray and turn the debate into something of a farce. There are legitimate questions that can be the subject of discussion, provided that discussion is principled and civil.

In 2019, after I had ceased to be a minister, the Cabinet Office published a circular entitled 'Te Tiriti o Waitangi / Treaty of Waitangi guidance'. This sets out guidelines agreed by cabinet for policymakers to consider the Treaty of Waitangi in policy development and implementation. There are a number of questions to guide policymakers, some of which are very helpful:

> How does the proposal/policy affect all New Zealanders? What is the effect on Māori (if different, how and why?).
>
> How does the proposal demonstrate good government within the context of the Treaty?
>
> What are the Treaty/Māori interests in the issue?
>
> How does the proposal demonstrate that policy-makers are meeting the good faith obligations of the Crown?
>
> To what extent have policy-makers anticipated Treaty arguments that might be made?[8]

I think these are good questions to ask at any stage of policy development. Importantly, the paper goes on to say that the treaty may justify different treatment of Māori interests or involvement of Māori in an issue, but it does not confer greater rights on Māori than the government owes to all New Zealanders. It is unfortunate that so often the arguments raised by those concerned about some policy developments focus on the alleged favouritism shown to Māori. Characterising these changes in that way is misleading and unfair. There may be particular interests of Māori that need to be taken into account in developing a policy or making a decision, but that does not mean that Māori necessarily have greater rights.

In my experience there will be particular issues where the Māori interest is distinct from the general interest, such as in the management of natural resources. But the distinction will be less apparent (if apparent at all) in many areas of government administration. For example, it is difficult to discern a particular Māori or treaty interest in the areas of national security, foreign affairs and defence.

As this debate continues in New Zealand, I hope that people concentrate instead on substantive points. It cannot be in the public interest for a debate on these sensitive matters to be diminished by hyperbole, half-truths and nastiness. I also think it is important that any extensions to the co-governance principle are challenged.

The new education curriculum

The other issue I want to refer to concerns the new education curriculum, which when introduced in 2023 will place much greater emphasis on the teaching of New Zealand history. When I was studying history in my last few years of secondary school, we focused on the United States between the wars and the Stuart kings in the seventeenth century, including the English Civil War. I found both areas interesting, but wonder whether learning about Warren Harding, Calvin Coolidge and Herbert Hoover was more important than learning about, for example, the New Zealand Wars. Teaching more New Zealand history can only be a good thing.

When I was minister for Treaty of Waitangi negotiations, I was always apologising for wrongs that had been committed by the Crown since 6 February 1840. Every deed of settlement contains an acknowledgements section that sets out the history of the interaction between the Crown and the settling iwi. It also includes a formal apology by the Crown for actions that are said to breach the Treaty of Waitangi and its principles. It is very important to note that these sections of settlements are not pro forma and nor are they rushed. They are the subject of very careful analysis by highly qualified iwi and Crown historians, and their contents are the subject of intense debate and negotiation. As a matter of principle, it is extremely important that the Crown apologises for real, not imagined, breaches.

One of the things that struck me in my time as a minister is that many historical matters seem to have been either suppressed or ignored in this country. This was especially the case in Taranaki.

The Parihaka negotiations in 2014–17 in particular revealed some very disturbing facts that even now I think are generally unknown in New Zealand. The raid on Parihaka in 1881 was probably the worst incident in our post-1840 history, yet for many years the truth was suppressed or ignored. It is as though the general community knew that wrongs had happened, but preferred to sweep these under the carpet. The negotiations over the Parihaka apology were probably the most intense in which I was involved, and it was the first time that the Crown actually apologised for rape. I was distressed after the ceremony when I received a number of most unpleasant emails and letters complaining that I had no right to apologise for rape and demanding evidence that it had happened.

Another example is the 2014 Ngāi Tūhoe settlement, including the disestablishment of Urewera National Park and the recognition of Te Urewera as a legal identity. Very few people knew the facts and simply assumed that Māori protesting in the national park were being disagreeable and criminal. They did not realise that Premier Richard Seddon's government entered into an arrangement with Tūhoe in 1896 that gave Tūhoe limited autonomy over Te Urewera, with a majority Tūhoe commission set up to make decisions about land sales. The legislation relating to the commission was then undermined over the next two or three decades and unilaterally repealed in 1923 without the consent of Tūhoe. Adding insult to injury, a national park was then created in 1954, again with no consultation with Tūhoe. That is why there was such a need for a just and durable settlement in Te Urewera.

The events that occurred at Parihaka and in Te Urewera are facts. They are not made up and all New Zealanders need to have a good understanding of what happened. That is why changing the curriculum so that these matters can be taught in schools is very important. In the twenty-first century, teaching New Zealand history must take precedence over teaching European or American history, but historical fact needs to be taught, not propaganda. Teaching history requires an objective analysis of everything that has happened, both good and bad. My fear is that those designing the history curriculum in this country are essentially propagandists who will overlook the good that has occurred and concentrate instead on the bad. Take, for example, the very good work of Christian missionaries since 1840, such as Mother Mary Aubert who founded Our Lady's Home of Compassion and ran a large mission at Jerusalem on the Whanganui River. There were many other positive interactions between Pākehā and Māori, and some early Pākehā settlers expressed real concerns over the way Māori were being treated.

Hopefully the Ministry of Education will do a good job in supporting the teaching of New Zealand history in the years to come. However, I have serious misgivings about their ability to do the right thing and worry that what, in my opinion, is a one-sided propagandist approach will be counterproductive.

Treaty settlements

The final issue I want to discuss concerns the durability of Treaty of Waitangi settlements. On more than 60 occasions I stood before settling iwi to apologise on behalf of the Crown for various breaches of the treaty and to promise a new beginning. When I made these grand statements, I always metaphorically had my fingers crossed because I knew only too well that Māori would honour their side of the bargain but that the history of the Crown's performance is one of great promises made that were broken shortly thereafter. In every treaty settlement it is important to ensure that all of government knows of the commitments that have been undertaken and equally that all of government honours those commitments.

To help ensure that commitments are honoured, the Post-settlement Commitments Unit was set up in 2015. Next, a database listing all commitments in the various settlements was established that could be readily accessed by government departments. This allows them to ensure that, before they take any action in relation to a particular matter, there is nothing in any deed of settlement that could impact on it.

When the *Cabinet Manual* was amended in 2017, it included a number of insertions to reflect the importance of treaty settlements and ensure that they are durable. The manual states that ministers should consult relevant ministerial colleagues before submitting papers that deal with significant or potentially controversial matters, or that affect other ministers' portfolio interests. So ministers have to consult, for example, the attorney-general on all proposals that raise significant legal issues, and in particular: 'the Attorney-General or the Minister responsible for Treaty of Waitangi settlement obligations, if there is one, on any proposal with potential impacts on existing Treaty of Waitangi settlements'.[9] In relation to bills, the manual says: 'Departments should assess the implications of Bills on existing Treaty of Waitangi settlements and consult the Ministry of Justice if they conclude there will be a potential impact. This is to safeguard the durability of Treaty settlements, and the renewed relationship that settlements have established.'[10]

When the new government was formed in October 2017, Kelvin Davis was made minister for Māori Crown relations and assumed responsibility for the Post-settlement Commitments Unit. I thought the idea of a minister for Māori Crown relations was an excellent one and was pleased to see Kelvin appointed to that role. As MP for Te Tai Tokerau, Kelvin had a good understanding of the settlements process and understood the importance of durability of settlements. I have had a number of dealings with him in recent years on behalf of iwi who have been concerned about various issues arising from their settlements, and Kelvin has always taken those concerns seriously and come up with just and practical solutions. He is held in high regard by settling iwi because of his careful stewardship of this portfolio.

That said, there are some real concerns about the durability of settlements. I know, for example, that Ngāi Tūhoe is concerned about its relationship with the Department of Conservation (DOC). The Tūhoe settlement created a board responsible for the stewardship of the area once known as the Urewera National Park, in which Tūhoe representatives outnumber Crown representatives. Unfortunately, there have been disagreements with DOC over maintenance and funding arrangements for Te Urewera, and it seems that DOC does not have a good grasp of the detail of the settlement. The department has to understand that it is no longer in charge of Te Urewera; that is the responsibility of the governance group set up under the settlement. There are some good people in DOC who have worked hard to make sure that settlements are a success, but in my opinion more needs to be done in Te Urewera to safeguard the Tūhoe settlement.

Sadly, the general misunderstanding around co-governance has led to unfair criticism of Māori who assume co-governance roles post-settlement. I have, for example, heard comments that, since Tūhoe have assumed responsibility for Te Urewera, flora and fauna there have dramatically declined. Stories like this can be symptomatic of observer bias, with complaints about ongoing issues made only after Tūhoe assumed management of the area. For example, trampers in the former national park have noted a lack of birdsong for some time. At its peak, DOC trapped up to 20 per cent of Te Urewera, and clearly restoration of wildlife there is an ongoing project.

While it is difficult to establish funding in the area, it is clear that less money goes into Te Urewera now than it did in the past. Tūhoe estimate that DOC previously spent $6 million in Te Urewera annually; the figure is now down to $2 million, allocated mostly to infrastructure maintenance according to DOC's priorities. If there is an issue, then it is perhaps that the public wants a particular level of service but does not want to pay for it. That is not an issue with co-governance or with Tūhoe, and it is unfair to blame Tūhoe for any problems.

There will also be an increasingly vigorous debate about things like teaching history in New Zealand. I hope the debate is principled and civil and does not degenerate to the levels experienced in, for example, the United States. There, statues of George Washington and Thomas Jefferson have been taken down in some cities because those two were associated with slavery in the early years of the republic. So, too, in the United Kingdom where historical figures' reputations have been trashed. A mature country should be able to look at these issues without that kind of extreme zealotry. Face the past, acknowledge that bad things happened, but acknowledge too that this country has endeavoured to address those issues and much good happened to all those who have lived in New Zealand since the Treaty of Waitangi was signed. Instead of pulling statues down, I like the idea expressed to me by one Ngāi Tahu leader: the current generation should simply put up statues to the people it respects alongside them.

There are many other examples I could give, but the Tūhoe settlement emphasises the importance of treaty settlements to New Zealand and the need for government departments to understand and accept their durability. If the Crown slips back into its old ways and ignores the legitimate aspirations of settling iwi, then we end up back where we were when the whole treaty settlement process started more than a generation ago.

Finally, I would like to comment on the Green party's suggestion that it will reopen treaty settlements and take private land under the Public Works Act 1981 for renewed settlements. I could not think of a better recipe for inflaming race relations in this country than these proposals. In my experience, Green MPs were great pontificators in the treaty settlement process, giving unctuous and nauseating speeches in Parliament on the subject. They were never satisfied with any settlement and adopted a holier than thou approach to issues, always implying they could do better and that my efforts were suboptimal. But the people of New Zealand will not tolerate a reopening of treaty settlements, and what the Greens are offering cannot come to pass. Treaty settlements are not perfect; they can never undo the injustices of the past. The amounts offered in settlements, although not nominal, are not full compensation for what has been lost. However, the system is the best that can be devised, bearing in mind the divergent interests of various sections of the community. In my view, to suggest reopening settlements after all the work that has been done by thousands of iwi members and the Crown is simply irresponsible.

For all its rhetoric on Māori issues, and its view of most Crown redress as inadequate and practically pointless, the Green party often runs into a fundamental problem in its approach to the treaty: they don't really believe in property rights. That places the Green world view at distinct odds with something that unites all iwi with whom I negotiated as a minister: the crucial importance of the control of whenua. The Greens also run into problems with rangatiratanga, authority guaranteed by article 2 of the Treaty of Waitangi. They more often than not ally themselves with non-Māori conservation groups, or endorse DOC as the critical player in protecting the environment rather than Māori. One member of Ngāi Tahu once told me of the abuse she saw hurled at tribal negotiators during the

1990s by Green conservation board members, who would turn up at public meetings and accuse Ngāi Tahu of not understanding how to care for the environment. And there is another problem, too. As signed-up members of the global environmental movement, the Greens are quite happy to prioritise international environmental goals, laudable as they might be, over the authority and aspirations of Māori.

Despite this, a 'we know best' approach continues to mark the approach of the New Zealand Green party to Māori issues. There is almost an arrogance in their certainty about their moral superiority on indigenous matters, an approach interestingly echoed by the Australian Green party, which is currently opposing a national referendum on indigenous representation in favour of a truth-telling and treaty process. Following the recent 2022 Australian election, one newly elected indigenous Labor MP described the Greens as a bigger threat to the idea than the coalition.[11]

CHAPTER 10 Overseas assignments

IN MID-2009, NOT LONG AFTER I BECAME attorney-general, Baroness Scotland visited me. She had been appointed the attorney-general for England and Wales by Tony Blair, and continued to serve in that position during the premiership of Gordon Brown. Over lunch, she suggested to me that it would be a good idea for the attorneys-general for England and Wales, New Zealand, Australia, Canada and the United States to meet on a regular basis to discuss important issues in their portfolios. I agreed and suggested that we commence such meetings while she was attorney-general. Thus was born the quintet of attorneys-general.

The first meeting was held in London some months later. President Barack Obama's attorney-general was Eric Holder, a man with a great deal of experience in both the judiciary and executive government. Rob Nicholson, MP for Niagara Falls, was the Canadian attorney-general. He had held a number of very important positions in the government of Stephen Harper and would subsequently go on to be minister of defence and foreign affairs. The Australian attorney-general was Rob McClelland, a senior member of the Rudd and subsequently Gillard governments. He was the son of a Whitlam-era cabinet minister.

The first meeting was a great success. We discussed not only criminal law issues, but also matters relating to promoting and protecting the rule of law. I thought the quintet should always set aside time to discuss rule of law issues because I considered my primary responsibility as attorney-general was to protect and promote the rule of law in New Zealand.

We had a subsequent meeting in Sydney in early 2010. That was the last one attended by Baroness Scotland, because the Brown government was defeated at the polls in May 2010 and Dominic Grieve became the attorney-general for England and Wales. Dominic became a good friend of mine, and I have enormous respect for his ability and integrity. He subsequently took a principled stand against Brexit, was deselected as MP for Beaconsfield (which he had represented since 1997) and, while he put up a very respectable showing, was defeated in the 2020 election and left politics.

Over the years the meeting of the quintet became more focused on security issues. Towards the end of my time as attorney-general, the various countries' security ministers also joined us. For example, the secretary of homeland security in the second Obama administration, Jeh Johnson, came to meetings, as did the then Australian minister of home affairs, Peter Dutton, who did not impress me. I have never liked Dutton since he referred to expelling New Zealanders as 'throwing out the trash'.

At one meeting of attorneys-general, I again emphasised the need to set aside time to talk about protection of the rule of law. By that stage I was receiving some rather odd looks, because at the time terrorism and the criminal law were regarded as the topics *du jour*. I always regret that we do not spend more time talking about the importance of the rule of law in our societies. It is not a theoretical topic, as I have said on a number of occasions in this book, but a very important feature of a liberal democracy, and it has been under threat in such great democracies as the United States and, more recently, the United Kingdom. One can never take the rule of law for granted.

I hosted the quintet in Auckland in 2013. It was a very successful meeting, marred only by the fact that Dotcom and his little band of supporters were protesting outside the venue because they wanted to embarrass Eric Holder.

After the change of government in Canada in 2015, the new Canadian attorney-general was Jody Wilson-Raybould. Jody, who had been elected as MP for a constituency in Vancouver, was an indigenous Canadian and had done a great deal of work on behalf of First Nations people in British Columbia. She was the first indigenous person to be appointed attorney-general and minister of justice in Canada. I was impressed with her when I met her and we obviously shared some common interests, particularly in the area of treaty settlements. I arranged for her to come to New Zealand as a prime minister's fellow, which she did a year or so later. I thought she had an excellent political career ahead of her, but her career was destroyed by Justin Trudeau in most unfortunate circumstances. The Ministry of Justice was prosecuting a Québec company, and Trudeau suggested to Jody that there could be ways of resolving the matter without the need for a criminal trial. She responded to him that ministers and attorneys-general should not get involved in day-to-day prosecutions and his suggestions were inappropriate. Trudeau undertook a cabinet reshuffle, where she was moved to a minor post and subsequently dismissed from government, then expelled from the Liberal party of Canada. Trudeau's actions were disgraceful, but Jody took a principled position and stood as an independent in her constituency. At the general election of 2019 she was re-elected, which was an amazing achievement given that very few independents ever succeed in a first-past-the-post system. She decided, however, that she did not want to continue in politics and retired at the most recent Canadian general election. Jody Wilson-Raybould is a woman of great ability and principle, and her loss to Canadian politics was tragic.[1]

After Donald Trump was elected, the former Alabama senator Jeff Sessions was appointed attorney-general, and I thought he would simply be a mouthpiece of Trump. When we had a quintet meeting in Ottawa in 2017, my initial view seemed to be confirmed because Jeff spent most of his time going on about China's lack of respect for the world trade order. It was not a contribution that was particularly relevant to many of the issues we were discussing. As it turns out, Jeff took a principled stand on issues on the rule of law with Trump, and the day after the mid-term elections in 2018, was summarily sacked. He was just one of many whose careers were ruined for standing up to Trump.

Looking back at the meetings of the quintet, I realise how precarious the position of the attorney-general can be. The two most egregious sackings were of Jeff Sessions and Jody Wilson-Raybould. I suppose one would expect such narcissistic and brutal behaviour from Trump, but one expected better of Trudeau, who prides himself as the apotheosis of modernity and liberalism. Dominic Grieve's fate was also unfortunate. As I noted earlier, he made the mistake of giving legal rather than political advice to David Cameron.

I count myself fortunate that my prime ministers were John Key and Bill English. They always respected the office of attorney-general and the independence that needed to be brought to many subjects.

International Court of Justice

One of the most interesting things I did as attorney-general was to represent New Zealand in the International Court of Justice (ICJ). On this occasion, New Zealand intervened in the case *Whaling in the Antarctic*, brought by Australia against Japan.

Australia's case questioned the validity of Japan's so-called 'scientific' whaling programme in the Southern Ocean. New Zealand's intervention allowed us to put our views on the proper interpretation of the International Convention for the Regulation of Whaling (ICRW) before the court. As a member of the International Whaling Commission (IWC), New Zealand has an interest in ensuring that the organisation works effectively and that the ICRW is properly interpreted and applied.

The ICJ was established in 1945 by the Charter of the United Nations as the 'principal judicial organ' of the UN. The court was the successor to the Permanent Court of International Justice (PCIJ), which was established within the League of Nations in 1921 and ceased sitting in December 1939. Both the PCIJ and the ICJ sit in the Peace Palace in The Hague, completed in 1913 as a home for the Permanent Court of Arbitration, a parallel international disputes body established in 1899 that continues to the present day.

The charter and the ICJ's statute confer competence over contentious cases — that is, inter-state disputes — and also advisory opinions, which the ICJ may give at the request of other UN bodies such as the UN General Assembly. The ICJ comprises fifteen permanent judges elected by parallel majority vote in both the UN General Assembly and the UN Security Council to nine-year terms. Where a party before the ICJ does not have one of its nationals as a judge, it may appoint a judge ad hoc — in the Australia–Japan case, Australia appointed Hilary Charlesworth, an eminent academic international lawyer.

The ICJ's jurisdiction depends upon the consent of each state, which may be given on a general basis — as 67 states have done at present — or in jurisdiction clauses in some treaties. In the case of Australia, Japan and New Zealand, each has accepted the general jurisdiction of the ICJ subject to various reservations: New Zealand's reservations relate to exclusive economic zone (EEZ) claims, and to cases in which either the parties have agreed on another dispute process or where the other state concerned has not accepted jurisdiction on a similarly broad and settled basis. The ICJ has no competence over individuals — unlike, for instance, the International Criminal Court, established in 2002.

The ICJ has determined 113 contentious cases and issued 27 advisory opinions. To give some illustration of the diversity (and also the workload) of the court in 2013, it had ten cases listed as pending, which in addition to the Australia–Japan case encompassed several boundary disputes, two claims of infringement of boundaries, a claim under the Genocide Convention and a dispute over a dam on the Hungary–Slovakia border.

Members of the ICJ have stressed the need to uphold its relevance, credibility and efficiency as a means of ensuring that states have confidence in the court as an institution. The former New Zealand member of the ICJ, Sir Kenneth Keith, commented that one of the strengths of the court is that states are increasingly likely to submit their disputes for decision — bearing in mind that, for instance, boundary delimitation cases can sometimes deter or even avert the outbreak of armed conflict (although Sir Kenneth also stressed that international law, and compliance with that law, both have their limits and tragedies continue to occur).

Prior to its intervention in the Australia–Japan case, New Zealand had appeared in one advisory opinion proceeding, *Legality of the Threat or Use of Nuclear Weapons* (1995–96) and one contentious case, *Nuclear Testing in the Pacific* (1973–74 and 1995). In the latter, the ICJ granted provisional measures in favour of New Zealand in June 1973, but France nevertheless proceeded to conduct a series of tests in July/August 1973 and June/September 1974. Before the full merits of the case could be heard, France announced that it would not carry out any further atmospheric tests after the 1974 tests had been completed. The ICJ decided that France's undertaking not to carry out further atmospheric testing meant that there was no longer a dispute between the parties. In 1995, after France resumed testing, New Zealand requested that the ICJ examine the situation and grant provisional measures to prevent France from undertaking any further nuclear tests. The ICJ dismissed New Zealand's application on the grounds that the basis of its earlier decision was France's undertaking not to conduct any further atmospheric tests, and that this did not extend to cover underground testing. However, France did reduce the number of tests it carried out from eight to six, and subsequently accepted a complete ban on all nuclear testing when it became party to the Comprehensive Nuclear-Test-Ban Treaty in 1998.

In October 2010, Australia began its case against Japan, alleging that the JARPA II whale research programme breached the ICRW and other international obligations. Shortly thereafter, Japan objected to the admissibility of the claim and its merits. Towards the end of 2012, Murray McCully, minister of foreign affairs, decided that New Zealand should become involved in the case. New Zealand then filed a declaration of intervention in its capacity as a party to the ICRW. The case was set down for a hearing from 26 June to 16 July 2013. New Zealand was given half a day to make its submissions on intervention.

Australia was represented by the Australian attorney-general, Mark Dreyfus QC; solicitor-general Justin Gleeson, SC; Professor James Crawford, SC of the Sydney and London Bars and Cambridge; Professor Philippe Sands QC of the London Bar and University College London; and Professor Laurence Boisson de Chazournes of the University of Geneva. Japan was represented by government lawyers and also Professor Alain Pellet of the Sorbonne, Professor Vaughan Lowe QC of the London Bar and Oxford, Professor Alan Boyle of the University of Edinburgh, and Professor Payam Akhavan of McGill University in Montreal. New Zealand was represented by me as attorney-general, the Ministry of Foreign Affairs and Trade (MFAT) international legal adviser, the deputy solicitor-general, and other internal and external counsel, including assistance from Professor Donald McRae, a New Zealand-born Canadian practitioner before the court, who was not able to appear at the hearing.

I was pleased with the New Zealand team. Although we did not have the resources of the Australian and Japanese governments, I thought our team was effective. I particularly want to mention the contribution of the MFAT international legal adviser, Penelope Ridings, and Elana Geddis, a Wellington barrister and former legal adviser in MFAT. Penelope, who had been our first ambassador in Poland, had a detailed knowledge of international law. This has been recently recognised by her election to the prestigious International Law Commission. Elana began her career in foreign affairs, then went to the Bar, where she has specialised in international law. She was largely responsible for bringing the submissions together and I thought her work was outstanding.

Both parties also called expert witnesses, who were examined before the court. Leading practitioners have suggested that ICJ proceedings cost at least US$10 million; New Zealand's costs were quite a lot less — in part because of New Zealand's limited role as an intervenor.

Australia took the position that the provision for scientific whaling under the ICRW required Japan to conduct any research on an objectively demonstrable scientific basis. Australia's basic point was, in short, that Japan's conduct of the JARPA II programme on a scale comparable to earlier commercial whaling, with limited research output and little engagement with scientific criticism, did not meet that requirement.

Japan opposed Australia's objective interpretation as imposing an improper restriction on the conduct of states party to the ICRW and, more colourfully, as culturally imperialist and as condoning protest activity by the Sea Shepherd group. Japan also contended that because some JARPA II whaling occurred in waters claimed by Australia, it was inadmissible because of Australia's reservation of maritime claims from its acceptance of the ICJ's jurisdiction.

New Zealand, as appropriate for an intervener, made submissions on the correct interpretation of the ICRW. In short, New Zealand advanced its view that the ICRW did impose both substantive and procedural obligations on states proposing to undertake lethal whaling research, relying on the collective character of the ICRW.

As one raised in the court system of New Zealand, I am used to judges firing questions at counsel within minutes of my starting a case. The ICJ could not be more different. The procedure of the court is very formal, with no spontaneous interaction between counsel and the court. If the judges had questions for counsel, they would prepare written questions that would be distributed at the end of the day. One could then work with the officials over the next few hours to prepare a response that would be filed with the court. It seemed a lot easier to be counsel in the ICJ than in the High Court of New Zealand.

The hearing was eventful in a number of respects, and at times there was more heat than light. The Australian solicitor-general cross-examined the expert witness for Japan to the point that another Australian counsel later felt obliged to explain that that was what cross-examination was and should be like. Professor Akhavan, for Japan, suggested that Australia had 'outsourced' its maritime law enforcement to the Sea Shepherd group, whose members were described as terrorists and/or pirates. Professor Pellet, also for Japan, suggested that the term 'scientific research' in the ICRW should be interpreted according to the sixteenth-century French philosopher Michel de Montaigne, who had said that true science was a knowing ignorance ('*une ignorance qui se sait*'), (to which I said that true scientific research was the 'immensely practical . . . art of the soluble'). And Professor Crawford, for Australia, concluded by describing Japan's submissions — in part following E.M. Forster — as 'a polemic against Australia's conduct within the IWC, on the one hand, and on the other hand, on purely legal arguments, seraphically free from the facts'.[2]

Because Parliament had adjourned for a fortnight, I was able to appear for at least ten days. During my time at The Hague, our ambassador to the Netherlands, George Troup, and his team were very helpful. In what must be a world first, one of my office colleagues, James Christmas, had his first-ever court appearance in the ICJ. It could only ever be downhill after that. Unfortunately for him, Mark Dreyfus QC was detained in Canberra because the Labor government was in trouble and was disposing of Julia Gillard and exhuming Kevin Rudd. I had dinner with him in The Hague the day he arrived. At the end of the dinner, he thanked me very much for not asking him any questions about the impending leadership spill in Canberra. He gave his address the following morning, then had to fly immediately back to Canberra.

A few months later, the ICJ indicated it would be giving its decision. Penelope Ridings was going to be present in The Hague for the release of the judgment. I suggested to the New Zealand-based lawyers that we should have dinner and then watch the result in my office. John Key sent me a number of texts during the evening asking how it was going. I responded that we had won on the jurisdictional issue (as expected), but that I was dubious about a substantive win. As the judgment continued to be read by the president of the court, it became apparent that Australia (and New Zealand) had won a great victory. We were successful in every respect. The Japanese were deeply distressed at the result and withdrew their recognition of the jurisdiction of the ICJ in relation to whaling.

A day or so later, the then leader of the opposition commented that it was a fabulous win for Australia, but 'Where the hell was New Zealand?' One of my staff posted on Facebook (and Twitter, I think) a photo of me sitting in the court at The Hague. Poor David Cunliffe. Even a rudimentary enquiry by him would have revealed that New Zealand had played an active and distinguished role at the ICJ.

The opportunity to represent New Zealand in The Hague only arises every twenty or so years, and so it was a real honour for me to have represented the country in such an august body.

The Vatican

In 2013, Bill English was responsible for giving me a very special overseas trip. I mention it here because it is not really related to my work as a minister but it was interesting nonetheless. I was sitting in Astoria in Wellington, March 2013 having my breakfast, when a barrister friend of mine told me that the cardinals had just elected a new Pope. They were meeting to determine who should replace Pope Benedict XVI, who had resigned a few weeks earlier. I went back to my office to see who the new pontiff would be, and learnt of the appointment of an Argentinian who would take the name Francis. A day or so later, Bill contacted me to say that he would not be able to go to Rome for the inauguration of Pope Francis and asked whether I would be interested. The answer to the question was obvious. My decision necessitated urgent travel arrangements, complicated by the fact that I needed to be back in Wellington a day or so after the inauguration to initial the deed of settlement with Ngāi Tūhoe.

Once in Rome, I was greeted by Trevor Taylor, the excellent New Zealand ambassador to Italy, and George Troup, who was ambassador to The Hague and also cross-accredited to the Holy See. We went down to the Vatican the following morning for the inaugural Mass. As people were milling around before the service, I saw Vice President Joe Biden and Nancy Pelosi, speaker of the US House of Representatives. I had no particular desire to meet Pelosi, but asked Trevor Taylor if it would be possible to go and say hello to Biden. We wandered over and introduced ourselves. I mentioned to Biden what an excellent ambassador the United States had in New Zealand, and he could not have been more affable and pleasant. It was interesting watching the great and the good at the inauguration. Also present was Robert Mugabe of Zimbabwe, whom everyone was avoiding.

At the end of the Mass, representatives of the various countries lined up in order to be introduced to the new Pope. I stood behind Angela Merkel, who was speaking to the president of the European Union and giving her views on a bail-out of Cyprus (I think). She spoke faultless English and it was obvious why she was regarded as the leading light in Europe. Within a few minutes, Merkel was moved to the front of the line, which hardly surprised me. I briefly spoke to the Pope, acknowledging his election and wishing him all the best, not knowing that his knowledge of English was very poor — I think he got the gist of what I was saying. Then after that it was a rush to the airport to fly home. Altogether, I spent about 40 hours in an Emirates plane and only 24 hours on the ground, but it was very much worth it.

A few months later, Margaret Thatcher died and Gerry Brownlee was asked to attend her funeral service at St Paul's Cathedral in London. (I think the decision for Gerry to go greatly distressed Judith Collins, who saw herself as an antipodean Thatcher. She hosted an evening in her office where we all watched the funeral, but I'm sure she would much rather have been there in person.) Some months later, I had the privilege of meeting the Polish foreign minister and his wife, Anne Applebaum, a leading writer and historian. I mentioned to her that I had attended the papal inauguration and that one of my colleagues, Gerry Brownlee, had attended the funeral of the sainted Thatcher. I said I thought I had won on points, but she profoundly disagreed with me. Clearly in her mind Thatcher was greater than the Pope. Actually, she's not wrong.

UN Security Council

In late 2016, the American ambassador, Mark Gilbert, contacted me. He said there was to be an urgent debate at the UN Security Council on terrorism-related issues and that the secretary of homeland security, Jeh Johnson, whom I knew from other meetings, wanted to know if I could attend. At that time New Zealand was a temporary member of the Security Council. It was the kind of invitation that was impossible to refuse, and so I naturally said I would be pleased to go. A few days later, Mark contacted me to apologise for speaking to me about the matter without talking first to the minister of foreign affairs, Murray McCully. I said he shouldn't worry about that at all and that I would be attending because it covered an area that I was reasonably familiar with and had been working on with the agencies.

A few weeks later I went to the Security Council, assisted by our then permanent representative to the UN, Gerard van Bohemen. I knew Gerard very well as we had studied law together. He had had a stellar career in foreign affairs and in private practice, culminating in his appointment to the UN, succeeding Jim McLay in 2015. (On his return to New Zealand in 2017, I made him a High Court judge.)

This meeting took place against the backdrop of recent serious terrorist incidents in Manchester, Sydney and Nice. More recently there has been some debate about whether the attention of the New Zealand intelligence agencies was too narrowly focused on Islamist terrorism and whether they should have been also considering white extremism, such as was manifested at Charlottesville, Virginia, in August 2017. I have always thought this criticism was unfair. The sad reality of the matter is that around the time I was the minister in charge of the intelligence and security agencies and was appearing at the Security Council with Jeh Johnson and others, Islamist terrorism was the issue of the day and needed to be confronted. It was not the only issue that was discussed at the Security Council that day, but it was an important matter that the council wanted to be engaged on.

Unfortunately, the trip home from New York was something of a disaster. My colleagues and I boarded a flight at JFK for San Francisco, where we were supposed to be on the ground for an hour or so before flying on to Auckland. However, the plane had broken down, which necessitated an extra day at a hotel near JFK airport and a delayed flight to New Zealand. The trials and tribulations occasioned by United Airlines, however, were relatively minor compared with the importance of the trip and the opportunity to meet very senior colleagues from around the globe who were dealing with these important security issues.

CHAPTER 11 Challenges

IN JULY 2020, SIR JAMES BEVAN, chief executive of the UK Environment Agency, gave an address. He began by reference to one of the best-known political quotes (which may not have been said!): 'You will probably recognise the quote. When Prime Minister Harold Macmillan was asked what was the greatest challenge for a statesman, he replied: "Events, dear boy, events." The same is true for most leaders and organisations. Events happen. When they do a lot of things are at stake: lives, livelihoods, reputation. So knowing how to respond is a key survival skill for leaders and organisations of all kinds.'[1] He then set out some top tips for dealing with events. Some of them warrant repeating here:

> **Lead:** If you are your organisation's leader, you need to lead the response to a big incident. Don't try to do the day job as well. The incident is the day job till it's over . . .
> **Move fast:** Flick the switch to put your organisation into incident mode . . . Establish . . . clear roles and responsibilities.

> **Get on the ground:** The absent are always wrong. Being present and visible at the scene of an incident is as important as what you do when you get there . . .
> **Have a strategy:** Be clear what your goals are and ensure everyone knows.[2]

He then ended with a quote from Bear Bryant, a well-known American college football coach: 'In a crisis, don't hide behind anything or anybody. They're going to find you anyway.'

That speech could have been written by John Key. Everything Sir James said was enacted by him and his ministers as they confronted some serious challenges between 2008 and 2017.

Members of the current government always say that, unlike other administrations, the Ardern government has faced a litany of natural and other disasters since it assumed office in 2017. While there is no doubt it has certainly faced challenges, it is equally true that between 2008 and 2017 we faced some extraordinary challenges, and as a minister, I was a witness to the way in which those challenges were confronted.

The global financial crisis

The Key government was born in the midst of adversity. The global financial crisis (GFC) was far and away the worst economic crisis faced by a government for generations — far worse than the Asian financial crisis of the late 1990s and even the crisis faced by the 1984 Labour government following the last few years of Robert Muldoon's reckless stewardship of the economy. In my opinion, New Zealand was very lucky to have John Key and Bill English as the leadership team guiding the cabinet and the country through this difficult period. Bill was born to be minister of finance in a crisis. From the time he assumed office in early November 2008, he was well aware of the severity of the situation and the need for the government to put its accounts in order. So every dollar spent had to be justified to him. As a cabinet minister in those times, I could take nothing for granted, and, as I have explained in this book, I was required to do my bit to ensure that all spending was justified and appropriate.

The GFC served as a bit of a welcome to the new government and probably characterised it in general. Shortly after he became prime minister, John went to an Asia-Pacific Economic Cooperation (APEC) meeting in Peru. The biggest part of the agenda was the GFC, and the countries attending agreed to work towards restoring confidence in their economies. Some of the steps made included enhancing regional economic cooperation and intensifying work on structural reform.

In early 2009 John convened the Job Summit. This was important because it took place during the GFC and because Bill was putting together a zero-sum budget. The summit underlined a lot of economic fundamentals and initiatives that proved very valuable later on. I did not attend but was aware of some of the discussions and the proposals put forward. One of those proposals was the prime minister's idea of developing cycleways. John asked for money for a national cycleway on the basis that cycling was becoming a popular recreational pastime and many small towns in New Zealand would benefit from a cycle trail. As expected, the Labour opposition made fun of the proposal. But the joke was on them, because it proved to be highly successful and towns like Ohakune in the central North Island found that they were being visited by hordes of cyclists, which in turn helped strengthen their accommodation and hospitality sectors. Cycleways have been a tremendous success and magnets for both international and domestic tourism.

The Christchurch earthquakes

No sooner was the GFC generally under control when the devastating Christchurch earthquakes hit. At the time of the first earthquake in September 2010, I was living in Kate Sheppard Apartments opposite Parliament. I remember the building shaking in the early hours of Saturday morning and I turned on the radio to hear that there was no tsunami risk. The next day, the full extent of the disaster became apparent.

The first priority was to show support and work with people on the ground. John was there first thing on the Saturday morning and walked around his home town with Mayor Bob Parker looking at the damage. The next priority was to save jobs as the earthquake had caused massive damage, resulting in either the temporary or permanent closure of a large number of businesses. Some of the policies the government used after this first earthquake were reapplied by the Labour government during the Covid pandemic.

It was important to have one person in cabinet primarily responsible for the aftermath of the earthquake. There was no debate that the obvious choice was Gerry Brownlee, then leader of the House and minister of economic development and energy. His economic portfolios were reallocated, and Gerry became minister for Christchurch, a job he carried out with great distinction. I saw first-hand his total commitment as a Cantabrian to seeing his beloved city recover. What is not understood or appreciated is that Gerry's own home was damaged in the February 2011 earthquake, and he used to stay with his mother-in-law when he was in the city. When he told me this, I said he should stay in a hotel, but he wouldn't have anything to do with such a proposition, saying that it would be wrong to be living in a hotel when his fellow Cantabrians were suffering.

The next task was the establishment of the Canterbury Earthquake Recovery Authority (CERA), which was established as a government department in 2011 to lead and coordinate the government's response and recovery efforts following the earthquakes. A huge amount of money was invested in the department to get things done.

I visited the city as soon as I could after the February 2011 earthquake as minister for arts, culture and heritage. The damage was devastating. Great buildings, once so beautiful and inspiring, were destroyed or very badly damaged, including the city's two cathedrals. I had only spoken a few days earlier in the Christchurch Anglican cathedral on Waitangi Day and was saddened to learn of its fate. The great Catholic cathedral in Barbadoes Street was in a much worse state and it has since been demolished — what was probably the most beautiful public building in New Zealand is no more.

This was the case right across the city, and there were some who were very critical of Gerry's forceful advocacy for demolition in certain cases. I know he irritated some people when he made the comment that 'old buildings kill', but he was haunted by what had happened to the organ repairers from Timaru who were killed in the Durham Street Methodist Church. He knew only too well that some buildings had not performed well in the earthquakes and simply had to go. That resulted in the inevitable criticism by certain heritage zealots in Christchurch, but tough decisions needed to be made in the public interest, and Gerry was prepared to make them.

Large parts of Christchurch that should never have been developed as housing in the first place were made uninhabitable. A red zone was declared, and the Crown purchased around 8000 properties from these areas after the earthquakes. Some people who had not been insured sued the Crown, and this both exacerbated and delayed the situation.

Insurance was another major issue confronting Gerry. Unlike Wellington, Christchurch was not originally on the quake radar. Due to the risk of future earthquakes, no one was willing to give

New Zealand primary insurance following the Christchurch events. Without primary insurance, there is no insurance for local businesses, so the government invested in more research into the science of earthquake risk to change the misunderstandings around it. Gerry and his team embarked on an insurance tour and presented in both London and Monaco to reassure insurance companies. He sought to convince the insurance market that they could trust in New Zealand due to the safe construction of our buildings. One insurer came to New Zealand to see the reasons why there should be investment in our country, and that resulted in more people trusting New Zealand, which in turn resulted in insurance support. All this work was overseen by Gerry.

This is but a superficial sketch of the Christchurch earthquakes. It does explain, however, that from the first few hours of the quake in September 2010, government ministers led by the prime minister were on the ground reassuring people, providing hope and providing a plan for rebuilding the second city of our country. Gerry, of course, has received no thanks for his work, and inexplicably lost Ilam in the 2020 election. I do not think his constituents or Cantabrians generally understand how much he did for them in the darkest days following those earthquakes. What has emerged in my opinion is the most beautiful city in New Zealand. There is, of course, still much to be done, but I hope that one day the people of Christchurch will see that Gerry's contribution deserves praise. A Royal Commission was appointed to investigate many issues arising from the earthquakes, and its report was outstanding.[3]

The Pike River Mine tragedy

In 1979 a geologist confirmed the presence of coal in an area on the West Coast not far from Greymouth, and in 1982 the Pike River

Coal Company was formed to hold exploration rights to the area. That company was purchased by New Zealand Oil and Gas Limited in 1982, and in November 2008 coal started to be extracted after the Pike River Mine was built. On 19 November 2010, at 3.44 p.m., there was an explosion in the mine following a build-up of methane. At the time of the explosion, there were 31 men inside the mine. Only two survived, the others most likely dying either from the explosion or from noxious gases. Just a few months before, a group of Chilean miners had been successfully rescued, and for days everyone hoped the Pike River miners would also be rescued alive.

John Key was intimately involved in the disaster from the very beginning. As soon as he could, he went south. When he arrived, there was a lot of uncertainty and a complete paucity of information. The whole situation seemed to be disorganised, as everyone was in shock. What was perhaps the saddest thing of all was the constant presence of the families of the miners, who were hoping against hope that something could be done. One could sense the shock of the community throughout the following days.

John was committed to the people of Greymouth during this dreadful period. He was very supportive and understanding of the needs of the families and made sure their voices were heard. In this he was assisted by the MP for West Coast-Tasman, Chris Auchinvole. In due course, a Royal Commission was appointed to inquire into all aspects of the Pike River operation. It made a number of recommendations, all of which were accepted by the government.[4] I spoke to the families on the day the report was released and went through the recommendations, in particular the recommendation to reform the health and safety laws of New Zealand.

I met with the Pike River families on a number of occasions thereafter. I felt for them, knowing how much they had suffered. I also had enormous respect for their lawyer, Nick Davidson QC, whom I subsequently appointed to the High Court bench. I tried to negotiate a settlement with the families and met with Nick Davidson's replacement, Peter Creany, in 2016. I thought I had reached the outline of an agreement about ways in which litigation could be avoided, but my proposal did not meet with favour from the inner cabinet and so went nowhere.

The Ardern government subsequently promised to set up an authority that would spearhead the entry into the mine to look for bodies. An enormous amount of money has been spent, with little return. I do not think that the welfare of the miners' families has been helped by promises made to them by politicians or by the establishment of a very expensive authority that has achieved very little.

The Pike River Mine site and surrounding area have been added to Paparoa National Park at the suggestion of a group representing the families of the killed men. A project to establish a great walk between the mine and Punakaiki was announced by Minister for the Environment Nick Smith on 14 November 2015. I always thought that was a good idea and was pleased to see it come to fruition.

Farming challenges

In 2013, there was a major food safety scare that had the potential to destroy, or at least seriously harm, New Zealand's export markets. In early August, Fonterra advised the Ministry for Primary Industries of the presence of confirmed *Clostridium botulinum* bacteria in whey protein concentrate manufactured at its site in Hautapu in the Waikato. International reaction to this news was devastating. Some countries closed borders to certain New Zealand dairy products, others began specific product testing and several announced product recalls. Exporters felt the impact almost immediately through rejected shipments, withheld payments and lost orders.

This incident had very serious effects on New Zealand's reputation as a producer of high-quality food and the economy. Nathan Guy, who had only recently been appointed as minister for primary industries, established an independent inquiry into the situation. This inquiry had to look at regulatory and best-practice requirements for dairy food safety, and then report on how the potentially contaminated product had entered the New Zealand and international markets and how this was dealt with. It produced two very highly regarded reports.[5]

Then in 2014 there was a very serious threat not only to the dairy industry, but also to the New Zealand economy as a whole. A warning had been received about the possible contamination of infant formula with the pesticide 1080. There was an emergency meeting of the Cabinet National Security Committee, attended by top civil servants. The police immediately started to investigate the incident and raided quite a number of properties. As a result, the offender was identified. It eventuated that he was not motivated by environmental concerns, but rather commercial interests as he had a similar product he wanted to sell. He was subsequently convicted and sentenced to a lengthy term in prison.

I considered that the work done across government on this issue was admirable. In particular, the police used all their skills to identify the offender, and they were assisted in this regard by a number of government agencies. It really was government at its best, acting swiftly and decisively in the public interest. As a result of this scare, security around the production of infant formula and sales was greatly stepped up. For example, cameras were installed in production centres and security guards posted in key places.

So in the space of a little over twelve months, Nathan faced two hugely significant biosecurity issues, which he dealt with very well indeed. He also had to deal with the issue of biosecurity and fruit flies following outbreaks in Auckland in 2012 and then in Northland in 2014. Nathan's ministry needed to move very swiftly to establish a lockdown that restricted the movement of fruit and vegetables within the areas affected.

In addition to the Christchurch earthquakes, the government also had to respond to the Seddon earthquake in 2013 and the Kaikōura earthquake in 2016, the latter causing very serious damage in Wellington. In these disasters and the others I have discussed, certain factors were always apparent. These were strong leadership from the prime minister, decisive action by the responsible minister, urgent law change where change was required, and excellent cross-government work to ensure that issues were addressed quickly and decisively in the national interest.

Any government is going to face what Donald Rumsfeld once called the 'unknown unknowns' that kept him awake each night.[6] The challenge is how to address them when the circumstances arise. I believe the National government between 2008 and 2017, besieged as it was by these innumerable problems, addressed them very well indeed. John Key ensured that government both handled the immediate crisis but also focused on the government's long-term goals. He did everything Sir James Bevan said had to be done in a crisis: he led, he was on the ground, he moved fast and he had a strategy.

CHAPTER 12 Change of leader

IT WAS A BEAUTIFUL DAY in Wellington on 13 November 2016. I started my day with the outgoing United States ambassador, Mark Gilbert, farewelling Secretary of State John Kerry at Wellington airport. Later in the day, I met the president of Hungary and spent a pleasant afternoon with the Hungarian community in Wellington, and at 9 p.m. I farewelled the president from Parliament and wished him a good sleep that night. A few hours later, at approximately two minutes past midnight, the Kaikōura earthquake hit. At the time, I was living in Kate Sheppard Apartments in Thorndon. I woke up thinking that it had been a good shake, and then it didn't stop. In common with most Wellingtonians, I found it to be the most horrifying event of my life. I immediately went over to the Civil Defence room in the basement of the Beehive to see if there was anything that was required of me as a minister. Gerry Brownlee came across a few minutes later. Some idiot reporter noted I was in my gym gear — an obsession with trivia afflicts some of the fourth estate even in the most serious situations.

I asked the officials whether they had contacted the Chatham Islands to warn them of the prospect of a tsunami, and they said they had not. So I phoned the mayor of the Chathams, Alfred Preece, to tell him that Wellington had had a bad earthquake and that the Chathams ought to be prepared just in case there was a tsunami. It was following that phone call that he alerted the citizens of the Chathams to move to higher ground. That is not the normal way of warning Chatham Islanders of disasters, and one would have expected Civil Defence to be more alert than that.

The next morning, we had an urgent meeting of cabinet to determine the nature and extent of the earthquake and what needed to happen. I could not go to my office on level 19 of Bowen House because inspections were being undertaken to check whether the building had been damaged. Some days later, the building was declared open, and so I tentatively climbed the nineteen floors to inspect my office. I was expecting chaos and was amazed to find nothing was out of place aside from my wooden Pitcairn Island turtle, which had fallen to the floor. It was a very strange earthquake, with damage occurring in unexpected places. Where one expected severe damage, such as in Bowen House, there did not appear to be any, whereas there had been a lot of damage in Kate Sheppard Apartments and, around the corner, Defence House was destroyed. Initially it looked as though it was going to be a repeat of the Christchurch earthquake, but thankfully the damage was not as extensive. Even so, the whole experience was very unnerving.

A few days later, I received a phone call from the prime minister. He said, 'Good morning, my legal beagle. Would you mind calling over to see me.' I did not think I had done anything wrong and so was not expecting to be sacked, but I was intrigued by the Monday morning summons. John Key told me he was resigning and I was obviously shocked. The more I reflected on it, however, the more I saw it was yet another stroke of genius from this amazing New Zealander. Most political careers end in failure because people stay too long, but John was leaving at almost the height of his popularity and power after a little over eight years in office. Once again, he was showing what a class operator he was.

The focus of the next few days was on the succession. Cabinet met as usual shortly after 11 a.m. I had a paper dealing with the detail of the intelligence reform legislation and was working through that methodically, but Paula Bennett interrupted saying that there was no need to deal with it in such detail in the face of the impending change in the leadership of the National party and the government. I joked that I could have obtained cabinet approval that morning to introduce water torture, because no one was focused on any of the detail of what I was proposing for the new legislation.

It soon became apparent that the inner circle had decided on the fundamentals of the succession. Bill English would step up to be prime minister with Paula Bennett as his deputy. It was then proposed that Steven Joyce would take over as minister of finance. I had no problem with Bill succeeding to the throne. He had been an outstanding deputy prime minister and minister of finance, and had been in Parliament since 1990. As the regional chair of the lower North Island during the dreadful 2001–03 period, I had witnessed first-hand the way in which Bill had been let down by the party machinery and his colleagues after he succeeded Jenny Shipley as leader in late 2001. He had been promised support by various MPs if he took over from Shipley, but having done so, he found that the promises were empty. The party organisation was so run-down that it could not effectively mount a credible election campaign in 2002. I thought Bill deserved another chance.

I was, however, concerned at the prospect of Paula becoming deputy leader. I mentioned my concerns to Gerry Brownlee and wondered whether it would be advisable to try to arrange an alternative candidate. We talked about Simon Bridges as a possibility and spoke to him about it. Simon agreed to put his hat in the ring, and then some days later was asked to go to a meeting with various people. He phoned me to say that he would not be proceeding with the challenge but 'had done very well'. He went from ninth to fourth in the ranking, picking up the portfolios of economic development and, a few months later, leader of the House. Not having a particularly strong ministerial resumé, Simon had risen without trace from being a junior minister to one of the most powerful ministers in government. When I suggested that he stand as deputy, it was not so that he could burnish his credentials by becoming a senior minister, but in order to stop Paula being the deputy leader.

I have reflected on this matter over the years and think I made a mistake in trying to persuade Simon to stand as deputy leader. I think there was an obvious candidate, although she never emerged at the time. That was Anne Tolley, who was then minister of social services. Anne had had an impressive career in Parliament, as I have outlined elsewhere in this book, and she was stable and dependable. Her breadth of knowledge and administrative abilities have been recognised by the Ardern government, which has made her one of the commissioners for the hapless Tauranga City Council. I think she would have been an excellent deputy prime minister and I regret not pushing her to stand for that position.

Anne was a good friend of mine and one of my favourite colleagues. I could always have sensible discussions with her on any issue. One day there had been a 'full and frank' discussion in one of the cabinet committees on reforms to domestic violence law being proposed by Amy Adams, then minister of justice. I was critical about one aspect of the reforms. A day or so later, Anne phoned me to ask me if I would like to meet with her. Over breakfast, she said that the ninth floor had not appreciated my criticisms of Amy's paper. I found that somewhat surprising and disappointing, given that Amy was only too pleased to be a critic of other ministers' papers. Indeed, she has been described to me as a veritable negative force of nature. However, when confronted with criticism over her own policy proposals, she could not stand the heat. That is one of the reasons why I could never support her for a leadership position.

Thus the transition occurred. Bill was elected unopposed and Paula became his deputy. The incoming prime minister made it very clear that he wanted commitments from ministers about their continuing in office, and that if there was any doubt they should see him immediately. Shortly after, Sam Lotu-Iiga and Craig Foss announced their intention to retire at the 2017 election. I was very fond of Sam and regret that he did not have a more enjoyable ministerial career. David Seymour once said to me that Sam had been in the top class at Auckland Grammar and also in the first XV, a very rare achievement for a student at New Zealand's best boys' secondary school. Sam had an excellent academic career, including a stint at Cambridge, and had worked at Russell McVeagh as a commercial lawyer. In 2014, in what I regard as a somewhat mysterious move, John Key had made him minister of corrections This is one of the worst portfolios and always fraught with difficulties, and needs to be held by a senior minister. After a year or so, Sam was transferred to local government. I think it is a shame that he was not given a portfolio like commerce where he could have shown his true strengths.

We all waited for the prime ministerial phone call advising us of the portfolio allocations in the new government. I was on the twelfth tee at Heretaunga one Sunday when I received my call. The prime minister simply said to me 'You can hold the same portfolios.'

I asked whether my focus was to be on treaty negotiations, and Bill responded, 'That's what you're there for.' After what I thought was a somewhat graceless telephone call, I resumed my golf. Most of the portfolio allocations were unsurprising, and Steven Joyce was confirmed as minister of finance. I was perhaps a little surprised that Nick Smith retained his portfolios. He was certainly a zealot as minister for the environment, but there had been problems in the housing area and I thought we needed a change in that portfolio. Nick had been in Parliament since 1990 and I thought his time was coming to an end. Unlike John Key, Bill did not appear to recognise that when it comes to being prime minister there are no friends at the top, and if a prime minister thinks someone ought to lose their job because it is in the party's interest, then that is the way it has to be. I know that Bill and Nick were very good friends, but I think a change would have been desirable. This was confirmed in my mind when, a couple of months later, Nick announced his clean water policy and managed to create chaos out of what should have been a very positive announcement. I was also a little surprised that Murray McCully was retained as minister of foreign affairs because I thought he was retiring at the 2017 election. He stayed on for a few months, leaving in May the following year.

A few months later, in April 2017, I was in Arras in France for the centenary of the Battle of Arras. My visit coincided with a number of ministerial meetings associated with the intelligence portfolio, and I subsequently received a phone call from Bill, saying that he was looking at a couple of matters before determining whether I could be minister of foreign affairs. That all sounded pretty good to me, but eventually it transpired that Gerry Brownlee became the minister of foreign affairs. Perhaps I was regarded as too pro-Israel.

I never really understood Murray McCully. On the one hand, he could be extremely supportive of his fellow ministers, and he and I worked very well together when he was minister of sport and I was minister of arts, culture and heritage. It was he who forced the minister of internal affairs to tell the Lotteries Commission to change their practice of retaining large reserves each year. As a result of his intervention, nothing was held in reserve and both sport and arts (which receive money from the proceeds of Lotto) had their funding greatly increased. On the other hand, however, he had a tendency to bear grudges against the Wellington establishment and also act unilaterally. I never really understood why he felt the need to conduct such a radical restructuring of the Ministry of Foreign Affairs and Trade. It resulted in a large number of people being made redundant and a lot of ill feeling being directed against the National government. While there is definitely a left-wing luvvie atmosphere in MFAT and some changes were justifiable, I felt that some of those Murray made were unfair and did not enhance MFAT's reputation or its ability to perform. Rather than appoint a senior MFAT official as secretary, for example, he chose my old friend John Allen, a former partner of MinterEllison and CEO of New Zealand Post. Some of Murray's ambassadorial appointments were also odd. For example, I never understood why Mike Moore was made ambassador to Washington or, having been appointed, was able to stay as long as he did. On the day of Moore's appointment, Michael Cullen walked up to me in Parliament and said, 'What have the Americans done to deserve that?' Moore left the embassy in Washington in something of a mess, and a very senior MFAT official had to be appointed as chargé d'affaires to sort things out before the new ambassador came on board.

I had had a busy start to 2017 as I needed to shepherd the intelligence and security legislation through the House. Thanks to Andrew Little, the Labour opposition were constructive. During the committee stages of the bill, Labour MPs asked a number of questions but they were not accusatory in any way; they were sensible and helpful questions and the MPs proposed a number of amendments that actually improved the bill. Denis O'Rourke for New Zealand First made a helpful contribution throughout the legislative stages, and Kennedy Graham for the Greens, while opposing the legislation, made a very measured and careful contribution. Because of the importance of the bill, I decided to take all the calls for the government in the committee stages — I did not want some junior National MP saying the wrong thing. The legislation passed and was enacted. I was very pleased that this major reform had been successfully concluded.

During my remaining months in office, I was preoccupied with treaty negotiations. I had reached the conclusion that trying to negotiate with Ngāpuhi representatives was a waste of time. They had promised that, if a settlement proceeded, the existing leaders would not create some kind of politburo. I had been adamant that there needed to be devolution in such a large and complex iwi. It was always one step forward and two steps back, and so I reluctantly decided in early 2017 that there was nothing much that I could do about the settlement and decided to ignore it to concentrate on more achievable goals. I was particularly focused on signing a deed of settlement with Ngāti Kahungunu ki Wairarapa and reaching the agreement in principle stage with Moriori, Ngāti Maniapoto and Whakatōhea, especially the latter two. Ngāti Maniapoto were once described to me as 'the sleeping giant' of central North Island. Leader of the iwi was Tiwha Bell, a wonderful man who lived in Te Kūiti. In all my time as minister for Treaty of Waitangi negotiations, Tiwha and the Ngāti Maniapoto team always showed great generosity of spirit, especially when dealing with the overlapping claims of other iwi. If they had adopted an intractable approach to the sometimes extremely difficult issues, then there would not have been settlements with, for example, Ngāti Tūwharetoa and Ngāti Raukawa. I felt I owed it to Ngāti Maniapoto to secure a settlement. At that time, their principal negotiator was none other than Nanaia Mahuta.

I was motivated to try to resolve the Whakatōhea negotiation. I had worked hard with Whakatōhea over at least five years to get them to a position where they could negotiate an agreement in principle. There had been many divisions in the iwi for some time but, under the excellent leadership of Robert Herbert and others, they were getting to a stage where they could negotiate, and the dissenters were declining in number and power. I signed an agreement in principle with the iwi in late 2017. I was upset when, some months after I went into opposition, the Waitangi Tribunal released a report criticising the approach of the Crown to negotiations with Whakatōhea and suggested that they had proceeded at pace for political considerations rather than in order to achieve a just and durable settlement with the iwi.[1] I regarded the tribunal's statements as extreme and unfair. The negotiations had not been rushed — there had been many years of quiet discussion with Whakatōhea.

And so once again a general election loomed, and I faced what for me was the miserable prospect of yet another campaign in Rongotai. Before Parliament rose, we had to endure the ritual of valedictories, some of which were incredibly good. First prize would have to go to Maurice Williamson, who gave a hilarious valedictory as he stepped down from 30 years of representing Pakuranga in Parliament. He went to Los Angeles as consul-general. Hekia Parata gave a very long valedictory. I listened to the first few minutes, and then went down to Copperfield's in the Beehive for an early dinner. Afterwards, I wandered back to the chamber and Hekia was still speaking. Annette King was also retiring after 24 years in Parliament. She had come back to Parliament in 1993 as MP for Miramar, and from 1996 as MP for Rongotai. She was a much-loved figure in Labour party politics and was greatly respected in the electorate. When I used to stand against her, I knew there was no way in which I could win the seat and my focus was always on the party vote. Her replacement was Paul Eagle, whom I had known for many years. A fellow St Pat's old boy, Paul is a nice guy and I enjoyed being on the campaign trail with him. The Green candidate was Teall Crossen, a serious (at least at the start) but competent candidate, and I found as the campaign went on that I had increasing respect for her. I cannot understand why she is not a Green MP. Many of the current line-up do not impress, whereas Teall would be able to represent Green environmental policies in particular with great skill.

Shortly before the campaign proper got under way, the Labour party leadership changed and this altered everything. I always liked Andrew Little, and my dealings with him over the intelligence legislation were excellent. He made a huge personal sacrifice in handing over the leadership to Jacinda Ardern at the eleventh hour. In doing so, he transformed the prospects for Labour in the election, and at one stage they even moved ahead in the polls. Rather than being a gentle walk to a fourth term (which I had been confidently expecting), we were in a serious fight. The campaign in Rongotai was boringly predictable. There was a crazy meeting in the most inappropriately named place on earth, Happy Valley, down near Ōwhiro Bay, where most of the people were to the left of even the Greens. At one stage, Paul Eagle leaned over to me and whispered, 'When is this dreadful meeting going to finish?' In contrast, the meeting in Brooklyn was delightful. All the candidates were asked a question about the arts and Paul wasn't sure what the Labour arts policy was so I told him *sotto voce*. Generally it was a pleasant campaign, although the usual raucous elements were not present at the Island Bay meeting. I think that had something to do with the lateness of the meeting in the campaign and the fact that so many people had voted early.

As expected, I was flattened in Rongotai a few days later. Paul won a convincing majority and recovered some of the party vote for Labour. All the seats in Wellington were bad for the National party, with the exception of Hutt South, which was won in a historic victory by Chris Bishop. I had known Chris's parents for many years and was delighted that, after his hard work as a list MP the previous three years and as a candidate, he picked up that seat in a difficult year for National.

On election night, National secured 58 seats, which looked tantalisingly close. Of course, the complexion of Parliament had changed because the Māori party had lost its seats and Peter Dunne had retired. Apart from ACT, we were friendless. It did look as though New Zealand First could hold the key to the Cabinet, and after the special votes were counted, we dropped two seats to 56 seats and Winston Peters was indeed the key player.

I was not invited to be part of the negotiating team, and was neither disappointed nor surprised. For one thing, I disliked Winston Peters and thought he was a malignant influence in politics in New Zealand. I had first had experience of him many years earlier when he was thrown out of the National party because of his behaviour, and witnessing him in Parliament from 2011 to 2017 only increased my dislike of the man. In my heart, I thought that retaining a fourth term was going to be problematic, and even if we did manage to hang on, there was no guarantee that I would continue to hold my positions as attorney-general and minister for Treaty of Waitangi negotiations because Peters and I had clashed over the years. I thought I would be one of the sacrificial lambs if National had to offer cabinet seats to New Zealand First. I was, however, surprised when our negotiating team was announced.

Among others, it included Paula Bennett and Steven Joyce, both of whom had a very bad relationship with Peters. I did not think that their presence would do much to advance the negotiation.

I was surprised at the lack of overtures to the Green party. I am sure John Key would have been on the phone to the Green co-leadership immediately to try to open up channels of communication. I would have been very happy to be part of a cabinet containing people like James Shaw. Many of the Green's policies, particularly in the environment and conservation areas, were attractive to me and I like James personally. I don't know whether any of those overtures were ever made.

Thus, as in 1996, the electorate was having to witness the spectacle of Peters strutting on the stage as he negotiated with both National and Labour. And then the inevitable came: Peters announced he was going with Labour and thus ended my ministerial career.

Going back to the night in 2008 that John Key phoned me to invite me to become a minister, I had no expectation during that conversation that I would be a member of cabinet for nine years, holding such interesting portfolios and doing such fantastic work. I was grateful for the opportunities that I had had. My portfolios of treaty negotiations and the GCSB and NZSIS were taken by Andrew Little. Because of his support during the intelligence reforms, I wanted to do whatever I could to be supportive of him, and I hope I have achieved that. I have never criticised anything Andrew has done in either portfolio. I was pleased when David Parker became attorney-general again. David is ideological but a nice guy, and it was because of him that the debate on the replacement for the foreshore and seabed legislation was principled and dignified. I said as much in the House. He had briefly been attorney-general from late 2005 to early 2006, but had to resign his portfolios after a former client had made some allegations against him. I felt sorry for him. He had come back into cabinet as minister of energy, but Helen Clark did not give him back the attorney-general's job, which was held by Michael Cullen for the remainder of Labour's term in office.

And thus it was that I left my office in the Beehive for the last time on 25 October 2017. I had a farewell dinner with some of my favourite officials and that was that. I was pleased with what I had been able to achieve and was ready for new challenges.

The last year in Parliament

One must always follow one's instincts, and after the new government was formed in October 2017, I failed to do so. That meant that 2018 was probably one of the worst years of my life. I should have notified the party leadership that I would not be taking up my seat after the Peters/Ardern government was sworn into office, but instead I decided to stay, mainly because there was a feeling that the government could collapse at any stage. I consulted people like Jim Bolger about whether I should go immediately, and he told me he thought doing so would make me look like a bad sport and that I should stay for a couple of months.

Nothing prepares a minister for the transition to opposition. The pain of leaving office was alleviated to a certain extent by my playing golf at Shandon on the morning of the changeover, and at some point on the course I ceased to be a minister and became an opposition MP. People say that former ministers regret losing the car. That is ridiculous. I never cared much for the ministerial limousines and losing them was hardly a problem. I handed back my self-drive Mini a few weeks later and then ordered a new car. After I walked out of my ministerial suite, I was, however, unprepared for what was to come. The then chief whip, Jami-Lee Ross, told me that my office would be on the second floor, and when I went to inspect it, it became apparent I had been given what was traditionally regarded as the waiting room for the crematorium. I was not on the third floor where all the action was; I was in a remote and forgotten corner of the National opposition offices. I went into the office on the Monday after the changeover to find piles of books in the office and then proceeded to try to make it habitable.

In due course Bill English and I had a discussion about portfolio responsibilities. I think he proposed that I continue in my existing roles as shadow attorney-general, and spokesperson for treaty negotiations and the intelligence agencies. I said that I thought it was time for a change and asked if I could pick up the commerce brief. I very much enjoyed commercial law and was interested in intellectual property and competition law. I felt that both those areas needed a bit of work and I was enthusiastic about working in this area. He asked whether I could work with Andrew Bayly, the then MP for Hunua (now Port Waikato). I said I thought Andrew was an excellent person and thereafter for a couple of months, Andrew and I formed a very good team visiting people and starting to talk about commercial law issues.

In February 2018, the National party had its caucus in Tauranga. I kept being asked by journalists why I was deciding to continue. I felt completely ill at ease at that caucus and simply didn't want to be there. Then slowly but surely the old team started to go their own ways. First up was Bill English, who decided to leave politics. That triggered an election contest. Paula Bennett decided not to stand for leader, and so the four candidates who emerged were Steven Joyce, Judith Collins, Amy Adams and Simon Bridges. While I was a strong supporter of Steven and felt he had been an excellent minister, I did not know whether he could make the transition to the leadership. I wondered whether, given the new prime minister, we needed a generational change. I decided to cast my vote for Simon. There was no way I could support Paula continuing as deputy leader as I had no respect for her. I decided to support Judith for deputy leader in the hope that she would be able to make a meaningful contribution. As it turned out, Simon was elected on the second ballot and Paula beat Judith for the deputy leadership.

A few days later, the new leader announced changes to the line-up. On the Sunday afternoon before the announcement, he phoned me to tell me that I was to be fifteenth in the line-up, and was to regain the treaty negotiations job. My brief sojourn in the commerce portfolio came to an end. Commerce went to the list MP Brett Hudson, who, in my opinion, proceeded to do nothing. I was very disappointed to lose that portfolio. I had told the new minister of commerce, Kris Faafoi, that I thought he was doing a good job in the portfolio and I was looking forward to working with him. He responded by saying that if ever I wanted any briefings or anything, just to give him a call. So it was back to treaty negotiations, which confirmed in my mind that I was stereotyped in a particular role and that my time in public life was coming to an end. I was sorry also to lose the intelligence brief. I had enjoyed being minister in charge of the intelligence agencies and was pleased with the reforms of 2017. Apparently Gerry Brownlee was upset at losing foreign affairs, and asked for and received the intelligence brief. As a postscript, a few months later Simon came into my office to ask me how I was, and I said I had been disappointed to lose the commerce job. He airily said he would give it back to me, and I replied that it was a bit late for that.

Things started off reasonably well for the opposition. It was apparent that the new government would have some issues settling down and that there were ministers who were clearly not up to it. The new spokespeople for the National opposition were generally making a reasonably good fist of things. The procedures meeting before question time in a sitting week was always interesting and I felt that National were dominating the House quite well.

However, it then became clear that there were emerging tensions. I did not really know Jami-Lee and had made no real endeavour to get to know him because I did not think he had much to contribute. I learnt subsequently that he was very angry that, having supported Simon Bridges for the leadership and been one of his closest confidants, he had not received the jobs he thought he was capable of doing. I was told he wanted to be chief whip, shadow leader of the House, hold a major spokesperson role and be on the front bench. Anyone who knows anything about Parliament knows that such a proposition is absurd — no one can do all those jobs at once. If a person is chief whip of a caucus as large as the National opposition, then that is a job in itself; a chief whip cannot also sit on the front bench and hold a major spokesperson position.

As the weeks and months went by, I was on the outer fringe. There were very few opportunities for me to ask questions in the House or speak, other than on treaty legislation, for which I required no preparation. The treaty bills going through the House were essentially mine, and I was very pleased to have a member's bill on the reform of the law of contempt pulled out of the ballot. I mentioned to the minister of justice that, while it was in form a member's bill, the issue was so important that it should be taken over by the government. Andrew Little agreed, and it became a government bill. I was seconded to the Justice Select Committee for submissions, and when I left Parliament, I thought it was in reasonably good shape. As I said earlier, I had not expected Nick Smith to try to undo the part of the bill that dealt with scandalising the court.

Apart from indulging my interests in the law of contempt, things were bleak. At one caucus I was chatting to people before the leader arrived to begin proceedings, and Amy Adams, who had just returned from the speaker's tour with an extended holiday tacked on, came up to me and said 'Oh are you still here?' I responded by saying that a lot of people were asking that about her and couldn't believe that, as the newly minted finance spokesperson, she had gone away on an extended trip in the period leading up to Grant Robertson's first budget. I said many people felt she had been derelict in her duty. Normally I would not respond so bluntly, but Amy is not a person who understands subtlety. This kind of ritual humiliation continued in 2018. The National conference was to be held in Auckland, and I found that Paula Bennett and Jami-Lee Ross, who were organising the speakers, excluded me completely — I had no role to play at all. This didn't particularly worry me, because John Key had invited me to play golf with him at Tara Iti, which was certainly preferable to attending the conference. I did go to the conference for about half an hour, but then went home. During this period I had been talking to Bankside Chambers in Auckland about joining them and was in the course of preparing for the transition, when one day I returned to the House after speaking on a treaty bill.

By this stage — October 2018 — Jami-Lee Ross had gone rogue. Problems with him had emerged a couple of weeks earlier, when he had started making all sorts of allegations about Simon Bridges and donations. He said he would be releasing tapes of conversations he had had with Simon that would show the extent of Simon's corruption. One of the tapes that was released was that of a conversation between Simon and Jami-Lee, which among other things concerned senior MPs such as David Carter, Nicky Wagner and me. Jami-Lee asked Simon about the three of us and what his thoughts were. Simon responded that he wanted us all to go, but not for a while; we could go at the end of the term. This was the conversation where Maureen Pugh was described as 'f***ing useless'. I was asked about my views, and I said I was not particularly troubled by it because I would be moving on reasonably soon. A lot of people thought I had been treated shabbily; indeed, one of the Labour press secretaries who had been a journalist told me that he was disgusted with what had been said. I never spoke to Simon Bridges again after that tape and dealt with the leadership through Gerry Brownlee. It was about this time that I decided there was no future for me in the National party, and a few weeks later I announced my departure. Looking back now, I should have told my colleagues myself, but I simply left it to Gerry to inform them. One day in the House, after I had interjected over something, the speaker said to me that I could make those sorts of comments in my valedictory speech. That was the first that many of my colleagues knew I was going.

I gave my valedictory speech in late December 2018. I loathe those experiences, particularly at the end of the speech when people come up and thank you and wish you all the best. So when I finished my speech, I simply walked out.

I left Parliament in early 2019 and began my new life as a barrister straight away. As I say, it was a serious error of judgement to stay the extra year. I achieved very little other than reform of the law of contempt, and felt I had been underappreciated and spurned by the new brigade.

Life after politics

And so for me it was back to the law. I enjoyed rebuilding my practice in 2019, although I found the commute between Auckland and Wellington rather tiring. In general, I would spend three days a week in Auckland, returning to Wellington for the weekends. While I was working out of an Auckland set of chambers, I had not wanted to leave Wellington for personal family reasons.

During this time I watched with horror as the National party brand was destroyed. I have described earlier in this book the huge efforts that were made after 2002 to rebuild the party, improve the brand and attract new candidates. The experience of being on the outside watching developments in 2019 and 2020 made me sick. All the old guard, with the exception of Gerry Brownlee, had either departed or had signalled their intention to do so. Jonathan Coleman had left reasonably early in 2018, and other members of the 2005 class indicated that they would do so in 2020. I was sorry to hear that Nathan Guy had decided to go. He had done a wonderful job as minister for primary industries and had also been a highly effective MP for Ōtaki. Like the rest of us, however, he felt he had made his contribution and wanted to get back to his farm and to business. His was a serious loss to National. Nicky Wagner was another I was sorry to see go. She had first stood in Christchurch Central against Tim Barnett in the 2002 election. She had been comprehensively trounced, then gradually lowered the majority and won the seat spectacularly in 2011, managing to hold on in 2014, before losing it to Duncan Webb in 2017. She was an effective Christchurch MP and worked very hard as a minister outside the cabinet. She was another one who was simply not appreciated by the new regime.

I knew that the Bridges–Bennett team was not effective, and like many in the party I was pleased to see Todd Muller take over the leadership in May 2019. He had always looked as though he would be a future leader, and his contributions in caucus and in Parliament were always measured and sensible. When I had asked Bill English for the commerce spokesperson role, he had asked me who could look after the Crown–Māori relations brief and I immediately named Todd. However, he did nothing in the portfolio, apparently thinking it would be a dead end for him politically. He was probably right — those who have served as minister for

Treaty of Waitangi negotiations generally find there is no future after that job. In any event, he held it for only a couple of months before I was given the job once again by Simon Bridges.

Just two months later, I was on my way to work one morning when a friend of mine texted me asking me what on earth was going on in the National party. He said that Todd Muller had resigned. I phoned him and said that was crazy, but indeed that is exactly what had happened. I think the sad reality was that Todd was simply not up to the job. This had become apparent to me when I was asked to meet with him to talk through Treaty of Waitangi issues before he had an interview on one of the Sunday morning programmes. He knew nothing about that area and couldn't even answer simple questions during the interview — it was an embarrassing performance. He has not made any substantive contribution to New Zealand politics and should probably go and rebuild his career. Todd's other problem was that he entered politics in the wrong cycle, becoming an MP towards the end of the Key government, so he was always going to have a spell in opposition. It is always best to try to enter Parliament at the end of a period of government, so that one has limited experience in opposition prior to being part of a government, hopefully as a minister.

I need not say very much about the 2020 election — the less said the better. Judith Collins took over the leadership in extremely difficult circumstances and Gerry became her deputy. The billboards around Wellington were not the best advertisement for the party — two very senior and experienced ministers were not projecting an image that people found comforting for the future. In addition, there continued to be a litany of leaks and mistakes, including the unfortunate budget errors made by Paul Goldsmith as finance spokesperson (there was an apparent $4 billion discrepancy). Everything was going wrong and it had the feel of 2002 all over again. I was invited to go on the TV3 panel on election night, and when the preliminary party vote figures emerged, I was devastated. I could not believe that we had sunk to 25 per cent. Like many in the party, I thought the figure would be around about 30 per cent.

Many electorates swapped hands. National party bastions such as Northland, Whangārei and Ilam were lost to the Labour party. I am still shocked Gerry lost his seat — Ilam and its predecessor seats, Fendalton, Riccarton and Christchurch West, have been held by the National party or the Reform party since the early 1920s. This was the home of leading lights of the centre right, including Gerry himself. How the seat was lost completely escapes me, but it was a metaphor for the rest of the campaign. While I knew that Andrew Falloon had caused immeasurable damage in Jo Goodhew's old seat of Rangitātā, I never thought it would be lost. When that result came up, with Paddy Gower making all sorts of comments in the studio, I knew the National party was in for a bad night.

The emergence of Christopher Luxon and Nicola Willis in 2021 has been a bright spot for the party. Nicola is a talented individual and I have known her for years — her father was one of my partners at Bell Gully and is a good friend. She is a formidable intellect and will make a significant contribution to government in the years to come.

The party itself is starting to rebuild after the tragic years of 2017–20. The old structures are being renovated and new blood is starting to emerge. There are some fine people who will contribute greatly to the National party and politics in the future. That said, however, the 2020 calamity was avoidable. Looking back, particularly given Covid, I suppose Labour was always going to win that election, but if the National party had kept its shape, the loss could have been less traumatic. The parliamentary party only has itself to blame for what transpired. The wrong people were elected leader and deputy leader at the beginning of 2018, and they failed to provide the mature leadership a great party like the National party expects. The generation who took command in 2018 were never really up to it. They had come into Parliament when John Key reigned supreme. Often they would fly into Wellington on a Tuesday morning and attend caucus, where, as I say, John was completely in command. They received a competent financial overview from the deputy prime minister, Bill English. The polls were always rosy and Steven Joyce was always on top of the politics. Then they would go to the House and possibly ask a few questions, which were prepared for them by the Government Research Unit. They would go to select committee on a Wednesday or Thursday, and generally have a great party on a Wednesday night after the House rose at 10 p.m. They didn't really work at all and thought that this was the norm. They considered they could do it as well as John Key, Bill English and Steven Joyce, but they were wrong. They weren't up to it, and when the tough times came, they couldn't cope. The National party is better off without them.

As for me, I enjoyed my time in politics. I tried to act as a minister according to the advice given to me by Professor Peter Norrish, one of my French lecturers at Victoria University. He stopped me once in 1979 when I was studying too many subjects as well as teaching part-time at St Patrick's College. He said to me, 'Christopher, do a few things and do them well.' It was sound advice, which I have too often ignored. As a minister, I felt it was important to focus on the big issues and try to get as many runs on the board as possible. I think I did that, particularly in the treaty negotiations area. But when the curtain came down in 2017, I should have moved on immediately rather than hang around. That was a mistake and I regret it. I am now back in the private sector, enjoying the arts, playing quite a lot of golf and thoroughly enjoying myself.

CHAPTER 13

Concluding comments

WHEN MY TIME IN PUBLIC LIFE drew to a close, I told my friends I wanted to write three books. The first book, *He Kupu Taurangi* (2021), co-authored with my former colleague James Christmas, is about treaty settlements. In it I endeavoured to explain the work undertaken by governments since the development of the treaty settlement process in the early 1990s under the leadership of Jim Bolger and Doug Graham, culminating in my own nine years in office. I also attempted to explain why the government repealed the Foreshore and Seabed Act and replaced it with the Marine and Coastal (Takutai Moana) Act 2011.

The second book (this one) is intended to be a sketch of my time in politics. I was very lucky to enter Parliament in 2005 and, after a three-year apprenticeship in opposition, serve nine years as a minister for the Crown. One of my favourite political figures is Rab Butler, who served in a number of governments in the United Kingdom from the 1930s to 1964 and held every political office except prime minister. After he left politics, he wrote an interesting sketch of his time in government entitled *The Art of the Possible* (1971). I have endeavoured in this book to do the same.

At some stage I also hope to write or co-author a third book, on the rule of law, with contributions from former attorneys-general around the globe. One of the greatest threats to liberal democracies is the declining respect for the rule of law. In its place one has the rule of politicians or, no less insidious, the rule of judges or, worse still, the rule of lawyers. The purpose of the book will be to explain what the rule of law is, how it is under threat from these various sources and what needs to be done to secure it.

My political career is now over and I watch the events of today from the sidelines. Occasionally I am asked to comment on an issue, such as the state of the National party in the period leading up to the 2020 election, or current controversies such as co-governance with Māori of natural resources or cooperation in some other area of government. Because my time is over, I do not want to tell the next generation what they should do, so what follows here are some general comments.

First, let me consider my political party. Many people who have read this book may think I have been too critical of the National party. If that is the case, then it is only because the party has been my political home since I left university in 1974 and I have invested a lot of time and energy in it. The National party means a lot to me. I am very grateful to its members who supported me, and appreciate that it has been the vehicle through which I have been able to contribute to public life in this country. It represents the best political traditions in New Zealand: the liberal and conservative non-socialist traditions. It has served this country very well over many years, and the point I have endeavoured to make is that it has been let down by certain individuals over the years. I was particularly critical of the Muldoon years, but reserved most of my criticism for what happened to the National party after Bill English left in 2018. As I write this in 2022, things are, however, looking up. The party now has new leadership, its organisation is being reinvigorated and it is relearning things. This can only result in better candidates and better-quality MPs at the next election. All parties have their ups and their downs, and some go through prolonged periods of turmoil. The National party has never been like that — when it trips, it gets up again quickly. I have every confidence that, under the leadership of Christopher Luxon, National will be successful and once again be a strong voice for liberal conservative New Zealanders.

The National party is not liberal or conservative: it is both. The organisation needs to ensure that both traditions are represented in the party caucus. In March 2022 the eminent American political scientist Charlie Cook wrote an article about the loss of political biodiversity in the United States.[1] He talked about how, over decades, the United States system developed into one with a centre-left party and a centre-right party, with a substantial overlap between the two. Up until the 1980s, the more liberal tendencies of the Democratic party were tempered by some of the conservative members from the American South or Midwest, whereas the conservative tendencies of the Republican party were tempered by the representatives from the Northeast and the far West. Unfortunately, that trend has been reversed. Cook talked about how, in political terms, it is healthy to have parties with internal diversity, not only along lines of gender and ethnicity, but also geography and ideology. As he said in his article 'Just as inbreeding can distort certain characteristics and nature, in politics it has an effect too, creating a certain tone-deafness or an inability to see how anyone else might see an issue differently.' This division has become increasingly bitter in the United States, where most Democrats think that the Republican party has been taken over by racists, and most Republicans think that the Democratic party has been taken over by socialists.

This group polarisation does not seem to have affected New Zealand to quite the same degree, but the seeds of it are there and the trend needs to be challenged. In all issues, be they race relations, the teaching of history or reform of the state, one hopes that there will be mature and reasonable debate focusing on the issues and not indulging in argument by epithet. To accuse those on the centre right who are concerned about co-governance of racism is unhelpful, but to condemn those in favour of increasing co-governance as anti-democratic is equally inappropriate. To achieve the best result for New Zealand, the issue needs to be examined and debated.

So what happens when the next National government is formed? What issues will it face? The biggest challenge will be how to confront the expanded state. In January 2022, for example, *The Economist* published a very interesting article entitled 'Beware the bossy state'. I grew up in the 1960s and 1970s, when the state was omnipresent. All that was swept aside in the mid-1980s, however, when David Lange's government unshackled New Zealand and liberalised the economy, and those reforms were continued by Jim Bolger and Ruth Richardson between 1990 and 1993. We hear a lot of gnashing of teeth and wailing about the legacy of the 1980s and 1990s, but the truth is that those reforms — enacted by both major parties — almost certainly saved New Zealand from decline into an economic basket case, as has happened to several South American countries that were prosperous once. The reforms have resulted in a New Zealand that is far stronger and more innovative than before. The same trend was apparent in the United States and the United Kingdom. I am an unabashed child of Margaret Thatcher and Ronald Reagan, who did wonders for their countries, as difficult as the transition was for many people.

The Covid-19 pandemic has caused the state to expand again. The experiences of governments since 1979 (when Thatcher became prime minister of the United Kingdom) are now being questioned, and so the challenge for any future National government is going to be how to unwind that state to make it lean and efficient once again.

A big state is not the answer to New Zealand's problems — one cannot solve issues simply by throwing money at them. Yet a view persists among a large proportion of the public that there is an unlimited pool of money and that announcing an injection of funding for something will improve it. The opposite is often true. One example, admittedly a very small one, comes from my experience as minister for arts, culture and heritage, when we managed to do some truly innovative and exciting things for the arts community with very little money. It always seems to be the lot of the National party to assume office when a period of austerity and fiscal discipline is required, and that pattern looks set to continue. The next National government is going to have to follow in the tradition of the Key and Bolger governments to try to turn the ship around after years of profligacy. It will not be easy but it has to be done.

The experience of the pandemic has illustrated another issue. Future governments will need to persuade New Zealanders that the state is not the answer to all their problems. The government cannot do everything for the individual; the individual needs to do most of it for themselves. Doing so will involve reversing a slow but seemingly inexorable decline in the idea of personal responsibility, probably begun in the 1930s but accelerated in the post-war years. In his famous essay 'Fretful sleepers', written in 1952 while he was studying in London, the great New Zealand novelist Bill Pearson said this about New Zealanders:

> The New Zealander delegates authority, then forgets it . . . There is no one more docile in the face of authority . . . partly because he wants to be sociable and co-operate in a wishfully untroubled world . . . No people is easier material for governing . . . Fascism has long been a danger potential in New Zealand . . . the ground is already prepared . . . a docile sleepy electorate, veneration of war-heroes, willingness to persecute those who don't conform, gullibility in the face of headlines and radio peptalks. New Zealanders may well wake up one day to find a military dictator riding them and wonder how he got there.[2]

The fear of New Zealand disintegrating into dictatorship was a common, and probably overblown, one after the war, influenced by a generation who had spent their youth fighting real dictatorships on foreign shores. But the core of the concern remains. New Zealanders place too much blind faith in the power of government, although they are not the only ones. A former lord justice of appeal in England, Lord Sumption, gave a very interesting lecture in late October 2020 entitled 'Government by decree: Covid-19 and the constitution'. Having criticised the government of the day for the actions it took during the pandemic, and in particular exercising coercive powers over its citizens on a scale never previously attempted, he offered this comment:

> Our society craves security. The public has unbounded confidence, which no amount of experience will dent, in the benign power of the state to protect them against an ever-widening range of risks. In Britain the lockdown was followed by a brief period in which the government's approval ratings were sky high. This is how freedom dies. When societies lose their liberty, it is not usually because some despot has crushed it under his boot. It is

> because people voluntarily surrendered their liberty out of fear of some external threat. Historically fear has always been the most potent instrument of the authoritarian state. That is what we are witnessing today. But the fault is not just in our government. It is in ourselves. Fear provokes strident demands for abrasive action, most of which is unhelpful or damaging. It promotes intolerant conformism. It encourages abuse directed against anyone who steps out of line, including many responsible opponents of this government's measures and some notable scientists who have questioned their empirical basis. These are the authentic ingredients of a totalitarian society.[3]

If such a person was an ordinary commentator, those sorts of comments could be taken with a grain of salt. But they are not; they are the comments of a distinguished judge and outstanding historian. What Lord Sumption describes in England was replicated in this country. Very few people seemed to be concerned about the unlawfulness of the first days of the lockdown in 2020, and those who questioned aspects of it were viciously criticised. Huge faith was placed in the so-called experts, with critical thinking put on hold in favour of uncritically accepting whatever was said on the Beehive podium, and treating as gospel the public pronouncements of people with agendas that were not always obvious. It will be a major challenge for any government to wean people off the notion of the cure-all state; it will take even more time to persuade New Zealanders that the future lies in their hands and that the government, far from being the answer to the problem, is (as Reagan used to say) the problem.

As minister for Treaty of Waitangi negotiations, I learnt a lot about this country. There is much that we should be ashamed of because of what happened in the past, which is why historical treaty settlements are so important. Any nation needs to confront its history, if necessary atone for past events, and then move confidently into the future. That is what treaty settlements are all about and why they have been successful. But they will continue to be successful only if government recognises that the landscape changes once a settlement occurs. The challenge for government into the future will be to honour the commitments it has made and not slip back into the old ways of doing things. Some commentators are suggesting that there needs to be a bonfire of government quangos and departments, including Te Arawhiti — The Office for Māori Crown Relations, which grew out of the Office of Treaty Settlements. I was in charge of that office for nine years as minister for Treaty of Waitangi negotiations. In my last term in office from 2014 to 2017, I created the Post-settlement Commitments Unit, which was established to ensure that all corners of government know the ongoing obligation on the Crown of treaty settlements. So often settlements would be signed and enacted, and then the Crown would start to ignore its obligations. If this continues, then those treaty settlements will not endure. The Post-settlement Commitments Unit and Te Arawhiti are essential organisations to ensure the finality of treaty settlements, and it would be irresponsible for any government to shut them down.

Treaty settlements are only one part of the equation, however, and there will be other issues that confront and challenge us all. The obvious contemporary one is co-governance and the extent to which central government should be sharing power with Māori. I made significant use of co-governance over natural resources when I was negotiating historical treaty settlements. The term has now been extended to a large number of other governmental activities, and people are beginning to say that it is not appropriate to extend it into certain areas so that, for example, a government agency has to have a board that is 50 per cent Pākehā and 50 per cent Māori.

Such boards should be appointed on the basis of experience and qualifications.

Since the Ardern government came to office in 2017, further types of co-governance have been introduced, not only in the area of natural resources in the context of treaty settlements, but also in other areas. The issue here is whether a co-governance model in those particular areas of administration is appropriate. Hopefully these matters can be debated publicly in a civil and productive manner, so that a consensus can be reached. One of the problems, however, is that there is not a very good understanding of the origins of co-governance and many people do not know what the term means. A better way of describing the arrangements is one I included in my time as minister, which is to call them treaty partnerships.

Another issue that has arisen recently is that there can be intense criticism of Māori who assume governance roles post-settlement. A very good example is the strident criticism of the stewardship of Te Urewera by Ngāi Tūhoe following its settlement. However, the problem here is not with co-governance and it is unfair to blame Tūhoe for the issues. As I said at the time the Tūhoe settlement was concluded, the new Jerusalem is not going to arrive in five minutes; it is going to take some considerable time, and patience is required on all sides.

I believe there will also be an increasingly vigorous debate on teaching history in New Zealand following the introduction of the new curriculum in 2023. Again, I hope the debate is principled and civil, and does not degenerate to the levels experienced in, for example, the United States. A mature country should be able to look at historical issues without the kind of extreme zealotry seen there and in the United Kingdom, where statues of historical figures have been trashed. It is important to face the past and acknowledge that bad things happened, but it is also important to acknowledge that

New Zealand has endeavoured to address those issues and that much good has happened to those who have lived here since the Treaty of Waitangi was signed. Instead of pulling statues down, I like the idea expressed to me by one Ngāi Tahu leader of erecting statues to the people it respects alongside the old statues.

There are a number of major reforms that I hope a future National government is prepared to address. In an earlier chapter, I spoke about my attempts to reform Te Ture Whenua Maori Act 1993. In my view, it failed because of unprincipled political opposition and a very poor decision of the Waitangi Tribunal. That reform of Māori land law has the potential to provide huge economic benefits to Māori landowners, and I hope that someone like Joseph Mooney, the new MP for Southland, who has a great interest in the subject, will have another go.

Speaking of the Waitangi Tribunal, it is not extreme to say that it has probably served its purpose. It was formed in 1975 to investigate contemporary grievances, and then its jurisdiction was extended to historical grievances. It has produced some excellent historical reports, but its contemporary reports are generally poor. One approach could be to say that the tribunal should be abolished and its jurisdiction assumed by the senior courts, but that is probably politically impossible. Why buy a fight like that, especially if one could be looking to the Māori party for support? The much better approach would be to remove Māori Land Court judges from the Waitangi Tribunal so that they can concentrate on the important work they need to do in the Māori Land Court. The chair of the Waitangi Tribunal should be either a High Court judge or a retired High Court judge (in fact, the legislation provides for that now). Reform of the Waitangi Tribunal in this way would mean a more effective body that is better able to address contemporary issues.

It is always easy to advocate the abolition of certain bodies but so often it creates controversies that a new government may wish to avoid. Take the Human Rights Commission, for example, which, I have always thought, is opposed to a National government when in power. The easy thing to do would be to abolish it, but in my opinion the more sensible path would be to appoint some non-ideological commissioners who can be relied on to be sensible in this important area. So often people are appointed and remain sensible and loyal only as long as it takes for the ink to dry on their warrant, and are captured by the organisation and end up doing its bidding. That comment applies across the board to a range of organisations.

When I was minister for Treaty of Waitangi negotiations, I used to be incensed at the attitude of Landcorp to assisting the Crown achieve its settlement objectives, and I was always going on about appointing directors who would be more understanding. More often than not, however, they were captured by the organisation as soon as they were appointed. There are many organisations within government whose existence is problematic, and Landcorp is a leading example. Why the Crown needs to have an SOE that owns thousands of hectares in farmland is questionable. There were discussions when I was a minister of making Landcorp sell its farms so that it could become a specialist land advisory company. Unfortunately, however, nothing came to pass. That reform is overdue.

Another major issue that is becoming increasingly concerning is the relationship between central and local government. One of the great litanies of the modern era is 'reform the Resource Management Act' to achieve better economic and environmental outcomes. However, the problem is deeper and more profound than that. One can reform legislation as much as one likes, but if those administering it are incompetent, then little good can be achieved. I am sure that the incompetence of local government lies behind the Three Waters Reform Programme. As one who has lived in Wellington all his life, I sympathise with the proposition that the Wellington City Council is incapable of doing anything well. There have been so many problems with Wellington water that fundamental reform is, of course, necessary, and water is not the only issue confronting the capital. What is clearly needed across the country is a careful review of local government, which is so obviously failing. We need a proper discussion about what can appropriately be performed by local authorities and what needs to be done by central government. For me, I would give local government as little to do as possible, because my experience in Wellington over many years has left me seriously jaded about its ability to get anything right.

At the heart of my concern is the growth of the professional local politician. The late Sir John Jeffries once told me about the Wellington City Council in the 1960s. He was a Labour councillor at the time and his opposite number was Dennis McGrath, a citizens' councillor. They both had very busy law practices in Wellington. At the end of most days, they would leave their offices and go down to the council at around 5 p.m., make key decisions on issues and then go home. In other words, they knew the difference between government and micromanagement. Quite simply, the growth of the modern professional local politician has resulted in micromanagement. The problem with local politicians is that they are paid too much. Instead, they should be paid a pittance so that they are required to have day jobs and will therefore approach their council duties in an economical manner. They will concentrate on the big issues and not get buried by pettifogging detail.

A whole range of economic challenges will confront a future National government. Its ministers will need to closely examine once again the relationship between the state and the individual.

The last major reform of the state was Tony Ryall's mixed ownership model in 2011. That created lean and effective mixed ownership companies that have done so well for the government over the years (with the exception of Air New Zealand, which has been negatively affected by the pandemic). But what about the other SOEs, which, as Bill English used to say, are basically dogs? I think the answer lies in what has happened in Singapore, where one large company administers a number of SOEs. A similar model could be adopted here — and I believe, with his abilities and attention to detail, Michael Woodhouse, National's SOE spokesperson, is the one to develop such an arrangement.

Fundamental change is also required in the public service, which has become increasingly political. It needs to regain its apolitical status. I have already mentioned my concerns about the Ministry of Education being able to do a competent, non-partisan job on the development of a New Zealand curriculum. My fear is that they will be propagandists. Other government departments are intrinsically left wing and cannot cope with a National government, and they will need to be tamed if a National government is to achieve much-needed reform. Some government departments are, however, not politically biased — they are simply incompetent. Te Puni Kōkiri is a prime example, and could provide next to no policy resource when Pita Sharples, Te Ururoa Flavell and I were working on Te Ture Whenua Maori Act reform. That is a department that needs fundamental change.

Many years ago, the United Future MP Gordon Copeland put forward a member's bill on reforming the Bill of Rights to provide for protection of property rights. It was an excellent idea but one that needed a lot of work and was beyond the scope of a member's bill. For that reason, National opposed the bill, much to the dismay of Gordon, but said it would do something when in government.

Unfortunately, we did not look at the issue and that was a mistake. One of the concerns about that is that it could have opened up the Bill of Rights for a general debate about whether, for example, there is an environmental right or a social right to housing and so on. Maybe there should be a debate on those issues, but there certainly should be careful consideration given to whether property rights should be included in the Bill of Rights. The group who would benefit greatly from the inclusion would be Māori. Lack of respect for Māori property rights is one of the reasons why this country had to develop a treaty settlement process. Māori rights were regularly trampled over by the state for many years. So, for example, if land needed to be taken under the Public Works Act for a road and there was a choice between taking Māori land or general land owned by Pākehā, the answer was obvious: Māori land was taken. There needs to be protection against that kind of abuse and the Bill of Rights Act should therefore be amended to include property rights.

Many important social issues will also need to be addressed. I have not endeavoured to begin looking at any of these topics because so many of them are outside my area of competence and require very detailed analysis. I was always very supportive, however, of the work Bill English did on the issue of social investment, which he developed in conjunction with various ministers of social development. It was all about providing intensive assistance to those in need at the start of their lives rather than leaving them to become dependent on welfare or find their lives ruined later on. In my opinion this work was the best example of compassionate conservatism I saw as a minister, and I was disappointed that the Ardern government discarded it when it assumed office in 2017.

In both my maiden and valedictory speeches, I said that other countries have problems but New Zealand has challenges. Some of those challenges are great, and some will irritate our community to a greater or lesser extent, but they can all be solved for the benefit of the country if we debate the issues vigorously (but politely) and then reach a consensus result. That is the way solutions have normally been achieved in New Zealand, and I hope that will be the way the many new issues facing the next generation of politicians will also be addressed.

Acknowledgements

Writing a book is always a time-consuming and difficult exercise. I was very grateful to have the assistance of some excellent research assistants, most notably Sunni Fredstad, formerly of Wellington and now back home in Norway. Her assistance in interviewing some of my former colleagues was invaluable. When she left to go home to Norway, I engaged a bright young law student from the University of Auckland, Hayden Rayen, who worked with me over the summer of 2021–22. He also interviewed some of my former colleagues and assisted with drafting and planning this book.

I have had the opportunity, with the assistance of Sunni and Hayden, to interview Wayne Eagleson (former chief of staff), Maurice Williamson, Anne Tolley, Wayne Mapp, Tim Groser, Kate Wilkinson, Phil Heatley, Nikki Kaye, Nathan Guy and David Farrar, and have also had discussions from time to time with Bill English about a couple of matters.

I also acknowledge the assistance of James Christmas and Peter McKenzie QC, who reviewed draft chapters and gave me valuable advice.

I particularly acknowledge the assistance of the team at Concept Secretarial, who worked with me in preparing the manuscript. They provided prompt and excellent service, and I am very grateful to them for their help.

The usual disclaimer: all errors and omissions are mine, as are the opinions and judgements expressed in this book.

Notes

Preface

1 Lord Bingham, *The Rule of Law*, London: Penguin, 2010, p. 38.
2 Quoted in ibid.
3 'Economics and the rule of law: order in the jungle', *The Economist*, 13 March 2008, pp. 95–97.
4 Jacinda Ardern, 'Why does good government matter?', speech to the Australia New Zealand School of Government, Melbourne, 18 July 2019.

1 Getting involved in politics

1 *Templeton v Jones* [1984] 1 NZLR 448.
2 Douglas Hurd, *Robert Peel: A biography*, London: Weidenfeld & Nicolson, 2007, p. 3.
3 Douglas Hurd, 'The Whig illusion', *Prospect*, 20 February 1997, p. 3, https://www.prospectmagazine.co.uk/magazine/thewhigillusion

2 Early days in the law

1 *Green v Broadcasting Corporation of New Zealand* [1989] 3 NZLR 18, [1989] 2 All ER 1056.
2 *Wilson v Broadcasting Corporation of New Zealand* [1990] 2 NZLR 565.
3 *Porirua City Council v Gerard Aloysius Wall*, M. 478/88, Decision of Judge D.A. Ongley, 17 March 1989.
4 For example, *O'Brien v Social Credit Political League* [1984] 1 NZLR 84 and [1984] 1 NZLR 68 (among others).
5 *Black v Taylor* [1993] 3 NZLR 403, and its aftermath, *Gazley v Lord Cooke of Thorndon* [1999] 2 NZLR 668.
6 *Fletcher Challenge Ltd v Commerce Commission* [1989] 2 NZLR 554.
7 *Holt v Holt* [1990] 3 NZLR 401.
8 *Governor of Pitcairn and Associated Islands v Sutton* [1995] 1 NZLR 426.
9 *Sodexo Pass International SAS v Hungary* [2021] NZHC 371.
10 *Dairy Containers v NZI Bank Ltd* [1995] 2 NZLR 30.
11 E.W. Thomas, *A Return to Principle in Judicial Reasoning and an Acclamation of Judicial Autonomy*, Victoria University of Wellington Law Review Monograph 5, Wellington, 1993.
12 D.F. Dugdale, 'A polite response to Mr Justice Thomas', *Victoria University of Wellington Law Review*, 1993, vol. 23, p. 128.
13 *VUWSA v Shearer* [1973] 2 NZLR 21, then [1974] 2 NZLR 138.
14 *Ngai Tahu Maori Trust Board v Director-General of Conservation* [1995] 3 NZLR 553.
15 R. Tomlinson, *The Big Breach*, Sydney: HarperCollins, 2001, p. 288.
16 *Attorney-General for England and Wales v Tomlinson* [1999] 3 NZLR 722.
17 *Attorney-General for England and Wales v R* [2002] 2 NZLR 91.
18 *Attorney-General for England and Wales v R* [2004] 2 NZLR 577.
19 *Attorney-General for England and Wales v R* [2007] 2 NZLR 347.
20 *A v Roman Catholic Archdiocese of Wellington* [2008] 3 NZLR 289.

3 In opposition

1 Margaret Thatcher, speech to the General Assembly of the Church of Scotland, Assembly Hall, The Mound, Scotland, 21 May 1988.

4 Becoming a minister

1 Cabinet Office, *Cabinet Manual*, Wellington: Department of the Prime Minister and Cabinet, 2017. As Bill English says in the Foreword, the *Cabinet Manual* is the primary authority on the conduct of cabinet government in New Zealand. I refer to this important document throughout this book.
2 *Cabinet Manual*, p. 28, para. 2.60.

5 My cabinet colleagues

1 Waitangi Tribunal, *Stage 1 Report on the National Freshwater and Geothermal Resources Claim*, WAI 2358, Wellington: Waitangi Tribunal, 2012.
2 Canterbury Earthquakes Royal Commission, *Final Report, Part One*, Christchurch: Canterbury Earthquakes Royal Commission, 2012.
3 Section 16 of the Policing Act 2008 makes it clear that the police commissioner is not responsible to, and must act independently of, any minister regarding, for example, the maintenance of order in relation to any individual, or the investigation and prosecution of offences.

6 The attorney-general

1 Sir Robert Buckland KBE, QC, MP, 'Foreword', in Conor Casey and John Larkin, *Crossing the Line? The Attorney-General and the Law/Politics Divide*, London: Policy Exchange, 2021, p. 5.
2 'Ministers, the law and inquiries', in *Cabinet Manual*, Wellington: Department of the Prime Minister and Cabinet, 2017, pp. 57–58.
3 There have been a number of papers on this subject, including *The Governance of Britain: A Consultation on the Role of the Attorney-General*, CM 7192, 2007, and *House of Commons Constitutional Affairs Committee, Constitutional Role of the Attorney-General, 5th Report of the Session 2006–7*, 19 July 2007, HC 306. A further inquiry is being conducted in 2022 by the Constitution Committee into the role of the lord chancellor and the law officers.
4 David Cameron, *For the Record*, London: William Collins, 2019, pp. 508–509.
5 Tom Bingham, *The Rule of Law*, London: Penguin Books, 2011.
6 *The WPC 80 Incident: Causes and Responses — Government Inquiry into the Whey Protein Concentrate Contamination Incident*, Wellington, December 2013, p. 31.
7 John Spencer, *Review of Public Prosecution Services*, Wellington, September 2011.
8 Miriam Dean, CNZM, QC and David Cochrane, *A Review of the Role and Functions of the Solicitor-General and the Crown Law Office*, Wellington, February 2012.
9 Legal Aid Review, *Transforming the Legal Aid System: Final Report and Recommendations*, Wellington: Ministry of Justice, November 2009.
10 Bingham, *The Rule of Law*, p. 37.
11 Murray Gleeson, *Courts and the Rule of Law*, Rule of Law Series, Melbourne University, 7 November 2001.
12 *Report of the Attorney-General Under the New Zealand Bill of Rights Act 1990 on the Sentencing and Parole Reform Bill*, Wellington: House of Representatives, 2009, s.15.
13 *Cabinet Manual*, p. 57.
14 Ibid., p. 58.

15 *Saxmere v Wool Board Disestablishment Company Ltd* [2010] 1 NZLR 35.
16 Michael Cullen, *Labour Saving*, Auckland: Allen and Unwin, 2021, p. 131.
17 Chris Corry, *Limitation Defences in Civil Cases: Update Report for Law Commission*, MP16, Wellington: New Zealand Law Commission, June 2017.
18 *Reforming the Law of Contempt: A Modern Statute*, Report 140, Wellington: New Zealand Law Commission, June 2017.
19 Douglas White, 'The Contempt of Court Act 2019: an intriguing tale of law reform', *New Zealand Law Review*, 2020, vol. 4, pp. 601–637.
20 *Cabinet Manual*, p. 59.
21 Rebecca Macfie, *Helen Kelly: Her Life*, Wellington: Awa Press, 2021, p. 333.
22 J.L.J. Edwards, *The Law Officers of the Crown*, London: Sweet & Maxwell, 1963, pp. 306–308.
23 John McGrath QC, 'Principles for sharing law officer power: the role of the New Zealand solicitor-general, *New Zealand Universities Law Review*, 1998, vol. 18, p. 221.
24 See, for example, *Isaac v Mills* (1887) 5 NZLR 122 (CA), where Sir Robert Stout acted for one party in a chancery case.

7 Minister for arts, culture and heritage

1 R.S.V. (Dick) Simpson, *Bring on the Music*, Wellington: Steele Roberts, 2002, p. 114.
2 Rebecca Macfie, *Helen Kelly: Her Life*, Wellington: Awa Press, 2021, p. 7.
3 Sir Peter Jackson and David Court, *Review of the New Zealand Film Commission*, report to the Hon. Chris Finlayson, MP, Minister for Arts, Culture & Heritage, June 2010.
4 Damian Fenton, *New Zealand and the First World War*, Auckland: Penguin Books, 2013.
5 *New Zealand Professional Orchestra Sector Review: Final Report*, Wellington: Ministry of Culture and Heritage, 2013. The reference group was chaired by Peter Biggs (now CEO of the NZSO) and independent expert advice was obtained from Avi Shoshani, secretary-general of the Israel Philharmonic.
6 *Growing the Pie: Increasing the Level of Cultural Philanthropy in Aotearoa New Zealand*, report of the Cultural Philanthropy Taskforce to the Minister for Arts, Culture and Heritage Hon. Chris Finlayson, December 2010.
7 Tricia Tunstall, *Changing Lives: Gustavo Dudamel, El Sistema, and the Transformative Power of Music*, New York: W.W. Norton & Co., 2012, p. x.

8 Minister for the spies

1 Learned Hand in a speech to Yale Law School graduates in 1931, quoted in Irving Dilliard (ed.), *The Spirit of Liberty*, New York: Alfred A. Knopf, 1960, p. 89. A similar point was made by Stephen Breyer, associate justice of the United States Supreme Court, in a speech to the annual meeting of the American Bar Association in Chicago, Illinois, in August 2007, where he talked about the lawyer as law reformer.
2 *Intelligence and Security in a Free Society: Report of the First Independent Review of Intelligence and Security in New Zealand*, Sir Michael Cullen and Dame Patsy Reddy, February 2016.
3 The remit of the United Kingdom Intelligence Security Committee of Parliament is covered in section 2 of that country's Justice and Security Act 2013.

9 Māori affairs and Treaty of Waitangi negotiations

1 Chris Finlayson and James Christmas, *He Kupu Taurangi*, Wellington: Huia Press, 2021.
2 *Growing the Productive Base of Māori Freehold Land*, report prepared for the Ministry for Primary Industries by PricewaterhouseCoopers, February 2013.
3 *Report of Māori Agribusiness in New Zealand*, Wellington: Ministry of Agriculture and Forestry, 2011.

4 *Discussion Document: Te Ture Whenua Māori Act 1993*, Wellington: Ministry of Māori Development, 2013. There were many examples of unbelievable fragmentation of Māori land, including an island off the coast of Pitt Island (Rangiauria) in the Chathams that is apparently owned by more than 1000 Māori.
5 Waitangi Tribunal, *He Kura Whenua ka Rokohanga: Report on Claims about the Reform of Te Ture Whenua Māori Act 1993*, Wellington: Waitangi Tribunal, 2016.
6 Waitangi Tribunal, *The Ngāpuhi Mandate Inquiry Report*, Wellington: Waitangi Tribunal, 2015.
7 Finlayson, *He Kupu Taurangi*, chapter 10.
8 Cabinet Office, 'Tiriti o Waitangi / Treaty of Waitangi guidance', circular CO (19) 5, 22 October 2019, p. 4.
9 Cabinet Office, *Cabinet Manual*, Wellington: Department of the Prime Minister and Cabinet, 2017, para. 5.14(f).
10 Ibid., para 7.34.
11 'Incoming indigenous Labor MP calls Greens a bigger threat to a Voice to Parliament than coalition', *The Australian*, 24 May 2022.

10 Overseas assignments

1 See Jody Wilson-Raybould, *'Indian' in the Cabinet: Speaking Truth to Power*, Toronto: Harper-Collins, 2021.
2 *Whaling in the Antarctic (Australia v Japan: New Zealand Intervening)*, judgment at the International Court of Justice, 31 March 2014, www.icj-cij.org/en/case/148/judgments, accessed 25 May 2022.

11 Challenges

1 Sir James Bevan, '"Events, dear boy": Managing incidents before they become crises', speech given to the Whitehall and Industry Group, London, 7 July 2020.
2 Ibid.
3 *Canterbury Earthquakes Royal Commission Final Report Vols 1–4*, 29 June 2012 and 10 October 2012.
4 *Royal Commission on the Pike River Coal Mine Tragedy Report*, 30 October 2012.
5 *The WPC80 Incident: Causes and Responses. Government Inquiry into the Whey Protein Concentrate Contamination Incident*, Wellington: Ministry for Primary Industries, 28 November 2014.
6 Donald Rumsfeld, US Secretary of Defense, US Department of Defense news briefing, 12 February 2002. Rumsfeld distinguished the known knowns, the known unknowns and the unknown unknowns.

12 Change of leader

1 Waitangi Tribunal, *The Whakatōhea Mandate Report*, Wellington: Waitangi Tribunal, 2018.

13 Concluding comments

1 Charlie Cook, *The Loss of Political Biodiversity*, The Cook Political Report, 31 March 2022, https://www.cookpolitical.com/analysis/national/national-politics/loss-political-biodiversity, accessed 24 May 2022.
2 Bill Pearson, 'Fretful sleepers', *Landfall*, 1952, vol. 23, pp. 201–230.
3 Jonathan Sumption, Lord Sumption, 'Government by decree: Covid-19 and the constitution', Cambridge Freshfields Lecture, 27 October 2020, Cambridge Private Law Centre, Cambridge.

Index

ما هذا البِناء؟

المُحْتَوَيات

بقلم: ريتشارد بلات

التصميمات: استوديو بالسار

Collins

ما هذا البِناء؟

ما هو ارْتِفاعُ أَيِّ بِناءٍ حَوْلَنا؟ ما شَكْلُهُ؟ ما هي وَظيفَتُهُ؟ لا توجَدُ إجابَةٌ مُوَحَّدَةٌ تَنْطَبِقُ على كُلِّ الأَبْنِيَة. فَبَعْضُ الأَبنِيَةِ، مثالاً، عُلَبٌ زُجاجِيَّةٌ عِمْلاقَةٌ، وبَعْضُها عُلَبٌ مُنْخَفِضَةٌ، بَعْضُها مُرْتَفِعٌ، أو مُسَطَّحٌ ... هناك أَبْنِيَةٌ مَبْنِيّةٌ بِخاماتٍ غَيْرِ تَقْليدِيَّة، وهناك أَبْنِيَةٌ غَريبَةٌ لِلغاية.

هذه ناطِحَةُ سَحابٍ في «تايباي»، في جَزيرَةِ تايْوان. هناك دَعائِمُ فولاذِيَّةٌ خَفِيَّةٌ تَدْعَمُ هذا البِناءَ منَ الدّاخِل.

المِساحاتُ الشّاسِعَةُ في بَعْضِ مَواقِعِ البِناءِ أَجْبَرَتِ العُمّالَ على اسْتِخْدامِ وَسائِلَ مُبْتَكَرَةٍ لِلتَّنَقُّلِ حَوْلَ المَوْقِعِ.

هذا نَموذَجٌ لِحِصْنٍ من حُصونِ «مارتيللو» المُسْتَديرةِ الّتي بُنِيَتْ بِالأَحْجارِ السَّميكَةِ لِتُقاوِمَ قَذائِفَ المَدافِعِ.

أَشْكالٌ خاصَّةٌ لِأَغْراضٍ فَريدة

حَظيرَةُ الطّائِرات

هذا البِناءُ أَعْلى مِمّا قَدْ يَبْدو عَلَيْهِ عَن بُعْد.

إنَّهُ مُخَصَّصٌ للطّائِراتِ العِمْلاقَة.

تَحْمي الأَبْوابُ العِمْلاقَةُ العُمّالَ منَ الحَرارَةِ أو البُرودَةِ في أَثْناءِ عَمَلِهِمْ في الدّاخِل.

يَجِبُ أن تَـتَّسِعَ الأَبْوابُ العِمْلاقَةُ
لِمُرورِ الجَناحَيْنِ العَريضَيْنِ.
شُيِّدَتْ أكبَرُ حَظيرَةٍ
لِلطّائِراتِ في دُبَيّ. إنَّها تَـتَّسِعُ
لِوُقوفِ ٦٧ حافِلَةً في طابورٍ،
واحِدَةً تِلْوَ الأُخرى.

المَنارَة

الغَرَضُ منَ المِصْباحِ المَوجودِ في أَعْلى المَنارَةِ هو إنْذارُ البَحّارَة. تَزيدُ احْتِمالاتُ رُؤْيَةِ المَنارَةِ كُلَّما زادَ ارْتِفاعُها. قُوَّةُ المِصْباحِ تُعادِلُ قُوَّةَ مَلْيونِ شَمْعَةٍ، ويُمكِنُ رُؤْيَةُ هذه المَنارَةِ من على بُعْدِ ٤٠ كيلومترًا. شُيِّدَتْ أَوَّلُ مَنارَةٍ في مِصْرَ مُنْذَ حَوالي ٢٣٠٠ سنة.

قَدْ تَبدو المَناراتُ صَغيرَةً،
إلّا أنَّ أَسْطُحَ مَناراتٍ عَديدةٍ
تَتَّسِعُ لِهُبوطِ طائِرَةٍ مِرْوَحِيَّة.
حينَ يَتَعَذَّرُ اسْتِخْدامُ القَوارِبِ
بِسَبَبِ الطَّقْسِ العاصِفِ والبَحْرِ
الهائِجِ، تَقومُ المِرْوَحِيّاتُ بِنَقْلِ
العُمّالِ لِتَنْظيفِ المِصْباحِ وصِيانَتِه.
شُيِّدَتِ المَناراتُ بِالأَحْجارِ
السَّميكَةِ لِتُقاوِمَ أَشَدَّ الأَمْواج.

بَيْتُ النَّخْلَة

بَيْتُ النَّخْلَةِ هو بَيْتٌ زُجاجِيٌّ ضَخْمٌ في حَديقَةِ «كيو» في لُنْدُن. بَيْتُ النَّخْلَةِ هو أشْهَرُ بَيْتٍ زُجاجِيٍّ في حَديقَةِ «كيو». تَحْبِسُ جُدْرانُهُ الزُّجاجِيَّةُ أَشِعَّةَ الشَّمسِ لِتَدْفِئَةِ النَّباتاتِ الاسْتِوائيَّةِ المَزْروعَةِ داخِلَهُ.

تَسْتَقِرُّ جُدْرانُ بَيْتِ النَّخْلَةِ الزُّجاجِيَّةُ فَوْقَ قُضْبانٍ حَديدِيَّةٍ مُقَوَّسَة. تَمَكَّنَ البَنّاؤونَ من تَوْسيعِ بَيْتِ النَّخْلَةِ لِيُناسِبَ النَّباتاتِ الضَّخْمةَ بِفَضْلِ قُوَّةِ هذه القُضْبانِ ومَتانَتِها.

وَصَلَتْ أقْدَمُ نَخْلَةٍ إلى حَديقةِ «كيو» عامَ ١٧٧٥، وهي لا تَزالُ مَوجودَةً فيها.

التَّخْزينُ والتَّصْنيع

بُرْجُ خَزّانِ المِياه

هذا الفِطْرُ العِمْلاقُ ليسَ لِلأَكْل! فَهو مَصْنوعٌ منَ الخَرَسانَة. الجُزْءُ العُلْوِيُّ هو خَزّانٌ لِلمِياه. تَمْتَدُّ الأنابيبُ من أَسْفَلِ البُرْجِ لِتَصِلَ إلى البُيوتِ المُجاوِرة. تَنْدَفِعُ المِياهُ إلى الأَسْفَلِ تَحتَ ضَغْطِ وَزْنِ المِياهِ المَوْجودةِ أَعْلى الخَزّان. المِضَخّاتُ تَسْتَطيعُ أن تُؤَدِّيَ المُهِمَّةَ نَفْسَها، ولكنَّها لا تَعْمَلُ إن اِنْقَطَعَ التَّيّارُ الكَهْرَبائيّ.

كُلُّ خَزّاناتِ المِياهِ عالِيَةٌ،
ولكنَّ تَصْميماتِها قَدْ تَخْتَلِفُ.
تَصْميمُ «الفِطْرِ الخَرَسانيِّ
العِمْلاق» اِقْتِصاديٌّ وسَهْلُ البِناء.

مِنَصَّةُ النَّفْط

تُصْنَعُ مِنَصَّةُ النَّفْطِ العِمْلاقَةُ منَ الفولاذِ والخَرَسانَة. إنَّها أضْخَمُ هَياكِلِ البِناءِ المُتَحَرِّكَةِ في العالَم. بِدايةً، يَبْني العُمّالُ، على اليابِسةِ، الأَجْزاءَ الضَّخْمَةَ الّتي تُكَوِّنُ المِنَصَّةَ، ثُمَّ يَسْحَبونَ هذه الأَجْزاءَ إلى المَوْقِعِ المُحَدَّدِ لها في المُحيطِ، حَيْثُ يَتِمُّ التَّجْميعُ والتَّرْكيب. تَرسو بَعْضُ المِنَصّاتِ طافيةً، وبَعْضُها يُثَبَّتُ في القاع.

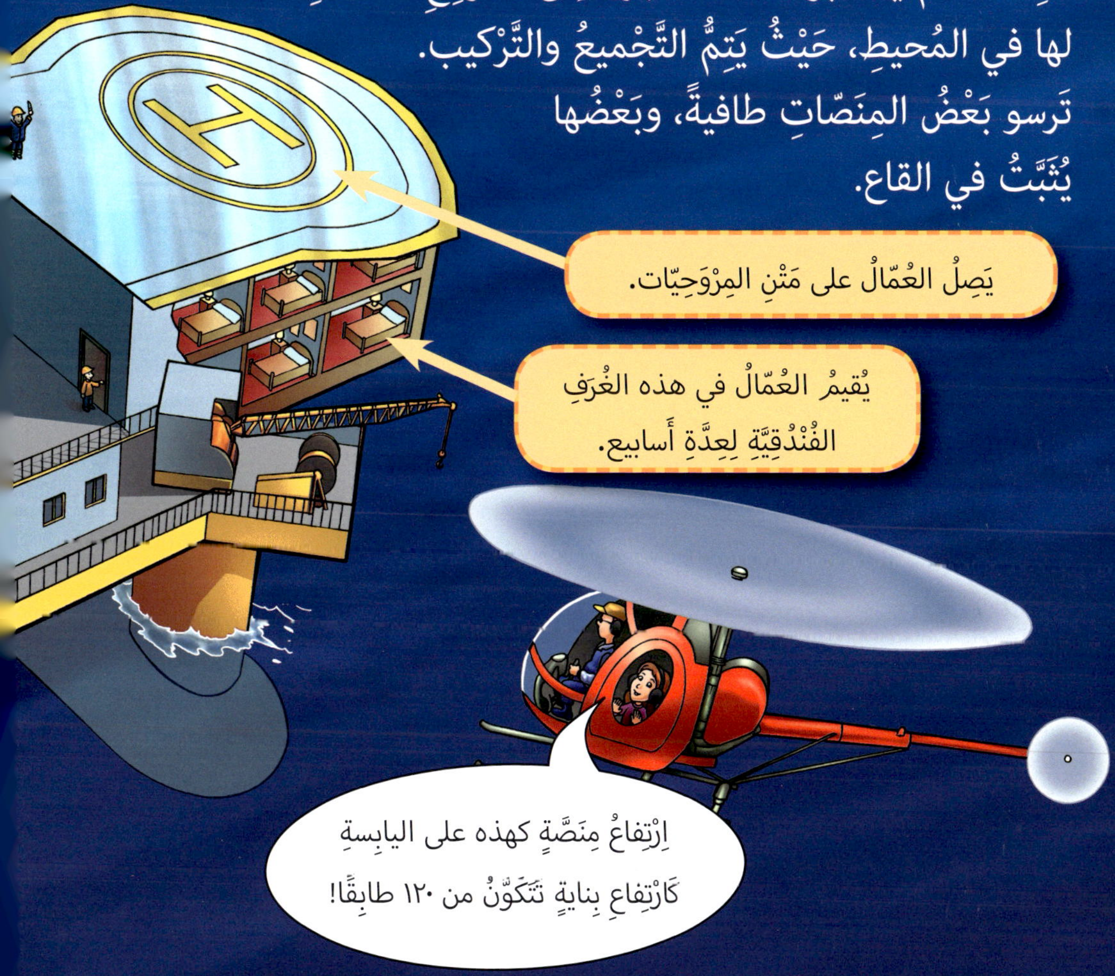

ضَخُّ الطّينِ في الآبارِ الجَديدةِ
يَمْنَعُ تَناثُرَ النَّفْط.

الطّاحونَة الهَوائِـيّة

مَتى يَكونُ البِناءُ آلة؟ حينَ يَكونُ البِناءُ طاحونَةً هَوائِيَّة! في يومٍ ما، كانَتْ هذه الأَبْراجُ الخَشَبِيَّةُ تَطْحَنُ الغِلالَ لِتُحَوِّلَها إلى دَقيق. كانَتْ أَشْرِعَةُ الطَّواحينِ تَدورُ بِقُوَّةِ الرِّياح، فَتَدورُ مَعَها أَحْجارُ الطَّحْنِ الضَّخْمَةُ المَوجودةُ داخِلَ البِناء. مُنْذُ حَوالي مائةِ عامٍ، اِتَّجَهَ بَعْضُ النّاسِ إلى اسْتِخْدامِ المُحَرِّكاتِ كَبديلٍ لِلهَواءِ في تَدْويرِ الطَّواحين.

توربيناتُ الهَواءِ الحَديثةُ أرْفَعُ وأطْوَلُ من طَواحينِ الهَواءِ التَّقْليدِيَّـةِ، إلّا أنَّها تُسْتَخْدَمُ في تَوْليدِ الطّاقَةِ الكَهْرَبائـيَّةِ، وليسَ لِطَحْنِ الغِلال.

تُديرُ التُّروسُ الخَشَبيَّةُ العَمودَ الّذي يُديرُ أَحْجارَ الطَّحْنِ الضَّخْمة.
يَدورُ الحَجَرُ العُلْوِيُّ، فَيَتِمُّ طَحْنُ الغِلال بينَ الحَجَرَيْنِ الضَّخْمَيْنِ.
دَفْعُ هذا العَمودِ يُغَيِّرُ اتِّجاهَ الطّاحونَةِ لِمُواجَهَةِ الرِّياح.

البِناءُ لِلحِمايَة

تَمَّ إخْفاءُ تابوتِ الفِرْعَونِ وَراءَ السَّراديبِ والأبوابِ السِّرِّيَّة.

في أَثْناءِ بِناءِ الهَرَمِ، راقَبَ الكَهَنَةُ البارِعونَ حَرَكَةَ النُّجومِ من سِرْدابٍ مُنْحَدِر. وبَعْدَ ذلك، قاموا بِتَحْديدِ مَواعيدِ المُناسَباتِ الدّينِيَّةِ لِتَتَطابَقَ وتَتَوافَقَ معَ مَوْضِعِ النُّجومِ في السَّماء.

هَرَمُ «خوفو»

يُطِلُّ هَرَمُ «خوفو» على الوادي والصَّحْراءِ بالقُربِ منَ القاهِرَة. مُنْذُ حَوالي ٤٥٠٠ عامٍ، أَمَرَ الفِرْعَونُ «خوفو» بِبِنائهِ لِيَكونَ قَبْرًا لَهُ. عَمِلَ ١٠٠,٠٠٠ مِصْرِيٍّ في البِناءِ الّذي اسْتَغْرَقَ حَوالي عِشْرينَ عامًا. يَتَوافَدُ الزُّوّارُ إلى هَرَمِ «خوفو» بلا اِنْقِطاعٍ مُنْذُ حَوالي ٢٠٠٠ عام.

القَبْوُ المُحَصَّن

تَصْعُبُ رُؤْيَةُ هذا القَبْوِ المُحَصَّنِ ضِدَّ القَنابِلِ الذَّرِّيّةِ لأنَّهُ مَدْفونٌ في أَعْماقِ جِبالِ «شايان»، في وِلايةِ «كولورادو» الأَمْريكِيَّة. الأَحْجارُ السَّميكةُ ذاتُ الخَصائِصِ اللَّوْلَبِيّةِ كَالزُّنْبُرُكِ تَحْمي مَن في الدّاخِلِ في حالِ التَّعرُّضِ لِهُجومٍ بالقَنابِلِ الذَّرِّيّة.

منَ الخارِجِ، قَدْ يَبدو وكأنَّهُ... جَبَل! ولكن، في الدّاخِلِ، فإنَّ هذا القَبْوَ المُحَصَّنَ هو مَدينةٌ صَغيرةٌ يَسْتَطيعُ ٦٠٠ شَخْصٍ أن يَعْمَلوا فيها.

في حالاتِ الطَّوارِئِ، يَسْتَطيعُ قادةُ الجَيشِ والدَّوْلةِ أن يوصِدوا أَبوابَ القَبْوِ، وأن يَبْقَوا داخِلَهُ لِمُدَّةٍ طَويلةٍ يَتعامَلونَ فيها معَ الأَخْطارِ الخارِجيّة.

مَسْجِدٌ منَ الطّينِ، مالي

هذا المَسْجِدُ، في مالي، هو واحِدٌ من أكْبَرِ دُورِ العِبادةِ في العالَم، رَغْمَ أنَّهُ مَبْنِيٌّ منَ الطّين. يَقَعُ المَسْجِدُ على أطْرافِ الصَّحْراءِ الإفريقيّةِ الكُبْرى. بُنِيَ هذا المَسْجِدُ بِبراعةٍ لِيُناسِبَ بيئتَهُ القاحِلَة. الجُدرانُ السَّميكَةُ تَمْنَعُ الحَرارةَ عنِ المُصَلّينَ في الدّاخِل.

ما هو دَوْرُ هذه الأَبْنِيَة؟

التَّصْنيع

التَّخْزين

الحِمايَة

أفكار واقتراحات

الأهداف:

- قراءة نصّ وثائقيّ معاصر بسلاسة، واستخلاص معلومات محدّدة منه.
- قراءة جُمَل طويلة نسبيًّا.
- التعوّد على استخدام قائمة المحتويات للعثور على المعلومات.
- قراءة المزيد من الكلمات الشائعة بدون تشكيل.

روابط مع الموادّ التعليميّة ذات الصلة:

- مبادئ العلوم الهندسيّة.
- مبادئ التعرّف على بعض أساليب البناء.
- مبادئ الجغرافيا والوعي التاريخيّ.

مفردات جديرة بالانتباه: بناء/أبنية، تصنيع، تخزين، حماية، ارتفاع، يتّسع/تتّسع، يُصنع/تُصنع

عدد الكلمات: ٩٥٠

الأدوات: الانترنت، ورق، أقلام

قبل القراءة:

- ماذا ترون على الغلاف الخارجيّ الأماميّ للكتاب؟ هيّا نقرأ العنوان معًا.
- مَن منكم يودّ أن يعمل في مجال البناء والمعمار في يوم ما؟ لماذا؟
- في رأيك، ما هي أجمل ثلاثة مبانٍ في مدينتكم؟ لِمَ هي الأجمل؟

أثناء القراءة:

- انظروا إلى الصفحة الأولى. ما هي قائمة المحتويات؟ (قائمة بأقسام الكتاب)
- كيف نستخدمها للعثور على معلومة معيّنة؟
- في أيّ صفحة سنجد بعض المعلومات عن البناء للحماية؟